Yiddish Plays for
Reading and Performance

SUNY SERIES IN CONTEMPORARY JEWISH LITERATURE AND CULTURE

EZRA CAPPELL, EDITOR

Dan Shiffman, *College Bound:*
The Pursuit of Education in Jewish American Literature, 1896–1944

Eric J. Sundquist, editor, *Writing in Witness:*
A Holocaust Reader

Noam Pines, *The Infrahuman: Animality in Modern Jewish Literature*

Oded Nir, *Signatures of Struggle:*
The Figuration of Collectivity in Israeli Fiction

Zohar Weiman-Kelman, *Queer Expectations:*
A Genealogy of Jewish Women's Poetry

Richard J. Fein, translator, *The Full Pomegranate:*
Poems of Avrom Sutzkever

Victoria Aarons and Holli Levitsky, editors,
New Directions in Jewish American and
Holocaust Literatures: Reading and Teaching

Jennifer Cazenave, *An Archive of the Catastrophe:*
The Unused Footage of Claude Lanzmann's Shoah

Ruthie Abeliovich, *Possessed Voices:*
Aural Remains from Modernist Hebrew Theater

Victoria Nesfield and Philip Smith, editors,
The Struggle for Understanding: Elie Wiesel's Literary Works

Ezra Cappell and Jessica Lang, editors,
Off the Derech: Leaving Orthodox Judaism

Nancy E. Berg and Naomi B. Sokoloff, editors,
Since 1948: Israeli Literature in the Making

Patrick Chura, *Michael Gold: The People's Writer*

Nahma Sandrow, editor and translator,
Yiddish Plays for Reading and Performance

Yiddish Plays for Reading and Performance

Edited and translated by
NAHMA SANDROW

Published by State University of New York Press, Albany

© 2021 State University of New York

All rights reserved

Printed in the United States of America

No part of this book may be used or reproduced in any manner whatsoever without written permission. No part of this book may be stored in a retrieval system or transmitted in any form or by any means including electronic, electrostatic, magnetic tape, mechanical, photocopying, recording, or otherwise without the prior permission in writing of the publisher.

For information, contact State University of New York Press, Albany, NY
www.sunypress.edu

Library of Congress Cataloging-in-Publication Data

Name: Sandrow, Nahma, editor.
Title: Yiddish plays for reading and performance / [edited by] Nahma Sandrow.
Description: Albany : State University of New York Press, [2021] | Series: SUNY series in contemporary Jewish literature and culture | Includes bibliographical references.
Identifiers: LCCN 2020024718 | ISBN 9781438481890 (hardcover : alk. paper) | ISBN 9781438481906 (pbk. : alk. paper) | ISBN 9781438481913 (ebook)
Subjects: LCSH: Yiddish drama—Translations into English.
Classification: LCC PJ5191.E5 .Y53 2021 | DDC 839/.12008—dc23
LC record available at https://lccn.loc.gov/2020024718

10 9 8 7 6 5 4 3 2 1

Contents

Preface: Yiddish Theater in Theatrical Context   vii

Plays

Mirele Efros; or, The Jewish Queen Lear by Jacob Gordin   3

Yankl the Blacksmith by David Pinski   91

Yoshke the Musician (*The Hired Bridegroom*, *The Rented Bridegroom*, *The Singer of His Sorrow*) by Osip Dimov, reworked by Joseph Buloff   185

Scenes

From *Uncle Moses* by Sholem Asch   261

From *Homeless* by Jacob Gordin   269

From *Safo* by Jacob Gordin   277

From *Carcass* by Peretz Hirschbein   283

From *Between Day and Night* by Peretz Hirschbein   293

From *Mishke and Moshke; or, Europeans in America* (*Mishke and Moshke; or, The Greenhorns*) by Joseph Lateiner   299

From *Khantshe in America* by Nahum Rakov   305

From *Riverside Drive* by Leon Kobrin   313

From *The 2,000* (*The Big Prize, The Big Lottery, The Jackpot*) by Sholem Aleichem   319

Appendix: How to Pronounce Yiddish Words and Names   335

Preface

Yiddish Theater in Theatrical Context

Yiddish theater, meaning theater in the Yiddish language, is a Western theater and participated in the developments and styles of Western theater since the Middle Ages. But the history of professional Yiddish theater was unique in that it was drastically compressed. Professional Yiddish theater did not appear till 1876; by 1976 it had lost much of its artists, audiences, and creative energy. In that one century, opera and costume operetta, melodrama, problem play, domestic drama, romantic symbolism, realism or naturalism, expressionism with or without political purpose—all those contemporaneous genres appeared roughly in the order in which they had developed in the various languages of Europe, but telescoped into less than a hundred years.

In addition to formal theater, low comedy (including revues and vaudeville) and musical entertainments have always been universally popular and were so on the Yiddish stage as elsewhere. And, of course, the repertory included not only plays written in Yiddish but also plays, classic or contemporary, translated into Yiddish from other languages. Finally, amateur biblical plays, analogous to those of the Christian medieval theater, were a Yiddish folk tradition long before 1876 and continue to this day. The result was that in the first half of the twentieth century, all kinds of theater were available to Yiddish audiences more or less simultaneously.

(I am aware that my verb tenses keep shifting. There's good reason for that. Yes, the golden era of Yiddish theatrical creativity was roughly 1895 to 1945. But Yiddish theater remained a lively institution on almost every continent till the end of the twentieth century, when it weakened considerably but did not disappear. Now it still exists and recently has even gathered energy. Shifting verb tenses reflect the historical reality. Besides, play texts endure, so discussing them demands the present tense.)

Yiddish theater never existed in isolation. In the nineteenth century, the mass of Yiddish speakers lived in Eastern European countries and naturally had much in common with their neighbors. Russia, where high culture was revered, produced most of the Jews who shaped Yiddish "fine" drama of the early twentieth century. The dark atmosphere and psychological thunder and lightning of many of the plays of Russian-born Jacob Gordin and Leon Kobrin call to mind Alexander Ostrovsky's *The Storm* (1859) and Leo Tolstoy's *The Power of Darkness* (1886). Naturalistic so-called cellar plays, like *Carcass* in this volume, came out of the same vision as did Maxim Gorky's *Lower Depths* (1902), which in fact was eventually performed in Yiddish translation. Serious Yiddish playgoers appreciated plays that were not so much stories about human characters as an acting-out of philosophical abstractions, the genre of Leonid Andreyev's *The Life of Man* (1907). Later, the American Yiddish actress Stella Adler traveled to Russia, birthplace of her matinee-idol father, Jacob, to study acting with Konstantin Stanislavski himself and carry his method home to New York Yiddish actors—who in turn served as conduit to American actors.

Similarly, Romanian Jews, whether in Romania or wherever they immigrated, tended to be reliably enthusiastic ticket buyers for light musical entertainments. And as a final illustration, it is not a coincidence that generation after generation of American Yiddish audiences got bigger and flashier musical shows than Yiddish audiences anywhere else in the world.

Actors, writers, and directors in other languages visited Yiddish theater because they respected the work of Yiddish playwrights and actors. Max Reinhardt's theater in Vienna and the Theatre Guild in New York presented contemporaneous Yiddish plays in translation, Leon Schiller directed Shakespeare's *Tempest* in Yiddish in Warsaw, non-Jewish critics reviewed local Yiddish productions, and Yiddish actors played on non-Yiddish stages. Of course, audiences were free to go back and forth. As one illustration, Sholem Asch dedicated his play *The Messianic Era* to the actress who created a role in the play's Russian production: Vera Komissarzhevskaya, star of Stanislavski's Moscow Art Theatre, the same actress who created the role of Nina in Chekhov's *Seagull*. More recent examples—all produced off-Broadway in the twenty-first century by David Mandelbaum's New Yiddish Rep, all directed by Moshe Yassur—have included Shane Baker's Yiddish translation of Samuel Becket's *Waiting for Godot*, which moved to the international Becket Festival in Ireland

and finally, triumphantly, to Paris; Joseph Buloff's translation of Arthur Miller's *Death of a Salesman*, which the *New York Times* praised for the "fineness of the performances"; and Eugene Ionesco's *Rhinoceros*, which *Theater Pizzazz* called "profound and touching."

On the other hand, Yiddish theaters all over the globe have tended to share certain repertory, production methods and values, attitudes and atmosphere—even individual actors and audience members, who moved from place to place in response to the same historical circumstances. To begin with, characters in Yiddish plays usually, though not always, were recognizably Jewish. Often playwrights were interested in the Jewish experience: pogroms, assimilation, search for identity, loss of faith. Religion itself generally served less as a subject in itself than as metaphor for secular culture or group loyalty. But religion is powerful when wielded onstage. When, at his wedding in act 1, Mirele Efros's son chants the prayer for his dead father to the traditional haunting melody, the atmosphere darkens, and the marriage seems ominous. When, in Sholem Asch's *God of Vengeance*, the brothel owner hurls to the floor the Torah scroll that represents his daughter, the sudden sacrilege makes a shocking stage moment. And when Lillian Lux, a popular entertainer in the 1970s, used to light Sabbath candles as part of a musical revue number, audience members who themselves practiced that ritual responded emotionally—while those members who only remembered their mothers doing it were probably even more profoundly moved.

Here there is an analogy to modern productions of Greek tragedies. No one now can respond exactly as did audiences who believed in the gods of Olympus—and as to Greek comedies, no one now gets all the jokes. Nevertheless, a good production evokes the power of the play, even in the twenty-first century.

Although Yiddish play plots were often simply about people and relationships, they often tackled social or political issues. When expressing such concerns, writers tended to construct their dramatic conflicts not so much between individual personalities as between social groups or generations, represented by characters that function allegorically. It follows that, when translating classic or contemporary plays, producers were likely to choose commentaries on society and social relationships: Yiddish theaters performed Gogol's *The Inspector-General*, Molière's *The Imaginary Invalid*, or Ibsen's *Ghosts* rather than *Twelfth Night* or *Oedipus*.

Melodrama and expressionism are the forms that remain especially associated with finer Yiddish theater. One reason is obvious: those forms were at their height in Yiddish drama's period of greatest creativity. Also, the two forms are congenial with Jewish culture's preference for art that teaches rather than art for its own sake. In melodrama virtue always triumphs, though if the dramatist is intelligent, the triumph may not be predictable or comfortable. Expressionism is a vehicle to express ideas, generally with a particular political lesson.

Certain theatrical qualities are generally characteristic of Yiddish theater. Yiddish theater is romantic rather than classical: colorful, lively, untidy, emotional, extreme. Serious plays are more often dark, heavy, and grotesque than bright and brisk. (Note the affinity to Russian theater.) Some of their weight comes from the abstract concepts that the characterizations may be carrying. Humor tends to come out of plot or character type rather than from verbal felicity, as illustrated by minor characters in this volume, such as Nokhemtse in *Mirele Efros*, Eti-Meni in *The 200,000*, and virtually all the townspeople in *Yoshke the Musician*. Speech has vigor and juice rather than elegance. In general, there is a fondness for largeness and risk, an almost operatic quality, rather than the smaller, lighter, more flexible tone that we associate with modern drama. Very often there is some musical component; popular audiences generally relished musical numbers, as in contemporary European operettas or American musical comedies, and even serious Yiddish playwrights often gave their public music, though preferably only when it could be integrated into the dramatic action with verisimilitude and, if possible, subtlety.

When Yiddish newspaper critics or ordinary theatergoers praised a performance, the adjectives that recurred were "truthful" and "full of temperament." Perceptions of truthfulness in art—and how to show it—vary over time, but the intensity, energy, and presence implied in both adjectives suggest that actors were understood to be an intrinsic part of the creative process—elevating the scripts and elevated by them. They also reveal how deeply traditional Jewish culture demands that art serve a moral purpose higher than aesthetic pleasure.

The birth of Yiddish professional secular theater was part of the nineteenth-century emergence of Yiddish as a modern secular high culture, with its own literary language. A birth rather than a rebirth, this period—known as "the Enlightenment"—nevertheless resembles aspects of the European Renaissance of the fifteenth and sixteenth centuries. In the Enlightenment, "Yiddishland" developed a sense of nationhood and established its vernacular as a vehicle for a new, modern, essentially secular literature. Many of the playwrights represented in this volume actually began by writing in Hebrew or a European language. For them, switching to Yiddish was an ideological shift, a commitment to a new ideal. Intellectuals felt urgently throughout the twentieth century that in order to be a respected modern culture, a community must possess fine theater. As a corollary, Yiddish theater that was vulgar or stupid, cheap or simply of poor quality, demeaned the language, shaming and undermining the entire culture.

There is an analogy here with the history of Poland, where many Yiddish writers grew up. Nineteenth-century Polish intellectuals responded to political impotence resulting from invasions and partitions by creating a literary culture and identity, consciously new but passionately loyal to national tradition, and valorizing Polish theater and poetry as a kind of spiritual patriotism.

In 1908, David Pinski wrote a monograph dividing the history of Yiddish theater into three "acts," starting in the nineteenth century: first folky operettas, then the literary melodramas of Jacob Gordin and his followers, and finally the work of modern playwrights and directors, including the avant-garde. Now, early in the twenty-first century, I would add a fourth act. For half a century now, few serious original plays have been written. There have been revivals and adaptations of classics, domestic dramas and comedies, and affectionate evocations of past generations, in Eastern Europe or wherever emigrants settled. These last, especially, offer an increasing proportion of dialogue in English or another local vernacular, with Yiddish words heard only in song lyrics—or sometimes conveyed wordlessly through old music. On the other hand, a new wave of intellectual interest has been leading to revivals and reworkings of Yiddish material, including innovative theater pieces that incorporate or rework Yiddish dramas and serious poems. And naturally plays in other languages appear in Yiddish translation.

Nostalgia for bygone Yiddish culture, in the Old Country or the New, still often centers around the image of Yiddish theater, and the stream of books, articles, and academic studies on the subject continues to flow. For intellectuals, the survival of high-quality Yiddish theater, whether professional or amateur, signifies the survival of Yiddish high culture—and their place in it—though this identification is less intense than it was a generation ago. For the mass Yiddish public, theater used to be a uniquely beloved social institution, with the result that in popular memory and imagination, the warmly cohesive atmosphere of Yiddish theatergoing has remained a touchstone and emblem of the Yiddish-speaking world. (For immigrants to America, in particular, plays reflected new realities while preserving the culture left behind.) It is no accident that Yale University Press's forthcoming ambitious ten-volume *Posen Library of Jewish Culture and Civilization*, encompassing all aspects of culture from ancient times to the present, both religious and secular, will include Yiddish theater—including a scene from this very translation of *Mirele Efros*!

This volume offers samples of most of the genres of professional early twentieth-century Yiddish theater. However, it does not constitute a complete survey of Yiddish drama. It does not include a serious play set in a significant period of Jewish history, such as the ancient world, medieval Europe, or fifteenth-century Spain. It does not include a scene in which the dialogue consists largely of extended speeches between several characters discussing history, politics, philosophy, ethics, religion, or the situation and fate of the Jews.

Several important writers are not represented. The "father of Yiddish theater," Avrom Goldfadn, is missing, though my translation of his beloved operetta *Shulamis; or, The Daughter of Jerusalem* (1881), in rhymed couplets, was performed at Harvard in 2009 and is scheduled for publication. The great Isaac Leib Peretz does not appear here, though some of his one-acters are available in translation elsewhere, and in 2017 an English-language music theater piece based on his symbolist "dramatic poem" *Night in the Old Marketplace* (1907) was performed at the National Yiddish Theatre–Folksbiene. (That score, composed by Frank London, is still available as a recorded album that critics have variously compared to jazz and to Berlin between the wars—an indication of the rich potential of the material.) Finally, of course it is impossible to include a glimpse of Yiddish theater's great actors.

In this connection, Motl Didner, Associate Artistic Director of New York's National Yiddish Theatre–Folksbiene—the longest continuously performing Yiddish theater in the world—considers that in our day there is no difference in acting styles between the Yiddish and the English-language stages. (I discuss performance styles specifically for nineteenth-century melodrama in my notes to *Mirele Efros*.) Didner points out a new reality, however. Although there were always occasional actors and even directors who did not speak Yiddish, now it is common to cast an actor who doesn't know Yiddish—and who may well learn only just enough to understand his own dialogue. Yet in order to "inhabit the character fully," he actually needs even deeper translations: of words and, beyond that, of cultural concepts. The example Didner suggests is the "abandoned wife," the character Makhle in *Mirele Efros*. Once the actress understands not only the word (in Yiddish: *agune*) but its full implications for the character, he explains, it "makes the stakes much higher." As for today's non-Yiddish-speaking audiences, the more dependent they become on supertitles (or on full translations, of course), the more they need the actress's emotion in order to "get" what's going on. There are no footnotes in performance. From Makhle's opening monologue, they may not get a precise understanding of the Jewish laws of marital status, but they definitely get the story that the actress is trying to tell. Thus, Didner thinks of the performer and audience as collaborators with the translator who provided the subtitles—collaborators in translation and even, I'd add, in interpretation. He adds parenthetically that there is a new wave of actors coming from the Hasidic world, people who know Yiddish language and culture but must learn the craft of acting.

The three directors whose reflections follow the three full-length plays have definite opinions, which I do not always share. All Yiddish-speakers, they have professional experience in Yiddish as well as non-Yiddish theater, and strong feelings for Yiddish theater. They talk about Yiddish theater as theater, not as a museum and not as a bar mitsve celebration featuring chopped liver and gefilte fish. The tone of their words, as well as the substance, belongs in a collection of Yiddish plays.

It is important to add that these three are not the only professional directors working in Yiddish in North America. At the National Yiddish Theatre–Folksbiene, Motl Didner has in the last few years directed several very successful musical pieces, old and new, as well as ambitious staged readings of several of H. Leivick's poetic dramas. David Mandelbaum, cofounder of New York's highly respected New Yiddish Rep, directed Clifford Odets's *Awake and Sing* in Yiddish translation to critical acclaim; other directors at his company have created fine productions of other plays from the serious modern repertoire, in Yiddish translation or in the original Yiddish. At the Saidye Bronfman Centre for the Arts / Segal Centre for Performing Arts in Montreal, and later at the Folksbiene, Bryna Wasserman has directed shows ranging from *Mirele Efros* to a Yiddish version of Gilbert and Sullivan's *HMS Pinafore*. Andrei Munteanu and Alexander Hausvater are among the directors active in Eastern European companies (notably, Teatrul Evreisc de State, the State Jewish Theater, in Bucharest, and Teatre Żydowski im. Estery Racheli i Idy Kamińskich, the Ester Rachel Kamińska and Ida Kamińska State Jewish Theater in Warsaw), and several fine directors have working relationships with the very lively Yiddishpiel company in Tel Aviv. Galit Klas and Evelyn Krape direct productions at Melbourne's Kadimah Yiddish Theatre, and there are still occasional shows in South Africa as well.

Picking individual scenes was the hardest part of making this book. There are so many to choose from! I took only pieces that can be made to work independently of the plays they're excerpted from. With some exceptions, I generally gave preference to scenes with a relatively light tone because that is more congenial to contemporary tastes and acting techniques, as well as to possible amateur performance. The casts are small, which makes production much easier. Finally, the scenes could work well together, so a company could present them all in a single event, in whichever order the director visualizes.

Plays

Mirele Efros; or, *The Jewish Queen Lear*

JACOB GORDIN

Introduction

Mirele Efros, "the Jewish Queen Lear," was one of the major roles in serious Yiddish theater. Jacob Gordin wrote the play in 1898 for Lower East Side star Keni Liptzin, who, though tiny and partial to sparkly jewelry, was known for her intelligence, intensity, and commanding presence. Having married a rich publisher, she was also one of the few performers who could afford to produce the vehicles she wanted: literary rather than low brow, primarily spoken rather than sung. A few years later, Ester Rokhl Kaminska, whom people called the Yiddish Duse, took on the role in her family's theater in Warsaw. Their interpretations differed because their personas differed. The most often reproduced photo of Liptzin in the role shows a handsome woman standing proudly erect despite the walking stick in her hand; the most popular photo of Kaminska shows her white-haired and gentle, leaning on her stick and her little grandson. In the rivalry between the divas, fans took sides passionately.

Soon Mirele became the role by which serious actresses were measured. I myself have seen three Mireles: Leonie Waldman Eliad with the Romanian State Jewish Theater, Zypora Spaisman with New York's Folksbiene, and Edit Kuper with Montreal's Dora Wasserman Yiddish Theatre. In every case, Mirele's chair, footstool, and stick are emblems of the woman and the play; the Montreal Yiddish theater actually sold T-shirts with a picture of an elaborate armchair. Opera star Rosalind Elias starred in a musical adaptation at New York's Jewish Repertory

Theatre in 1985. The first to play Gordin's Mirele in English was Valerie Leonard, who starred in this translation at Theater J in Washington, DC, in 2019, at which time Nelson Pressley, critic for the *Washington Post*, described the "thump of her scepter-like cane" and called her "imperious and elegant." Mireles have performed in Spanish, Ukrainian, and a number of other languages, including a Russian-language film in 1912, and Berta Gersten played Mirele in the 1939 American Yiddish film, which has English subtitles.

Though Mirele's grandson appears only in the last act, a number of Yiddish actors got their start in the little role. Celia Adler played Shloymele in her father, Jacob's, production. Ida Kaminska played him in her mother's production.

Mothers often figured in Yiddish plays, though not so much as in Yiddish popular songs. Especially in America, where people had in fact left their mothers behind, far away, and might never see them again, mothers were the focus for guilt and longing; they also embodied guilt and longing for the entire traditional life immigrants may have left behind. Popular plays and songs about mothers tended to sentimental tear-jerking. More literary theater, however, offered a range of interesting mother characters, dramatic or comic, including steely heroines, shrews, criminals, and fools.

I disagree with Allen Rickman's analysis following the play of long-suffering Mirele. Overweening pride—hubris, as in Greek tragedy, and not merely maternal sacrifice and a scheming daughter-in-law—is what brings her low. In the Aristotelian formulation of the nature of tragedy, pride is her fatal flaw. Battling for control of the world (both household and business) that she built and intends to keep, she is a woman who struggles, falls, and rises wiser than before.

In *World of Our Fathers*, Irving Howe suggested that the power of the plot goes beyond the protagonist herself:

> *Mirele Efros* spoke to the common Jewish perception, grounded in a sufficiency of historical experience, that the survival of a persecuted minority required an iron adherence to traditional patterns of family life. [The character] Mirele represents the conserving strength of the past, which alone has enabled the Jews to hold together in time.*

---

*Irving Howe, *World of Our Fathers: The Journey of the East European Jews to America and the Life They Found and Made* (New York: Harcourt Brace Jovanovich, 1976), 495.

And yet Gordin began his career as an enemy of all traditions, especially the Jewish: as a revolutionary in Russia, he worked the land alongside the peasants and wrote in Russian under the pen name Ivan. He left for America in 1891, just in time to escape arrest by the czarist police. Throughout his career, he remained true to the ideological missions of his youth, above all socialism and women's rights. He wrote plays to support his large family—nobody knows how many plays he turned out, including many potboilers under pseudonyms—but he also wrote and lectured on the political and literary subjects closer to his heart. And he was influential not only through his words but also because he was a very handsome man, tall and straight "as a palm branch [*lulav*]," as another playwright recalled, with dark intense eyes and great personal charisma.

Gordin was a revolutionary in theater as well. Like the other Russian Jewish intellectuals who arrived in America in the late 1800s, he knew fine Russian theater and at first scorned Yiddish theater, which had only appeared in 1876 and in 1891 was still primarily popular fare for uneducated audiences. But when a committee of Yiddish stars approached him in the hopes of a finer repertory, he sat down, "as a scribe sits to copy a Torah scroll," to elevate Yiddish theater and thereby the young modern Yiddish literature.

Melodrama was the form of the times, and it suited his goals. Melodrama may have taken its name from the invariable use of music in the action to heighten emotion. Music in *Mirele Efros* includes not only moments when characters are playing some kind of instrumental music, heightening the effect of the action, but also the sounds of specific prayers (traditional chants and even the Hebrew words themselves). It's true that nowadays producers may find it hard to pay musicians, but music deepens and darkens the action emotionally, enlarging the universe of the action from bourgeois parlor to eternity. It's also true that most actors will probably be unfamiliar with the way prayers should sound, but the prayers in this play can be heard on YouTube as well as at any traditional Ashkenazic synagogue. Naturally, the effect of the melodic chanting will be stronger and more specific on theatergoers familiar with the prayers' associations, but all hearers will respond consciously or unconsciously to performers who make it their business to find and listen to the real thing, however exotic, and imitate it musically.

Typically, melodrama includes certain other elements as well, such as suspense, splendid curtain speeches, and a mix of high intense moments with comic "low" characters. Above all, melodramatic plots depict the battle of good and evil. Virtue always triumphs, reestablishing order in the universe. This pattern has led us moderns to dismiss melodrama as simple-minded, and many popular melodramas are just that. Besides, nowadays people so pride themselves on tough-minded irony and cynicism that the very term *melodrama* is an insult. But for intelligent playwrights like Gordin, the story and characters are too nuanced, too real, to be simple-minded, and the underlying implications give the story a deeper resonance. For all those reasons, melodrama has been getting more respect in the academy lately—while on the stage (and television, and movies), it never went away! Note also that for a long time Yiddish theater preserved the nineteenth-century European acceptance, and indeed approval, of tears as a profound response to truth in art.

Just as Shakespearean actors must not only enunciate the sixteenth-century words but also rise to the sixteenth-century sensibility, so too Yiddish actors—even actors playing a Yiddish drama in translation—must carry roles written a century ago or more. (When a Yiddish play seems old-fashioned, that is a factor of when it was written as well as its Yiddish-ness.) Stirring declamations, sudden shifts in tone, embodiment of characters who are real and yet larger and more meaningful than real—melodrama roles give marvelous scope to actors who can make the most of them. Performing melodrama is perhaps analogous to performing baroque music. Authentic period instruments make clear the composer's intentions by making the composition beautiful in the original way. However, some modern ears find the sound alien, and for their sake a twenty-first-century musician may search for a more modern instrument and playing style in order to convey the beauty of the piece. Similarly, a director can choose to make the performance of a melodrama low-key, the words spoken as colloquially and informally as possible (and possibly the musical enhancement pruned away), and this does make the play more accessible to modern audiences. Still, when this diminishes the potential dramatic effect down to just another family story, what's the point in doing the play at all? Responding to Theater J's 2019 production of *Mirele Efros* in English, the *Washington Post* critic reflected that nowadays acting such "high relief drama" requires "a particular kind of tact," which he associated with cast members' "simplicity and power." I think by "tact" he meant the ability to serve the original, though in a way accessible to modern sensibility. Not easy.

In stage practice, Gordin insisted on verisimilitude unbroken by adlibs or distracting musical numbers; on ensemble acting rather than, to use the Yiddish term, *starizm*; and on a spoken Yiddish unpolluted by German (an affectation of the time), so that actors spoke only the Yiddish (or occasionally Hebrew or Russian) appropriate to their characters. He had a gift for creating vivid minor characters, sometimes for specific actors who remained identified with the role forever; actors feared him but adored him because his plays stretched them and let them shine. And in general, because his reforms drew audiences that were more refined and educated people, he transformed Yiddish serious theater. Naturally, popular theater continued to thrive, as it does in all cultures, but from then on, Yiddish intellectuals considered the state and level of Yiddish theater a touchstone of modern secular Yiddish culture as a whole. From 1890 to 1910 is remembered as the Gordin Era.

By the early twentieth century, the more intellectually ambitious Yiddish art theater projects shared the visions of the European and American avant-garde as a whole. It was Gordin who had drawn Yiddish theater into the larger sphere; yet, ironically, his own plays were becoming old-fashioned. Yiddish art theaters began to scorn such warhorse melodramas as *Mirele Efros* and *God, Man, and Devil*. All the same, popular audiences kept asking for them, laughing and crying till the final curtain, and actors continued to choose Gordin's plays as vehicles. Several of the best, including *Mirele Efros*, have remained repertory staples till this day.

Mirele Efros; or, The Jewish Queen Lear

JACOB GORDIN

1898

Characters

MIRELE EFROS	Successful businesswoman, forty or fifty.
YOSELE	Mirele's older son, mild, passive, twenty.
DONYE	Mirele's younger son, self-centered, eighteen.
MAKHLE	Mirele's devoted maidservant, forty.
REB* SHALMEN	Mirele's business manager, intelligent, dignified.
SHEYNDELE	Yosele's bride, pretty, clever.
REB NOKHEMTSE	Sheyndele's father, weak, a bit of a scholar.
KHANE-DEVOYRE	Sheyndele's mother, greedy, vulgar.
SHLOYMELE	Yosele's and Sheyndele's son, clever, thirteen.†
CANTOR‡	

MUSICIANS, WAITERS, CHORUS, GUESTS, BUSINESSMEN, RABBI

---

*Reb simply means Mister, not Rabbi.
†Characters age fourteen years between acts 1 and 4.
‡There were no female cantors then.

PLACE	The action takes place in Eastern Europe.
TIME	Around 1900.
ACT 1	A hotel in Slutsk, a provincial Polish town.
ACT 2	Three years later. Saturday evening at sundown as Sabbath is ending. The parlor of Mirele's comfortable, prosperous home in the city of Grodno.
ACT 3	A year later. Mirele's parlor.
ACT 4	Ten years later. Grodno. Mirele's parlor and Nokhemtse's humble house.

Act 1

A very big public room in a hotel. Many boxes and trunks set about. Russian porters make several trips in and out, bringing boxes in through a door upstage. MAKHLE moves ahead of each carrier showing where to put the boxes down and keeps hushing them, "Shh, Shh." Porters leave.

MAKHLE. Well, thank goodness, we finally made it to Slutsk. If I get through this wedding, I'll say the blessing you say for when you almost die but then you get better. (*With a cloth, wipes away the porters' footprints.*) Dear father in heaven, how long is it now since Yosele was a little boy, running around in short pants? Now here he is having a wedding day—in a lucky hour, please God, amen. (*Looks out window.*) A downpour. From Grodno to Slutsk we traveled like kings. Such nice weather, warm and dry. We get here, dark and wet. Exactly on purpose today the skies in Slutsk have got to let go. What a place. It shouldn't—God forbid—ruin the celebration. Children dear, what a trip, I'll never forget it. You could say Mirele Efros traveled to her son's wedding like a czarina. A whole train, five big wagons, all of them packed with everything good. In every town where we stopped, we handed out honey cake and brandy and gave charity. Shh. She lay down to rest, and the boys are chatting quietly off by themselves in their room. The bridegroom, poor thing, his little heart is beating hard. Of course, I know, I had a wedding day once myself. Oh, I trembled, and I shook. And where did it get me? My husband deserted me and for fifteen years now, it shouldn't happen to you, I'm an abandoned wife. Not a girl and not a wife, not a widow and not divorced. Not this and not that. He should burn. Such a nice wedding it was. Mirele gave my dowry and bride gifts. The boss, rest in peace, was the best man. So how long has it been now since the boss died? Sixteen—no, fifteen years. Mirele's husband died and mine ran away. Mirele Efros is my husband now, my family, my household. I grew up in her home, and it's probably my destiny to die in her home. Shh, who's there?

SHALMEN enters.

God be with you, Reb Shalmen, where were you? She called for you several times. You know very well without her head-of-staff she can't go to sleep.

SHALMEN. I was with the in-laws. Ah, Makhle, the bride is really something. But paupers! Poverty whistles in every corner, sweet heaven.

MAKHLE. Really? Our clever Mirele made a mistake?

SHALMEN. What are you talking about? The opposite. She specifically wanted a poor girl from a nice family. She herself sent the money for clothes and the wedding expenses, and she'll need to keep giving, too. The bride's father is on his way here. They want to suck out the bones of the rich in-law. Listen, Yosele could have had a bride with a thirty-thousand-ruble dowry. Who wouldn't want Mirele Efros's son? And what he himself wanted was an educated bride from a big city. But she didn't want that. And when she says no, you know yourself—shh, what is she doing now?

MAKHLE. She lay down for a rest. She is not satisfied somehow. I'm afraid that the day will end badly for somebody.

SHALMEN. Maybe it's just because the groom's side is supposed to be standoffish. Makhle, we have to clean up a little. She hates a mess.

Takes off his jacket and with Makhle drags the boxes. From other room, Mirele's voice: "Makhle! Makhle! Come here!"

MAKHLE. (*Wipes face with her apron.*) Right away. (*Runs out.*)

SHALMEN. (*Looks around.*) I didn't expect I'd pick up so many coins along the way. Big expenses: oats and hay for the horses, and in the inns. A little here, a little there. She doesn't mind. She likes everything done with an open hand. It's like her eyes see everything, but sometimes she decides not to see. She doesn't begrudge anybody.

MAKHLE. (*Returning.*) Reb Shalmen, the boss is calling you.

SHALMEN. Immediately. (*Puts on jacket, fastens it, clears his throat, wipes his feet on the threshold, and goes in.*)

MAKHLE. Our Madame Efros wants tea. (*Opens upstage door.*) Hey, Yurka! Put on the samovar right now.

NOKHEMTSE enters, his clothes and shoes wet.

And Yurka, the samovar better be sparkling, or you'll get it. (*Turns.*) Oh, the father-in-law. I recognized you. Congratulations.

NOKHEMTSE. You brought Yurka to the wedding too? Well, fine, as it is written.

MAKHLE. Naturally. Oksana and Yevdokhe are here too. Anton the coachman, Yurka—all of them. You know our lady likes things to be like at home. Our samovar, her drinking glass, her shawl, her teaspoon, her knife and fork. What more does she need? We even brought her chair. (*Shows a big armchair.*) You probably want to see your new in-law? Right away. (*Exits.*)

NOKHEMTSE. A Jewish housewife, that's all she is, really, and all the same it feels exactly like an appointment with his honor the chief of police. (*Fastens his jacket.*)

MAKHLE. (*Returning.*) She says, would you please do her the favor of coming back later.

NOKHEMTSE. What do you mean "later"? This is important. The betrothal banquet is tonight. God be with you, what do you mean? I have to see her now. I'm asking you please.

MAKHLE. That works with me, but when she says no, it's the commandments down from Sinai. (*Exits.*)

NOKHEMTSE. I should have sent my Khane-Devoyre here instead. She would have argued it out with her better.

MAKHLE. (*Returning.*) Mirele says: "If you don't have the time to wait, then you may go in good health."

NOKHEMTSE. What do you mean "go"? Help! Woman, there are still a lot of things to buy. We simply don't have money and . . . and . . . the musicians are standing in the rain. They came to play the welcome march. Some welcome. I'm begging you, tell her people are waiting.

MAKHLE. I'm afraid to drive her crazy. She hates that. (*Exits.*)

NOKHEMTSE. Here's a welcome for you. Lord of the world, I make a vow: if I survive this, I'll learn thirty commentaries. As it is written.

MAKHLE. (*Returning.*) She says the musicians don't need to stand in the rain. Bring them inside. She's coming right away. (*Cleaning up.*)

NOKHEMTSE. (*Opens the door.*) Come in, excuse me.

> MUSICIANS *enter.*

Sit down. The mother-in-law is on her way.

> *Makhle gives them chairs. They sit.*

Aha!

> KHANE-DEVOYRE *enters, drenched.*

Khane-Devoyre, God himself brought you here. I've been tearing my hair out for not bringing you along. Shh, she's coming any minute.

MAKHLE. Oh, is this Yosele's mother-in-law? (*Shakes her head.*)

KHANE-DEVOYRE. Yes, what's the matter, I'm not good enough for you? (*To her husband.*) I knew that you're a fool, and she, our Countess Pototsky, would say no. Never you mind, I've got nothing to be ashamed of in front of her. Put her family connections up against mine! Shh!

MAKHLE. (*Looks at door.*) She's coming.

> *Musicians get ready. Shalmen opens the door. Musicians play a fanfare.* MIRELE *enters, leaning on a stick. Gray hair but blooming face. Makhle moves out her chair. Mirele sits down, and Makhle puts the little stool under her feet.*

NOKHEMTSE and KHANE-DEVOYRE. Congratulations, congratulations, Mother-in-law. May it be for a blessing.

Mirele bows her head. Sarcastic little smile on her lips.

NOKHEMTSE. Arrived safely, thank God.

KHANE-DEVOYRE. It's raining today, Mother-in-law dear. When it rains, that's a sign of blessing.

MIRELE. When it rains, that's a sign of mud. Have the musicians play.

KHANE-DEVOYRE. The bridegroom and your other son should come in too. It's a march for the whole wedding party.

MIRELE. Your younger in-laws will probably not be impressed by your Slutsk music. They're musicians themselves. The elder plays the flute, the younger boy the violin. Play for us older generation. Shalmen, open the door to the kitchen. Let Yurka and Oksana hear our in-laws' wedding march.

Shalmen runs to open the door. Musicians play wedding march.

MAKHLE. May God send good fortune; may God send our Yosele happiness. (*Weeps.*)

MIRELE. What are you crying for, silly? (*Strokes Makhle's head.*) Shalmen, give the musicians twenty-five and treat them with honey cake and brandy. And give them sweets to take home for their children.

MUSICIANS. (*Astonished, as Shalmen gives them money.*) Twenty-five rubles! Twenty-five rubles!

They bow and leave with Shalmen. Mirele writes something in a little notebook.

NOKHEMTSE. What did you expect? Our in-law, you get me, is Mirele Efros. As it is written.

MIRELE. Makhle, you go out too.

Makhle off.

Now I will permit myself to ask: You couldn't have found a worse neighborhood for us to stay?

NOKHEMTSE. My dear Mother-in-law, this is practically the finest house in Slutsk. It's an honor for the bridegroom to stay here. The proprietor is a wealthy aristocrat.

MIRELE. Really? Slutsker wealth and Slutsker aristocracy: "Who is like unto thee, Lord, among the mighty?" It's dreadful. I sent a rider ahead and I waited two hours outside the city. Why didn't you come out to meet me?

NOKHEMTSE. You mustn't be offended, Mother-in-law, my dear. First, the rain. And to tell the truth: for hiring a pair of covered wagons—we simply didn't have the money. And going on foot wouldn't look nice for the family, you must understand that for yourself. Fine, as it is written. Ah, I am weak from hunger.

KHANE-DEVOYRE. Why do you need to make excuses to her like that? The mother-in-law knows us. It's true that we've come down in the world, but we haven't lost our family name. Brides like my daughter aren't lying around under the oven waiting to be picked up. Don't forget, my grandfather was Reb Menakhem Mendele.

MIRELE. The grandfather can be Moses; it is worth nothing if a person is nothing himself. Makhle.

Bangs her stick lightly and Makhle comes.

Serve him a carafe of brandy with a piece of honey cake.

Makhle off.

KHANE-DEVOYRE. But now is not the time to measure families. We have more important things to talk about. There's nothing to be embarrassed about—there's nobody here but us. Mother-in-law, we need . . .

MIRELE. I know, you need more sugar. I have already heard what kind of practical use you made of my money. You remember how much I sent you for wedding clothes for the bride? Three hundred rubles you were to spend on linens.

NOKHEMTSE. Yes, you should be healthy. But for me, and my wife—our little necessities—we're all part of the wedding party, and we needed new clothes for the wedding. And besides, as soon as your few kopeks arrived, the creditors fell on us like dogs on a carcass—not to compare human beings with animals. But as it is written—once you get her home, you'll see for yourself what Sheyndele needs.

Makhle enters with brandy and snacks.

MIRELE. Oh really? My daughter-in-law, in other words, will be—
How does that little song go, Makhle? "Dressed in suits like dancing
bears, four with patches, four with tears." Very nice. Makhle, wipe
the floor under their feet. Look, they tracked in genuine Slutsker
mud.

Makhle wipes up the floor with a cloth.

Khane-Devoyre's Reb Nokhemtse, you may eat.

Nokhemtse drinks and eats.

KHANE-DEVOYRE. I don't understand. You thought I'd hand my
daughter over to you for free?

MIRELE. Oh, not free? What do I owe for the cow and the rope all
together?

KHANE-DEVOYRE. We have to pay the grocery stores and the shops.
Everything you need for a wedding we took on credit. Everybody
knows that our in-law is good for it. Today the money for the musicians
is due, and the cantor, the waiters, the beadle, the attendant in the
ritual bath. And Panye Yanushevski, the professor of the forteplee-ano,
is coming. You yourself wrote us that she shouldn't stop learning to
plink, right up to the wedding.

MAKHLE. (*Apart.*) Oh, what beggars these Slutskers from good families
are. Whoever saw such a thing?

MIRELE. I see already that we are not going to find any bargains here
in your Slutsk. All right, I will tell Shalmen to give you two hundred.
Is it a bargain?

NOKHEMTSE. Mother-in-law dear, what do you mean? No one's
bargaining. Don't forget, our Sheyndele—may she be healthy—is
Reb Mendele's great-granddaughter, after all. All Slutsk considers
her a treasure.

MIRELE. All Slutsk? I have no idea why your town is called Slutsk.
It is Chelm, I give you my word—the town of fools in the story-
books—Chelm, precisely.

NOKHEMTSE. Ha, ha. You should be healthy—you consider us Chelm
fools? Fine. As it is written.

KHANE-DEVOYRE. (*Sarcastically*) Oh my, my left earlock feels hurt. What do they say? "You can call me Fool, just give me honey cake." Instead of talking, let's see your gifts. You promised diamond earrings, with a brooch, with a brooch-alet, and then we'll see. You're not going to start quibbling over everything now.

MAKHLE. Don't get offended. They don't understand.

MIRELE. (*Stands.*) No, of course not. How can they be offensive? They are Reb Mendele's grandchildren, after all. Enough. The welcome is over. You can go. (*Shows the door with her stick.*)

MAKHLE. (*To them, quietly*) Better to go in good health. She could, God forbid, get angry.

Nokhemtse drinks down a glass in a hurry and starts out.

KHANE-DEVOYRE. What do you mean: Go? And the money?

MIRELE. (*Bangs stick angrily.*) The money? Money? Money? Ha? Shalmen will give you money. What Miryam Efros promises is as good as gold. Just like your grandfather's name.

NOKHEMTSE. Khane-Devoyre, why argue? The mother-in-law promised, so it's a promise. It is fine, as it is written.

KHANE-DEVOYRE. (*Imitates him.*) "Promised, as-it-is-written"? Some luck. From the two hundred, what will be left for us? After the wedding, they take away our Sheyndele and leave us the poverty. No! We settle everything now, before the wedding.

NOKHEMTSE. Khane-Devoyre, enough. (*Quietly*) You're going to make things worse, God forbid.

KHANE-DEVOYRE. What are you so scared about? Didn't you say yourself: "We've got to get at least three hundred rubles out of her for ourselves, if we're going to make any profit at all"? Didn't Sheyndele herself say: "Don't let them get away with anything"? You idiot, if we don't drag it out of them now, hard, after the wedding will be too late. Mother-in-law, we want, in addition to everything, three hundred rubles cash. Before the wedding.

NOKHEMTSE. Getting past that was harder for me than crossing the Red Sea but thank God we're on the other side now. And after all, the mother-in-law herself understands. (*Drinks brandy.*)

MIRELE. Oh really? Cash, and before the wedding? Hm.

KHANE-DEVOYRE. Yes, in Grodno you're a sure thing, but here the money before the wedding.

MAKHLE. (*Wrings her hands.*) Oh, my, oh my, why are you making these problems?

MIRELE. (*Good-humoredly*) Problems? Ha, ha, you are a fool. Who has problems? Shalmen! (*Bangs stick.*) Shalmen!

Shalmen enters.

Have them harness the horses this minute and pack up our things. We are going back to Grodno.

All astonished.

SHALMEN. What do you mean? How—how—I don't understand. Right away? Back?

MIRELE. Right away! Now! We are going back. I call off the match.

SHALMEN. Forgive me, but the horses haven't rested yet. Such mud.

MIRELE. The horses are to be harnessed. Now.

Shalmen rushes off.

Makhle, call in the children.

Makhle off.

Khane-Devoyre's Reb Nokhemtse, you have nothing more to do here. The match is off. (*Shows the door.*)

NOKHEMTSE. Mother-in-law dear, what do you mean you call off the match? I don't understand. Lord of the whole world!

KHANE-DEVOYRE. Mother-in-law dear—God be with you—why are you talking like that? It's like that with in-laws; so what? In-laws fight.

MIRELE. I hate fighting. (*Opens the door.*)

NOKHEMTSE. What do you mean? The engagement contract is at the bridegroom's. He's a fatherless orphan. You can ruin our child, God forbid.

MIRELE. He will break the contract with full compensation. Now.

KHANE-DEVOYRE. Don't you think we'll keep quiet. We'll tell the world. I'll stir up the whole town.

MIRELE. (*Tranquilly*) Tell the world. Turn the town upside down. I do not like the match, and we are going home. Eh, I hate arguments. Go in good health.

Khane-Devoyre and Nokhemtse off.

They say the apple does not fall far from the tree. A tree like this will produce a dreadful apple. No. I do not want it. I am sorry. A battle early is always better than a battle late. People are often embarrassed to ruin a wedding—but to ruin a whole life? No. No.

MAKHLE. (*Entering and lighting lamps.*) The boys are on their way. Oh, Mirele, don't be mad at me. I believe you shouldn't dare mix in, in a thing like this. Maybe the match is destined by God?

MIRELE. You go help pack up the clothes.

Makhle off.

God does not destine something crooked. People make themselves miserable, and then they reproach the lord of the world. No, I will not allow any reproaches against him. Aha, here is my wedding party.

YOSELE and DONYE enter, dressed richly in old-fashioned style.

Children, get ready to be on our way, we set out at once.

DONYE. Now who's right, Yosele? I told you we'd go get the bride right away. He sits there all dreamy-eyed, and he shakes. His hands and his feet are jumping around. He wants to see her. He's dying.

YOSELE. (*Embarrassed*) No, no, Donye, stop it. Mama, are you coming with us too?

MIRELE. Little silly, of course I'm coming too. But not to the bride. We are going home, back to Grodno.

Yosele stares at her.

DONYE. What do you mean? What about the wedding?

MIRELE. No more in-laws. No more wedding.

YOSELE. Mama, no wedding at all? Why?

MIRELE. Because I simply do not like the match.

DONYE. If we'd only known beforehand. And he was shaking, the fool.

MIRELE. Go, change your clothes and pack, at once. Well?

Donye off.

Yosele, why such a sad face? I wanted you to have a bride from a family that is poor but good. A girl from a family like that will be a quiet and innocent child. But a daughter-in-law from a household of beggars and spongers? No. I will look for the kind of bride you wanted: educated, and from a big city.

YOSELE. Before, Mama, I wouldn't have cared, but now—now—

MIRELE. What "now"? Send her back her picture with the engagement contract and be done with it. Makhle, give me my jewelry box there, and my pen and ink.

Makhle gives them to her. Yosele takes from his breast pocket a picture and contemplates it a long time.

(*Mirele searches in the box.*) Here, here is the contract.

YOSELE. A whole year I've thought of her as not a stranger, and now here we are strangers again. (*Hands over the picture to her.*) Don't be mad at me, Mama, but it is so hard.

MIRELE. I know, what you like is her pretty face. Don't worry, little silly, it will not be hard for long. What do you say to him, Makhle? He is a real man already. Here, write her a few words on the contract.

He takes the contract and remains sitting at the table with the pen in his hand.

No. You are still a child. A pretty little face is not everything. Well, why aren't you writing?

YOSELE. I don't know what I should write, Mama.

MIRELE. Write: (*Dictates.*) "I am returning the engagement contract.

He stealthily wipes at a tear and writes.

"I forgive you and your parents for doing me an injustice. I hold nothing against you, and I ask you to forgive me as well."

YOSELE. (*With a trembling voice.*) "And . . . I ask you to forgive me as well." (*Falls on both arms on the table and weeps.*) Mama, we don't have to, we don't have to. I'm begging you.

MIRELE. (*Tenderly*) Oh, is that how it is? You silly, you just come over here, come to me.

He goes over to her.

Well, tell me, what are you crying for?

MAKHLE. You'd have to be stronger than iron not to cry. (*Wipes her tears with her apron.*)

YOSELE. I don't know. It pulls at my heart.

MAKHLE. Oh my, oh my. Nothing—just take young children and tear their hearts. For Mirele Efros, that's nothing.

Mirele remains seated deep in thought. Enter Shalmen.

SHALMEN. The horses are harnessed.

MIRELE. Ha? Harnessed already? Shalmen, have them unharnessed. We are staying in Slutsk.

Makhle kisses her hands.

Well, bridegroom, you just come over here.

Wipes his tears with her scarf.

Will you look, wet tears. Ah, you silly boy. (*Kisses both his cheeks.*) My child, I want you to be happy.

A noise. Khane-Devoyre and Nokhemtse enter, depressed.

You see, we don't even have to send for them. They are here already.

KHANE-DEVOYRE. Mother-in-law dear, what do you want from us? Because we're poor people, so it's all right to suck out our blood? Back in Slutsk, guests are already collecting for the betrothal banquet. The bride is crying.

YOSELE. You hear, Mama, she's crying. Oh, she's crying.

NOKHEMTSE. You're supposed to be so smart, you tell us, what do we do now?

MIRELE. What you do? Hm. Shalmen, have them bring the bride and all the guests here to us. The horses are harnessed anyway.

Shalmen off, returns immediately.

Here where I am—that is where the banquet will be, right here. I do not want to step through your Slutsk mud. No, I am not going to Slutsk, Slutsk must come to me. Never mind, your grandfather—may his memory be a blessing—will not be shamed. I brought enough roasted meat and baked meat, liquors and wines. And not only the betrothal: we will put up the wedding canopy too, at the same time. Celebrate everything all together, here, all in one day. We will do the bridegroom a favor and say the short form of the prayer.

YOSELE. (*Covers his face.*) Oh, Mama, what are you saying?

KHANE-DEVOYRE. This is news! Since when does the bridegroom's side make the wedding?

NOKHEMTSE. The wedding now? But the couple haven't fasted.

MIRELE. A very great sin indeed, but I take the guilt on myself. Have them set the tables up here and get everything ready. See that everything is the way it should be.

NOKHEMTSE. Fine. As it is written. Meanwhile, Yosele, take my hearty greeting and my great congratulations. (*Kiss.*)

MIRELE. Yosele, go, tell Donye to dress up all over again. Makhle, come, you get dressed too, you're part of the wedding party. I make you a present of my new silk dress, and get me out my good black mohair.

Mirele and Makhle off.

YOSELE. Did she cry very hard? Oh my. Tell her that she'll never have to cry again, never in her whole life. (*Exits.*)

KHANE-DEVOYRE. Now I don't even know where I am on earth. She mixed me all up.

SHALMEN. Trust me and don't ask any questions. It'll go smoother for you if you do what she wants. You don't get stubborn with Mirele

Efros. Go home. All our wagons are there at your place. And you, Mr. Father-in-law, help me set up the table.

KHANE-DEVOYRE. Dear heavens, if we survive all this craziness, make it at least worth our while. (*Exits.*)

SHALMEN. Well, Father-in-law, roll up your sleeves.

> *Both take off their coats. They carry in tables. Nokhemtse sings a Hasidic tune. Then WAITERS enter and prepare everything: brandy, wine, snacks.*

NOKHEMTSE. A little liquor wouldn't be a bad idea at all just about now. (*Looks at the decanters.*)

SHALMEN. Time enough for liquor. Listen here, if you're not a fool, you can start making a few coins. You'll soon see that it's nice and warm up close against a stewpot. Listen. She will certainly want to make donations to all the charities in Slutsk. You need the sense to keep good receipts. How many charities do you have here in town?

> *They both sit downstage at a little table.*

NOKHEMTSE. Which charities? The Committee for Visiting the Sick, the Torah School Committee, Hospitality to Strangers—

SHALMEN. (*Writing.*) Yes, Hospitality to Strangers, the Widows and Orphans Committee.

NOKHEMTSE. Widows and Orphans? No, not a trace of that one.

SHALMEN. Don't be a fool. (*Writing.*) Widows and Orphans. And?

NOKHEMTSE. Oh. I see. "The wise student understands his teacher's littlest hints." Dowries for Poor Brides, Burying Dead Paupers.

SHALMEN. (*Writing.*) Burying Dead Paupers, and Cemetery Maintenance, and Comforting Israel's Mourners—

NOKHEMTSE. Comforting Israel's Mourners too? Fine. As it is written. In that case, write Committee for Clothing the Naked, Freeing the Captive, Raising Up All Those Who Are Bowed Down, and Healing the Afflicted. (*Laughs.*) Committee for Causing the Blind to See! A toast to life!

> *Both drink.*

Reb Shalmen, if you can stand her, you are a hero.

SHALMEN. Father-in-law, you are—forgive me—an idiot. Hard to find anyone in the world as fine as she is. And a clear head with straight sense: absolutely unbelievable that she's a woman.

Noises off.

Shh, who's this driving up? Father-in-law, crawl into your coat.

They put on their jackets.

Aha, brought the musicians already. Here, this way!

Musicians in.

NOKHEMTSE. First of all, put down the zithers, and I'll make a toast in your honor. I'm one of those people who are "swift to say and swift to do." Do it now, do it later, as it is written.

He drinks a toast with them. Shalmen organizes a place for the musicians in the corner. More noises off.

SHALMEN. Aha, the first travelers have finished traveling. Father-in-law, once business starts moving, it moves!

NOKHEMTSE. May the travelers bring good fortune! As it is written. Aha, the cantor with the singers, welcome.

CANTOR and CHORUS enter. All cry, "Mazl tov, mazl tov."

SHALMEN. Shh. Don't yell like that.

NOKHEMTSE. (*Drinking with the cantor.*) You don't forget for one minute that Mirele Efros is there.

Another group arrives: men, women, girls.

SHALMEN. I should tell her that the guests are here. (*Clears his throat, buttons up his jacket, goes off to Mirele's room.*)

NOKHEMTSE. (*To a guest.*) If she says the canopy right there, that's where it better stand. When you're rich—no evil eye—you can have everything your own way. Fine. As it is written. Have a little. "If I am not for myself, who will be for me?" (*Drinks.*)

SHALMEN. (*Returning.*) The mother-in-law is on her way. Shh, I beg you, behave like decent people.

Musicians get ready.

NOKHEMTSE. (*To musicians.*) A pretty, a proper entrance for our Madame In-Law, Madame Miriam. Hooray.

Music plays. Mirele and Makhle enter.

MIRELE. Congratulations. Congratulations. Good fortune to you all. (*Sits on her chair.*) The bride not here yet? Drink and have something to eat in the meantime. Shalmen, we haven't forgotten anything?

SHALMEN. You will certainly donate something to the local charities? Here, the father-in-law and I made a list. (*Gives her a list.*)

MIRELE. (*Looks, laughs.*) Dowries for Poor Brides, that means doing ourselves a good turn: what they call burying yourself. Burying Paupers: also burying. Cemetery Maintenance: burial again. Widows and Orphans: one more time buried. They are good at burying here in Slutsk. (*Laughs.*) Shalmen, here's my signature on every groshn. (*Shows him her checkbook.*) So what, you stole a little bit there from expenses, from fodder and hay, for example, it does not bother me. You stole from my horses, but from the Slutsk horses, however, I will not let you steal. (*To Guests.*) Drink, please, and enjoy yourselves.

SHALMEN. (*Stammers.*) Forgive me. I . . . I . . .

MIRELE. Don't be embarrassed. All right, we are old friends. I know you. Go drink and be part of the wedding party.

SHALMEN. You should be healthy. What did I want to ask? Yes, the landlord here wants to sell four thousand pounds of flax.

MIRELE. Here on the spot I do not buy, only if he handles delivery to Riga.

General movement.

Look, who is coming? I think this is the bride.

NOKHEMTSE. (*Tipsily*) A nice fine entrance for the bride Madame Sheyndl, daughter of Reb Nokhem.

Musicians play processional. SHEYNDELE enters with her mother. From the other door, Yosele with Donye.

MAKHLE. Oh, I should have such a year, what a beautiful couple this will be. (*She kisses the bride.*)

All cry, "Mazl tov, Mazl tov."

MIRELE. (*Remains seated.*) Well, come over here to me, Sheyndele.

They bring her over.

Sit down next to me. Yosele dear. He is shy, poor thing.

Yosele comes, embarrassed.

DONYE. I'm not a bridegroom, so I don't have to be embarrassed. (*Goes over to the guests and eats cake.*)

MIRELE. Look at him. You see? An innocent, a good boy, with clean thoughts and a good heart.

SHEYNDELE. You'll be my mother. You'll teach me. I'll do whatever you say.

MIRELE. You're no fool; that I can see from your answer. Here, this is for you. (*She kisses Sheyndele. Takes off brooch and earrings and puts them on her. Then she kisses Yosele and Khane-Devoyre.*)

Meanwhile the cantor and chorus sing a merry wedding tune.

YOSELE. (*Quietly to Sheyndele.*) How I wish the fuss would be over fast.

SHEYNDELE. Yosele, we'll survive this too. Isn't it better that there won't be a groom's betrothal banquet first?

YOSELE. I don't know. I . . . Oh, you're not scared at all.

MIRELE. Well, Father-in-law, I will take a drop with you. Shalmen, give me a glass of wine. To life! May God send happiness. Makhle, to life, my dear member of the wedding party. (*Kisses Makhle.*) Well, Sheyndele, to life! Let us hope that we will be good friends. One rule: in my house, no arguments. You see my sons? When they are both old Jews with beards, I'll call them over and say, "Let's have your cheek, Sir, so I can slap it." (*Raps lightly with stick.*) Respect one's elders. But you don't need to be scared. I am not a bad woman.

MAKHLE. "Bad!" If God were only bad like that to his people Israel!

SHALMEN. My children should be so lucky—the jewel of a heart that she has.

MIRELE. Well, I say no delay: lead the children straight to the canopy.

KHANE-DEVOYRE. Yes, girls, now seat the bride so the groom can veil her.

MIRELE. No need for seating. Everyone is seated enough already. There is a custom among us Jews, a very nice custom, to remember one who should have been here and cannot be here because God took him before his time. He was not blessed to have that joy from his children. (*Covers her eyes.*)

NOKHEMTSE. Yes, yes. Cantor, chant "Compassionate God" for the bridegroom's father, Reb Shloyme, may his memory be for a blessing.

MIRELE. (*Sadly*) No, no, not a stranger, not somebody hired. His own child should honor his memory. Yosele, I want it to be you to say, "Compassionate God."

Guests become very serious.

YOSELE. Me? Mama, I don't know if I can.

Positions himself, starts chanting, Mirele occasionally singing along or injecting bits of translations.

"El moley rakhamim, shokhen bam'romim" (Who dwells in the heavens). "Hamtsey m'nukha al kanfey ha-shkhino" (Grant rest in the shelter of your presence).

All weep.

"B'malos k'doyshim oot'horim k'zohar harokeeo maz'heerim" (With the holy ones and the pure ones who shine like the firmament). "Es nishmas avi mori" (For the soul of my dear father).

Yosele cries hard. The cantor ends it, with chorus.

MIRELE. (*Wipes away her tears.*) And now, in a lucky hour, to the canopy. To the canopy. Under the sky, in the rain, that's where I want the canopy to stand. (*Laughs and cries.*) The mother-in-law says rain is a good omen. Probably she learned that from her grandfather.

Musicians strike up a merry tune. People exit in pairs. Shalmen and Nokhemtse embrace, and Khane-Devoyre dances alone. Makhle leads Mirele.

END OF ACT 1

Act 2

Very richly furnished large salon in Mirele Efros's home. A piano, a violin lying on it. Many flowers. By a small table, Mirele's armchair with a little footstool. Light sparkles from lamps and chandeliers. It's dark, and moonlight comes in through the window. Mirele enters. She has aged a great deal. She walks about the room a few times, deep in thought. She is wearing shoes with a light squeak. Then she moves her chair to the window and sits down. All is still. Yosele's flute can be heard playing a melancholy Jewish melody in a minor key. Pause.

MIRELE. A beautiful night, and Yosele's tune sounds so sad. It seems to me that sweet, sad notes suit a quiet thoughtful evening, exactly the way that loud and lively noises suit the radiant beams of the hot sun. Light affects all of our senses. (*Thinks.*)

MAKHLE. (*Opens the door looking for her.*) A good week! You're sitting there all alone in the pitch dark? Oh, what I've lived to see in my old age.

MIRELE. Why didn't you turn on the lamps, Makhle?

MAKHLE. Sheyndele said we don't need the lamps on in the parlor. No one will sit there today. Oh my. Do you remember how lively and happy it used to be around here Saturday evenings after Sabbath? The children used to give a concert, you played chess with somebody, in the kitchen the chopping knives kept on chopping. Every little corner was full of energy for starting the week. Oh, what we've been through these three years since she arrived. You yourself don't see how you've changed.

MIRELE. There you go, you're crying. Upon my word, Makhle, a person might actually think you were an old lady. So. Light all the lamps at once.

MAKHLE. (*Lighting the lamps.*) I don't understand. Why do you give in to her the way you do? Aren't you Mirele Efros?

MIRELE. Makhle, you are a fool. Fight over every silly thing and make a scandal in the house? (*Crossly*) Ah, if Yosele did not love her so much, I would have shown her who Mirele Efros is. I would deal with her, at once. (*Raps her stick.*) But he adores her. A man in love is deaf and blind. He sees nothing and understands nothing. And I will not break his heart and ruin his life. Makhle, they are young children. Better for me to give way.

MAKHLE. She sees that and digs herself in deeper and deeper. She's taking over everything. You know yourself how much misery we suffer from her father and her mother.

MIRELE. (*Laughs.*) You don't like them? Simple, Makhle: when you are governor of Grodno, you can send them into exile. Silly, if smart people from Grodno could become stupid in Slutsk, Slutsk fools can become wise in Grodno. (*Stands up.*) I am going to balance the books for the week. When Shalmen comes, send him in to me. (*Merrily*) Makhle, strength means more than forcing someone else to do what you want. It is also a mighty feat to force yourself to do what someone else wants. For you, better to pay attention to the dust on the table there. (*As she exits, sings traditional end-of-Sabbath song.*) "God of Abraham, of Isaac, and of Jacob. And may your people Israel live to praise you. The holy Sabbath goes away, the week should come with good fortune to blessing and to success. Amen." (*Exits.*)

MAKHLE. (*Wipes table.*) In the beginning, when I was even sillier, I used to be afraid of her. And now, if I could, I would give my soul for her. She is as dear to me as a mother, and I love her like a child. And in fact, as wise and strong and dignified as she is, that's how much of a child she is, too.

Nokhemtse and Khane-Devoyre look in through the door.

NOKHEMTSE. Look how much light. Like back home in synagogue on Yom Kippur. A good week to you, Makhle. Sheyndele isn't here?

KHANE-DEVOYRE. What are you doing standing in the doorway? If lamps are on in the parlor, that's where Sheyndele will be, probably.

Both enter.

I told you we should stay in our Sabbath clothes. Maybe we're supposed to sit out in the hallway with the guests? You see, I was right all along.

MAKHLE. Why skimp on clothes? You spend so much? You in your whole lifetime won't wear out all the clothes that Mirele Efros gives you from her own wardrobe. And you, Reb Nokhemtse, Yosele's coats fit you perfectly.

KHANE-DEVOYRE. Some bargain. When I was a girl living with my grandfather—may he enjoy paradise—I had a better wardrobe than your duchess. You remember, Nokhemtse, when I was a bride, I had a silk tunic, fur-trimmed, with yellow flowers?

NOKHEMTSE. As it is written. Ay, Makhle, a glass of tea, I'm dying—it shouldn't happen to you. Saturday evening, after the Sabbath stew, I always get heartburn.

MAKHLE. (*Aside.*) Now that the daughter's an aristocrat, plain Sabbath stew gives the father heartburn. (*Sharply*) Reb Nokhemtse, we don't drink tea in here. Go into the dining room, there's a samovar on the table. You know perfectly well that in this house, whoever wants can drink tea and have something to eat. So long as this is the household of Mirele Efros.

NOKHEMTSE. In the dining room, you say? Whatever you say. As it is written.

Exits. In doorway meets Shalmen, who carries account books.

Ah, my dear, dear Reb Shalmen, a good week.

SHALMEN. A good week, my dear, dear Reb Nokhemtse. A good week, Makhle. Is Mirele home? Have to do the accounts for the week.

KHANE-DEVOYRE. We know how you do the accounts, Reb Shalmen. Sure, what does she understand, the senile stuck-up old blowhard?

MAKHLE. (*Aside.*) You should blow up—lord of the world.

SHALMEN. Madame Khane-Devoyre, she blows away the dirt so it won't fall on her. What has the world come to when one asks what Mirele Efros understands? If only all old ladies understood as much as she does, it would be an honor to be an old lady. Even your husband wouldn't be embarrassed that they call him Khane-Devoyre's Reb Nokhemtse. (*Clears his throat, buttons up his coat, and goes in to Mirele.*)

KHANE-DEVOYRE. The duchess's adjutant! An ulcer in his throat—lord of the world—for every groshn he's stolen from our children.

NOKHEMTSE. As it is written. You, my missus, had better be quiet. Reb Mendele's grandchild ought to know that the sages say, "Kalbo b'lo matyo sheva shonim lo novo-akh" (A dog in a strange city waits seven years to bark) and you haven't been in Grodno long enough to talk. Shh. Here comes Sheyndele, and she can read you the sorrows of Jerusalem.

Sheyndele enters.

A good week to you, Sheyndele.

SHEYNDELE. (*Doesn't answer.*) Look how bright. Showing all our many guests the way, maybe? (*Goes to window.*)

MAKHLE. Mirele ordered all the lamps on.

SHEYNDELE. Oh really? Very nice. Just look, the window open at night. Whose smart idea was that?

MAKHLE. The lady of the house opened the window. It's a warm night. It wouldn't do anybody any harm, God forbid. (*Closes the window.*)

SHEYNDELE. (*Moves the armchair angrily.*) No other place for the chair, it's got to be here. Sure, it goes perfectly in the parlor, dresses it right up.

NOKHEMTSE. It's fine. As it is written. Why fight with her?

SHEYNDELE. Who's fighting? Makhle, I've told you more than once, this old rag does not belong in the parlor. Haul the armchair into the dining room where it won't bother anybody.

MAKHLE. What are you saying, God be with you? Where will our Mirele sit? You know she's used to . . .

SHEYNDELE. Where do other people sit? It won't kill her to get used to sitting like the rest of the world. Get it out of here.

Makhle can't lift the chair by herself.

Papa, if you don't mind, would you help her drag out Mother-in-law's bathtub.

NOKHEMTSE. Honored. As it is written.

MAKHLE. (*Sighs.*) Lived to old age, lived too many years.

They carry out the armchair together.

SHEYNDELE. (*Sits.*) You've got to be stronger than iron to live with her under one roof. Mama, do me a favor, bring me—there's that little stool over there.

Khane-Devoyre puts the little stool under her feet. We hear Yosele's flute.

KHANE-DEVOYRE. Who says you have to be a fool and suffer because of her? Who is obligated to put up with all her craziness? A general! Countess Pototsky! Sheyndele, her lieutenant Shalmen is in there with an account book like hers. He steals from you and robs you. Why should he get away with it? It's a bitter sin. Your husband, no offense, is a dope. He sits by himself and toots, and Shalmen-the-thief is going to toot you all. You mark my words.

SHEYNDELE. I hate that Shalmen. I can't stand to look at him. Listen, this can't go on forever, I'll take it just so long. Shh, stop, who's coming?

Donye enters, dressed in modern, fashionable style, rather than in a kaftan like a traditional Jew.

Nice. That's your new outfit? It's becoming.

KHANE-DEVOYRE. Wear it in good health.

DONYE. A good week. Nice, right? But what will Mama say when she gets her first look at me? I'll tell you the truth, I'm a little bit shaking in my boots.

SHEYNDELE. Just look how scared. So it was really true what she said: she'll be giving you spankings when you're an old Jew with a beard.

DONYE. We'll see about that.

KHANE-DEVOYRE. What's the big fuss? When a person is rich—no evil eye—he can permit himself whatever he wants. For a pauper it isn't suitable to cram himself into narrow trousers, and other high style. But if God helps you—Look, there's my Sheyndele, a married woman—goes around with her hair uncovered and does other things. And I don't mix in.

SHEYNDELE. You see? Also a mama, heart and soul, and Reb Mendele's grandchild into the bargain, and nevertheless she does me a favor and doesn't mix in. Trust me, Donye, let it go. Sit down. Let her come see. She's in there with the prime minister, Reb Shalmen. He looks like a fool, Reb Shalmen, but he leads you all by the nose.

DONYE. The man's been in the house for thirty years, runs all the business.

SHEYNDELE. At your age, grown-up sons don't dare to interfere? The whole fortune in a stranger's hands. What are you, little children?

KHANE-DEVOYRE. God shouldn't punish me for saying so, but all Grodno holds you up to ridicule and to scorn. Shalmen is stuffed with money, he should only vomit it up—Lord of the world.

SHEYNDELE. Here comes the cursing already. Let's talk seriously. How long will the two of you let yourselves be led around on a leash? My Yosele is weak. Let him play his flute, and he's satisfied. But you—

KHANE-DEVOYRE. It's a sin, a great sin. My grandfather Reb Mendele was, after all, a somebody. Nevertheless, as soon as his children were just barely grown up, each of them already had a mind of his own. A person doesn't get embarrassed, a person simply goes up to her and says—

Mirele and Shalmen enter.

Mother-in-law dear, a good week to you.

MIRELE. A good week. Donye, what is this? Well, come here.

Donye goes to her.

So, off with the Jew and on with the modern man. You know, Shalmen, in our house we get tailored like aristocrats. I don't mind. If it suits you, it is all right with me. But you might have asked first.

DONYE. Ask about every silly little thing? A person has to have some independent mind of his own, after all.

SHALMEN. (*Apart.*) Since when does buying a suit require a mind? (*Aloud.*) A good night, Mirele, and a good week. (*Starts out.*)

MIRELE. Wait, Shalmen, tonight we will play a game of chess.

SHALMEN. With my head? After three moves you're already taking my queen. Some player I am.

Donye sits down beside Sheyndele.

MIRELE. Never mind, stay. Sit down, Shalmen. (*Looks for her armchair.*) Where is my chair? Ha? What is this? Please. Makhle! Makhle!

Makhle runs in.

Where is my chair?

MAKHLE. Sheyndele had it carried into the dining room.

MIRELE. Carry it back.

Makhle exits.

I like things to stay where I put them. (*Bangs lightly with stick.*) That, Shalmen, is precisely the way they want to escort us out to the dining room, and from there it is not far to the kitchen.

Makhle drags the armchair back as far as the door. Shalmen helps her put it next to the little table.

SHALMEN. If you're in the kitchen, the kitchen will be the parlor. Only my enemies shouldn't live to see that. And I myself shouldn't live to see it.

SHEYNDELE. I didn't mean us to fight over such a silly thing: where a chair should stand.

MIRELE. Fight? So. "Fight." "Fight."

Shalmen sits down and lays out the chess pieces while she walks about thoughtfully.

SHEYNDELE. Makhle, go bring in—on my table there's a new deck of cards. And tell Yosele I want him. Donye, we'll play a hand.

Donye places a little table near her chair. Makhle exits.

KHANE-DEVOYRE. Fight? Who needs to fight? Isn't peace in a house better than fighting? What does the peasant say? The opposite: "Khata pokrishka": my roof is thatched.

Mirele isn't listening but walks around deep in thought. Makhle brings in the cards.

SHALMEN. (*Quietly*) Yes. Reb Mendele's granddaughter has gotten her own roof nicely thatched, all right.

YOSELE. (*Entering cheerfully, dressed as before, with a little beard.*) Mama dear, a good week. A good week, Reb Shalmen, a good week. (*Puts his flute down on the piano.*) Makhle, I wished you a good week already, I think. Just look, Mama, Donye is a modern man of the world, no less. Did you call me, Sheyndele?

SHEYNDELE. Yes, we want a hand. (*Takes up the cards.*)

MIRELE. Cards, now? I don't like card-playing in my house.

SHEYNDELE. If you like chess, you play chess, and if you like cards, you play cards. Yosele, sit here next to me so Donye can't look at my hand.

Yosele looks around.

What are you looking for? Sit down.

Yosele sits down. Sheyndele deals cards and puts down silver coins.

MIRELE. Well, Shalmen, we are lucky we are still allowed to play chess. (*Sits.*) Makhle!

Sheyndele has her feet up on Mirele's footstool. Mirele looks around for it.

MAKHLE. (*Runs over to Sheyndele, says quietly.*) Sheyndele, don't get mad, her footstool.

SHEYNDELE. (*Ignores her.*) Donye, your two jacks don't scare me a bit, not one bit.

KHANE-DEVOYRE. (*Quietly*) Sheyndele, give her the footstool—May she choke!

SHEYNDELE. (*Ignores her.*) I'm in three coins for three cards.

MIRELE. Makhle, come here. Take the keys. Upstairs in my bureau you will find the jewelry box with the diamonds. Bring it here.

Makhle exits.

Shalmen, begin.

They play. Her hands are shaking badly.

SHEYNDELE. (*To her mother.*) What does she need her diamonds for all of a sudden? (*Loudly*) Yosele, you're staring at the cards like a hen stares at the butcher. If you're playing, play.

YOSELE. Oh, Sheyndele, I . . . I . . . What did I want to say? Yes, how much have I lost?

Makhle brings in the box.

MIRELE. Put it down under my feet.

MAKHLE. Should I take out the jewelry?

MIRELE. No, just the way it is, with the jewels, the diamonds, the pearls, put it under my feet. I am Miriam Efros.

Makhle puts the box under her feet.

Shalmen, we're playing . . . One . . .

Plays. Makhle stations herself behind her armchair.

KHANE-DEVOYRE. Jewelry under the feet? Oh, a plague—I'm having a stroke—

SHEYNDELE. There, you see: fine and strong and crazy. (*Loudly*) Yosele, say something. Cat got your tongue?

YOSELE. Sheyndele, I can't play. I know it upsets Mama. Let's be nice and play the Mozart piece she likes instead. We used to play for her every Saturday night, and now we're in the house like enemies, God forbid. I'm begging you, Sheyndele, please. Donye, come on, the modern man will enjoy himself.

SHEYNDELE. Sure, play a little concert, that's all I have to do.

YOSELE. Trust me, darling, if you're nice with Mama, she'll do anything for you. You'll see. I'll talk to her today about your father, Sheyndele.

(*Tickles her with a finger.*) Mr. Modern Man, don't make us beg you. (*Pushes Donye to the piano.*) Wifie dear, don't be naughty. (*Leads Sheyndele by the hand.*) Mama dear, would you like us to play your favorite kind of concert?

MIRELE. I don't know other people's tastes, but I think that playing Mozart is much nicer than playing cards. Shalmen, you've never played better.

SHALMEN. You don't want to admit that you've never played worse. Where are the inspirations, the famous moves? No, your mind is not on chess, I can tell.

MAKHLE. (*Turns her back and wipes a tear with her apron.*) You see, Reb Shalmen, how her hands are shaking. Oh my, oh my.

Yosele, Sheyndele, Donye play classical music.

KHANE-DEVOYRE. Singing something Jewish, that I can understand. But when they start this—what do you call it? Motzi-Matza piece? Might as well go see what's doing with my old man.

Exits. They play Mozart trio. Mirele listens, propping her head on her hand.

MIRELE. Don't you sometimes feel, Shalmen, that music is precisely like a balm, like an ointment, for wounds in the heart.

SHALMEN. Forgive me. I understand very little of such things. Checkmate!

Takes her chess piece. Enter Khane-Devoyre and Nokhemtse.

NOKHEMTSE. A good week, Madame Mother-in-law. Sheyndele, I had cream in my tea, and some strange kind of cookie. Sell the shirt off your back: whatever it takes—it's worth it to be rich. Yosele, I'll bet you've got a good cigarette.

YOSELE. (*Opens his cigarette case.*) Yes, Father-in-law, first class. Sobranie tobacco.

Donye takes cigarette too, plays cards with Sheyndele.

NOKHEMTSE. What did you say? Sour Brandy tobacco? Funny names the gentiles go in for. (*Smokes, throws the ashes on the floor.*)

MIRELE. Reb Nokhemtse, there is an ashtray on every table. There is no need to throw dirt around.

KHANE-DEVOYRE. Nokhemtse, really, don't be a pig.

NOKHEMTSE. Fine. As it is written.

SHEYNDELE. Don't you worry, Papa, it's not such a terrible tragedy. There's somebody to clean it up, isn't there? Makhle, if you don't mind.

Makhle takes the whiskbroom and cleans up.

YOSELE. Mama dear, you're getting mad at my father-in-law, and here I was just about to ask you to do him a favor. He sits around in Grodno with nothing to do. Why shouldn't he have a job? I don't mean take Reb Shalmen's place, God forbid.

DONYE. Look how he looks out for Reb Shalmen. Our servant, and—

MIRELE. Silence! Shalmen is an elderly man. Show respect.

DONYE. He certainly is an elderly man, but if he's robbing us—the whole town knows it—then it's high time—

Mirele bangs her stick. Donye falls silent. Shalmen stands.

SHALMEN. I've been in this household over thirty years and have never been treated with such disrespect. Your father, may he rest in peace, did not insult me. Mirele Efros never used such words to me. Donye, I carried you and Yosele in my arms when you were small children, and I have lived to old age to hear you call me a thief.

YOSELE. Oh, no, Reb Shalmen, may God punish me if I meant to insult you, God forbid. Donye, you should be ashamed. You used to be so different. It's not decent. Who taught you to act like this?

MAKHLE. (*Looking at Sheyndele.*) He has a good rebbe.

SHALMEN. I don't deny what I take, God forbid. Mirele knows every kopek. Yes, sometimes there's a chance to earn something on the side, but steal from you, God forbid? I don't take what belongs to anybody. I don't have to serve here. I'm an old man and thank God my old age is provided for, from before Mirele, and then with Mirele as well. I've held on here for only one reason: because I was sorry to leave

Mirele here alone. She is used to me. Not everybody understands that she—Mirele, I'm going. Good night and be well.

MIRELE. Go in good health, Shalmen.

Shalmen off.

SHEYNDELE. A saintly thief.

MIRELE. "A thief"—and which of you is not a thief? Nokhemtse, in his position—he wouldn't steal? He would not know how to run a business, but to steal—that he could figure out. Shalmen took what I permitted him to take. A person who serves the Efroses, in their household, a full thirty years—by the time he is old, he ought to be rich. That is what I think. And when a good opportunity appears, I tell him to put in a share of the capital, and often he earns a nice few hundred. Why not? He is an honorable man, an industrious worker, our truest friend, and as long as I live, he runs all our business. (*Pounds her stick.*) He and nobody else.

SHEYNDELE. Yes, he and you. And when will your sons have something to say? Shouldn't they get started in the business? What do you think—a person lives forever?

MIRELE. Don't worry. I won't live forever.

MAKHLE. Oh my, oh my, oh my.

SHEYNDELE. What is Makhle doing here? Why aren't you in the kitchen?

MIRELE. She will be in the kitchen when I tell her to be there.

KHANE-DEVOYRE. The Countess Pototsky with her adjutant.

NOKHEMTSE. Madame In-law, the sages say: "Lo kol odom" (Not every man merits two tables). And you—

SHEYNDELE. Mama, if you don't mind, go on into the house. Papa, you too. (*Opens the door.*)

NOKHEMTSE. As the sages say: "It is written."

Nokhemtse and Khane-Devoyre off.

SHEYNDELE. Mother-in-law, now that we've finally started to talk, I want you to know what all of us in this household really feel. You're getting old. It's time for you to take a rest. And besides, frankly, you hold the entire estate in your two hands, and we have no security in life. You could take it into your head some time, on a whim, if someone flatters you a little, or shows you a pretty dimple, you could throw the money away into the mud. Sometimes already—you know it yourself, the things you do—I don't know: a box of jewels under your feet? Five hundred rubles to support Talmud scholars? Well, fine, whatever you say, but you must admit, hasn't the time come for your children to begin to breathe freely?

MIRELE. No, the time has not come.

DONYE. Don't think, Mama, that you can lead us around on a leash forever.

YOSELE. This is awful, stop it, please. Mama, don't think we mean to upset you, God forbid. If Sheyndele would just listen to me—

SHEYNDELE. If I listened to you, we'd be nose to nose with the facts soon enough. Mother-in-law, as I see it, you don't intend to let go of the reins. Run things the way you want to, but I'm not staying here. Divide up the estate and give us our share.

YOSELE. Yes, Mama, what can we do? It will be very hard to leave you, God knows that is true. But what can I do if Sheyndele just can't live with you in peace, and I can't live without her?

MIRELE. Divide up? No. The greatest unhappiness for human beings is that everyone wants to divide up, each with his own share. People must live together. Together.

SHEYNDELE. It's high time for me to run my own household. Bad enough to have a Khane-Devoyre over my head before the wedding. I don't want a new Khane-Devoyre over me. I want to be free. A poor laborer's wife is luckier than I am. She does what she pleases in her own home and nobody gives her an opinion. Why should I be cheated? No. Better just be nice about it and give Yosele the inheritance that his father left him. His father left him a fortune. It doesn't belong to you.

DONYE. Yes. Yes. It's time, high time, to know how much father left us. No one knows what's in the accounts.

YOSELE. Sheyndele, I'm begging you, don't be like that. Come on, enough for today. We'll talk more some other time. Sheyndele, are you coming?

MIRELE. No, Yosele, it is not enough. She is right. You are no longer little children, and it is time you should know. Eighteen years ago your father died. You were still little tiny children. (*Falls silent.*)

MAKHLE. Mirele, I'd better leave. (*Exits, weeping.*)

MIRELE. I was not old then, and many fine and rich people sent matchmakers. I did not even listen. I thought a widow should not marry. If she was happy, she must understand that one does not find happiness a second time. If she was unhappy, why should she be so foolish as to gamble with her freedom and risk winning sorrow? Especially when there are little children! I had two children, and I determined that I would live only for their sakes, to rejoice in their joys and to share in their happiness. I—but enough, I know that your mother interests you very little. What you want to know is how much your father left you. I will show you the books. No one in the world, except for Shalmen, knows the secret: your father died from sorrow and shame, because he had to go bankrupt.

ALL. Bankrupt!

MIRELE. Yes! Sixty thousand rubles: that is the debt he owed when he died. That is your inheritance. I did not sleep days and nights. I set myself to saving his name. I did everything so the house of Shlomo Efros would continue as it had before. I showed the men how stupid they are when they believe that a woman is a weak creature, who can only be a servant or a wife. All his creditors I paid, a ruble on a ruble, and that is why my credit is unlimited now. I brought you up as was proper for Efros's children, with tutors, with music teachers, with every luxury. What I suffered, nobody knew; how many times my heart poured blood, nobody noticed. You lacked for nothing. Certainly, now we have a great fortune. But all of it comes from me. Yosele, what your father left you, you may take it and go, with your dear wife. You too, Daniel, you can have your share. You are right, the time has come for you to live according to your own judgment.

SHEYNDELE. So that's how it is? In other words, I married a pauper, who can be thrown out on the streets tomorrow, with his wife and child, without a penny. Why didn't you tell me this before? You should be ashamed.

YOSELE. Sheyndele, I beg you, don't be so harsh. Mama dear, I didn't know there was no estate. But it's just what I said: I want to divide up for Sheyndele's sake, to share with Sheyndele.

SHEYNDELE. Meanwhile he's still dividing up! I ask you. Disgusting! You cheat! For shame, you old liar.

YOSELE. (*Beside himself.*) What did you say? (*Pulls at her hand.*) I will destroy you. Who do you think you're talking to? Shut up. If you want to get out of here alive, shut up, I tell you.

SHEYNDELE. (*Weeps.*) Yes, now I'll be quiet. I'll be quiet now. Oh lord, oh lord, I'm ruined.

MIRELE. Leave me.

Raps with her stick. All go to the door.

Ah. I wanted to say one more word. Now your heads are hanging, hah? It wasn't for my own sake that I accumulated the money, and I don't need it. You want to be the bosses? You feel mistreated? Fine, I won't ruin your lives. My happiness is when you feel happy. And my satisfaction is when you feel satisfied. Tomorrow morning early, I will hand you over all the books, all the documents, and everything that is in the safe. Now you can sleep in peace. Good night.

All leave. She walks around in thought, takes a prayer book, reads extracts of Psalms, sighing and chanting quietly to a traditional sad tune.

"Lam'natseyakh al shoyshanim l'dovid."

Makhle enters quietly and remains in the doorway.

"Hoshee-eynee elokim kee vaw-oo mayim ad nofesh" (Save me, Lord, for the waters rise about me). "Tovasee beeveyn metsoole v'eyn mawmawd. Vawsee b'm-amakey mayim, v'shiboles shtofawsnee" (I sink in deep mire, where there is no foothold . . . in deep waters . . . and the flood sweeps over me). (*Lays her head down onto the prayer book and weeps bitterly.*)

Makhle wipes her tears with her apron.

END OF ACT 2

Act 3

Same parlor. Furniture has been moved. All is in great disorder. Mirele's armchair and little stool stand in a corner near the door. Nokhemtse enters in a white linen duster carrying a big travel bag, which he throws on the piano. He shakes dust off himself.

NOKHEMTSE. Foo. So, as it is written, we went and we came. (*To tune of chanting from Torah.*) And lo they journeyed from Slutsk and they encamped in Slonim. I'm still dizzy in the head. We sucked up all the liquor in Slonim. In Slonim, the Hasids are exactly the same kind of Hasids as all the other Hasids in the world. As it is written. (*Shakes off dust.*) Once, if our Madame Mother-in-law saw—God forbid—where I've been dusting off dust, I'd have been dusted till the dust flew. And today, it's dust here, dust there. As it is written. Ah, my head is turning like a mill wheel. (*Sits in Mirele's armchair with the stool under his feet.*) So Khane-Devoyre's Reb Nokhemtse has become a businessman. I go bouncing from tribe to tribe. I've done Volkavitshki business, Prozshene business, Sokalke business, and now I'm coming from Slonim. It used to be Shalmen that was the manager. Now it's me. Well, that's fine, as it is written. I managed all right. Never mind who, what, why—why not take a little nap? It's cool and quiet and peaceful here. (*Gradually falling asleep.*) And they journeyed from Mashmine and they encamped in Prozshnane. And they journeyed from Smorgan and they encamped in Babroisk. And they journeyed from Babroisk and they encamped in Slonim. And they journeyed from Slonim and they encamped . . .

He remains quiet. Mirele enters from her room. She has aged greatly. Poorly dressed. She is leaning on her stick, walks several times slowly around the room. When she approaches her armchair, she notices the sleeper.

MIRELE. My place is taken. That is how it goes in the world: as soon as one person stands up from his place on the bench, someone else sits down in it. He who grabs, can sit. Grabbing is how it works. When something good takes your place, that you can bear. But when your place is taken by a jewel like this one here, for example, and the world says "fine" and "it is written"?—feh, that is very painful.

(*Walks about.*) He sleeps soundly, and I go nights without sleep. I cannot find a place for myself because I have nothing to do. It seems to me, somebody with nothing to do should not exist in the world.

Goes to the door and meets Makhle, who is wearing a shawl on her head and carrying a little bundle of things in her hand.

Makhle, what is this? Where are you off to?

MAKHLE. My dearest boss, Mirele, my mother! I've come to say: Be well. (*Kisses her hand.*) I can't stay here anymore. Sheyndele is pushing me out. It breaks my heart to leave you now.

MIRELE. What? You are leaving too? Who will be left for me here, Makhle? What are you saying, God be with you?

MAKHLE. What can I do? For a long time already she has wanted me out. But today she said to me: "Out of my house this minute. Don't leave a trace. You're an abandoned woman," she said, "so go look for your husband. I have enough servants." Oh, I'm ready to put up with everything here, just to stay with you, but if you're fired, you have to go. It's bitter for me. Who will take care of you when I'm not here? (*Weeps.*)

MIRELE. Don't talk foolishness. Staying here without you will be very hard for me. Is Yosele home? Send Yosele straight to me. I know that good is normally repaid with bad, but surely I didn't do them all that much good, after all. (*Bangs angrily with stick.*) Feh. What an ugly, low, vile little world it is.

MAKHLE. Lived like a favorite child all these years, and now in her old age— (*Weeps aloud.*)

MIRELE. (*With a little smile.*) Shh, silly, don't cry. You might—God forbid—wake the father-in-law. (*Exits.*)

MAKHLE. Oh, an evil has struck me. That a Jew lets himself act like this. Ever hear of such a thing? (*Drags Nokhemtse out of the chair and with her shawl wipes the place where he was sitting.*)

That's how they live at his grandmother's in Slutsk. (*Exits.*)

NOKHEMTSE. (*Sits down elsewhere.*) And there you have it. And they journeyed from Ramses and they encamped in Sukkes. And they journeyed from Mashmine and they encamped in Prozshnane. And they journeyed from Slonim and they encamped . . . Aha. Here comes my wife's grandfather's grandchild.

Khane-Devoyre enters from street.

The sages say, "Eesha kley zayne ale-ha" (A woman comes with her own weapons).

KHANE-DEVOYRE. There, Makhle was right, here he is, sure enough. Weapons, ha? A violent death on you and your weapons. You came from Slonim, why didn't you stop at home first?

NOKHEMTSE. Idiot. As it is written . . .

KHANE-DEVOYRE. You come here and snore, and they stare at you. Their eyes crawl out of their heads.

NOKHEMTSE. Fine. As it is written. Fool, because of you, do you understand me, the Slonim Hasids treated me almost like a rabbi's grandchild. We carried on. A banquet, as at the right hand of the king, and we did drink royally.

KHANE-DEVOYRE. Banquets is what you're good for. If Shalmen had gone on that trip, he'd have brought us home a nice bone to lick. You lick up the schnapps. I wish you were licked up, dear God in heaven.

NOKHEMTSE. So go on and lick me up. As it is written.

KHANE-DEVOYRE. You should be burned, you and your as-it-is-written together. Shh. Pull open your drunken eyes. Yosele's coming.

Yosele and Makhle enter. He is dressed half-European, that is, worldly, not in a caftan like a traditional Jew

Good day, Yosele.

YOSELE. Good day. Whom do I see? The father-in-law has been found. We didn't know what to think. I just telegraphed to Slonim, in fact. Makhle, would you mind calling in Sheyndele? Tell her that the lost item has been recovered.

Makhle off.

Oh wait, forgive me, one minute, Mama wanted to see me. Yes, yes, yes, you played a nice wedding feast there in Slonim. They say a mother-in-law is a misery. Father-in-law, I'm afraid you're worse than a mother-in-law. (*Off to Mirele.*)

NOKHEMTSE. As it is written.

KHANE-DEVOYRE. What's this new misery? Miseries should darken your eyes, you drunk. Let's see what you have left from your travels. Let me see. (*Searches in his pockets.*)

NOKHEMTSE. (*Laughs.*) Stop, Khane-Devoyre, it tickles.

KHANE-DEVOYRE. The angel of death should do the tickling, God in heaven.

YOSELE. (*Reappearing in doorway.*) Be calm, Mama, and don't eat your heart out over nothing. I assure you—

> *Sheyndele, Donye, and Makhle enter from the other door. Donye is dressed in a fashionable European, that is, assimilated style.*

Here's Makhle. What do you mean you're going away? Don't you know that Mama can't manage without you? Who in the world knows all her little ways and everything she needs the way you do?

SHEYNDELE. Don't worry, we can manage without her. Papa, are you drunk again already? Congratulations.

NOKHEMTSE. And congratulations to you, Sheyndele.

YOSELE. All right, never mind. Makhle, listen to me. You're staying here.

SHEYNDELE. She is not staying here. Don't worry. The old princess will manage without her old adjutant. But what do you need to bother with such foolishness? Have you talked to Papa yet? That's more important. What's going on with that?

YOSELE. I don't consider this a foolishness. Sheyndele, I swear by our only child that Makhle is not leaving here. Makhle, go to my mother.

SHEYNDELE. Oh, is that right? Well, well then, we'll let it go for now. (*Leads him to one side and talks to him angrily.*)

MAKHLE. I've lived to be something they let go for now. (*Off to Mirele.*)

DONYE. Well, Mr. Jew, speak up, spit it out. You acted like a boss in Slonim, right? A fine businessman, everyone can see that.

NOKHEMTSE. As it is written. (*Takes out of his pocket a flat silver tobacco case and rolls a cigarette.*)

YOSELE. You're wrong, Father-in-law, it is not written at all. I received a telegram that the entire shipment of flax that you delivered from Slonim is rotting and wet. They're afraid it might catch fire in the wagons.

KHANE-DEVOYRE. Your bones should catch fire, father in heaven.

NOKHEMTSE. As it is written.

SHEYNDELE. What do you say, Mama? We're about to lose eight thousand rubles. If you had a sober head, you'd realize. Eight thousand rubles, dear lord in heaven.

KHANE-DEVOYRE. Your eyes crawled out of your head; you couldn't see what kind of merchandise they were selling you?

NOKHEMTSE. I thought they made me a banquet in honor of your grandfather, but looks like they did it so I wouldn't see the merchandise. Feh. Can it be? That's a sin.

YOSELE. It can be. It is a sin. And all we can do about it is yell, "God of Ages." Upon my word, it can drive you crazy. Look, Sheyndele, my silver tobacco case. I've been looking for it.

NOKHEMTSE. As it is written. (*Hands it over.*)

SHEYNDELE. Mama, what in the world do you say to him? We'll be paupers, for sure. He can ruin us all.

KHANE-DEVOYRE. (*Screams.*) What is the matter with you? You should be eaten up and spit out, you should be dropped in a pit, a riot should destroy you—

SHEYNDELE. Wasn't it worth it to be a little careful, you old drunk?

Both women scream. Yosele walks about agitated. Donye looks in the mirror. Makhle enters.

MAKHLE. Don't be mad. Mirele asks would you please not yell like that.

SHEYNDELE. Let her stick cotton in her ears. (*To Nokhemtse*) Thief, murderer, what have you done? How can we stand this?

MAKHLE. What goes on in this house! A new tragedy every minute. (*Exits.*)

YOSELE. Enough. Father-in-law, where are the accounts, and the cargo transport receipts from the railroad?

NOKHEMTSE. I must have written the accounts down somewhere or other. But the lod—the led—what do they call it?—the bill of lading—that I don't have. I was plain and simple scared to go over to the official there in the station. First of all, you understand me, I don't have a pass and he is after all such a lord, with gold buttons. And second of all, all I can say in Russian is, "No pipe, no tobacco."

DONYE. There's someone to depend on.

SHEYNDELE. How can you dare to trust such an imbecile with business?

KHANE-DEVOYRE. Peasant-brain, what use are you in the world?

SHEYNDELE. (*Looks at Donye.*) On one side thieves, on the other side robbers. It's too much, I can't stand it. (*Screams.*) I can't stand it.

MAKHLE. (*In doorway.*) Oh dear lord, you're making her sick with your screaming.

SHEYNDELE. How do you like the nerve? Not allowed to talk the way you want to in your own house. They can drive you crazy.

MAKHLE. In her house screaming is called talking. And it is her house. (*Exits.*)

SHEYNDELE. Get him out of here. I can't look at him. One robbed us in Riga. (*Looks at Donye.*) The other made us paupers in Slonim. Business is moving right along, thank you very much.

KHANE-DEVOYRE. Come on, you drunk. Come on, you idiot. With your head in the ground, that's how you should come.

NOKHEMTSE. As it is written.

Khane-Devoyre drags him out.

DONYE. If we don't get Shalmen back, we'll be done for, and fast.

YOSELE. Nowadays, Shalmen is in business for himself. He won't come back. He was willing to serve for Mirele Efros, but not for Daniel Efros.

DONYE. And not for Mr. Yosef Efros either. Reb Yosef Efros has a thief and a drunk for a father-in-law.

SHEYNDELE. We don't know yet who's the thief here. Why not explain where your accounts are, instead? You've been back two weeks from Riga and no reckoning yet.

YOSELE. Brother dear, you're making a mistake. It's not your money and not my money, it's our money. You got a great sum in Riga. We have to know how much you laid out and how much is left.

DONYE. I didn't go to Riga to fast and remember Jerusalem. I lived there in the style appropriate to Daniel Efros.

SHEYNDELE. I've been telling you all along, Yosele, watch out, he's making paupers out of us. He steals and he robs.

DONYE. You, My Lady Slutsk, are better off keeping your mouth shut.

YOSELE. Shh. Better let's see where we stand without yelling. I'm not going to bother asking you how much is gone. Just hand over what's left. You had yourself a good time—why else be modern, after all? I just don't understand how a person can spend thousands and there's no merchandise and no money.

SHEYNDELE. Nice merchandise he deals in, the crook.

DONYE. It's not your father's money.

YOSELE. It's our mother's money.

DONYE. Put it all down on my account. There's nothing left.

SHEYNDELE. He's lying. He's still got money. Thief. Crook. Hand over the money. Hand it over. Better give in and just hand it over nicely.

DONYE. How do you like her? A ragpicker, a fishwife from Slutsk—she demands an accounting.

YOSELE. Quiet. Enough now. God help me, I can't stand this. I can't bear this. (*Hits his own head with both hands.*)

SHEYNDELE. Right, go and cry like an old lady. Why don't you speak up? I saw for myself his wallet is stuffed with hundreds. Such a barefaced hoodlum. Such a gangster. I'm not letting him out of here. He's not getting away with the money. (*Struggles with him and grabs the wallet full of money out of his breast pocket.*) See? Here's the money. Our money. Our blood.

DONYE. Shameless. Tramp. Drag it out of my pockets? Witch!

Tries to take it back. Both are screaming. Mirele appears.

YOSELE. Let go of her, Donye. Stop it. You know she's right. (*Pushes him back.*)

DONYE. Get away from me, you idiot. Only you could think such a wild animal is right.

YOSELE. (*Shoves him.*) I'm telling you, stop it. I'm telling you stop it. Oh, you animal. You don't want to listen? (*Throws him to the ground and falls on him.*) I'll show you how to be a gangster and a loudmouth.

Struggle.

SHEYNDELE. A crook. A thief. Give it to him, Yosele, so he never forgets.

MIRELE. (*Raps hard with stick. Silence. Yosele and Donye stand up.*) So, you are running the business for yourselves according to your own judgment. Very nice, very nice.

YOSELE. Oh, it's awful, Mama, you're here? Don't be angry at me. I don't know. They're driving me out of my mind.

SHEYNDELE. Be proud of your darling. He's Mirele Efros's son too.

MIRELE. Yes, I am proud of you, very proud, very, very proud. Donye, I do not want to mix into your account books, but there, it seems to me, you have become a little too modern. What is this: take money without accounting for it?

DONYE. None of your business. You go sit over there by yourself and read your old ladies' prayer book. Nobody's asking you.

SHEYNDELE. Well, you're the great wise one, you're Mirele Efros after all, why don't you teach him any respect?

MIRELE. Whom can I teach now? No, he is right. It is not my business. Now I have to be silent like the wall, mute like a stone. A rider who cannot stay on the horse must lie under the horse. Yes. And the horse can kick him, stamp on him, strike him with his hooves. (*Reflects.*)

Donye suddenly grabs the wallet from Sheyndele's hands.

Give Yosele the money. (*Bangs the stick angrily.*) Give the money to Yosele, go on.

Donye gives Yosele the wallet.

How easy it is to destroy what took so much effort to build. How quickly one can ruin what was accomplished with so much difficulty and tended for so many years.

SHEYNDELE. The crook practically tore off my brooch. (*Settles the brooch.*)

MIRELE. (*Gazes at Sheyndele's jewelry.*) Tell me, if you don't mind, what is that? I didn't pay attention till now, and I never noticed. Yosele, just tell me. Your wife wears my jewelry?

SHEYNDELE. All of a sudden she noticed. I took it all long ago. What does an old lady need with jewelry? You're not going to wear it, are you?

MIRELE. What do you mean: you took it? Without my knowledge you took my keys, you secretly unlocked the cupboard, broke open the jewelry box, and without my knowledge you took—So in plain words, you two robbed the old lady? Yosele, now you've gone too far.

SHEYNDELE. What do you mean robbed? Are we strangers? You see I'm not hiding anything.

YOSELE. Mama, may God punish me if I know what to say. I have no idea what I bought her and what you gave her. Oh, Sheyndele, what did you need this for? I'm embarrassed to look you in the eye.

SHEYNDELE. What's the fuss? If not today, tomorrow. It'll be ours anyway. And besides, if I could only butter her up like other people do, she would have given it all to me herself anyway. The whole problem is that I can't make little compliments and flatter her. At your age, you still want to dress up? Take it back. (*Wants to give back the jewelry.*)

MIRELE. No, no. I don't need it. You are right. After all, if not today, tomorrow it will come to you. And what does your father say: fine, what's the difference, as it is written. I was frightened because I thought that Yosele had also become equally enlightened. But so long as he did not know about it, I am satisfied. (*Raps with the stick.*) One must accustom oneself to everything. Once gold and silver lay here in the house, and no thieves appeared, not even strangers. Today, thank God, we provide our own thieves.

SHEYNDELE. That an old person should have such a mouth.

YOSELE. Quiet, I beg you.

SHEYNDELE. According to her we're all thieves.

YOSELE. Stop, I'm begging you, stop.

SHEYNDELE. And we're all fools, according to her. All bad people. She's the only good one, the smart one, the fine one, the—the—

Makhle runs in.

MAKHLE. Let it be, for pity's sake. Businessmen are coming, important people. They want to speak with Mirele.

Moves Mirele's chair. Mirele sits down.

DONYE. Since you've got the money now anyway, let's go over the accounts.

All three sit at a little table, counting money and doing accounts. Shalmen comes in with a few BUSINESSMEN.

SHALMEN. God's greetings, Mirele. Managed a chance to see you. What's the matter? Cut yourself off from the whole world? (*Looks at her hard.*) Oh my, how you look. What's going on with you?

MIRELE. Sit. Sit. Makhle, bring another few chairs. What have you brought me? I thought Grodno forgot long ago that once upon a time there used to be a Mirele in the world. Sheyndele, would you perhaps send for brandy and something to eat? Shalmen is such a guest for me, after all. What are you doing then, my old, faithful, good friend? It feels as if I haven't seen you in a world of days.

SHEYNDELE. Mother-in-law, we don't have any brandy in the house. You know Yosele doesn't drink, so who would we keep brandy for?

SHALMEN. Why go to any trouble? Mirele, you know why we've come? The congregation has finally decided to build a Jewish hospital. Well, who else among us has such a good heart and a broad hand as Mirele Efros? As a matter of fact, we came to you before anybody else. We're expecting a windfall from you—a few thousand.

Mirele remains sitting thoughtfully.

SHEYNDELE. (*Aside.*) He had to come with a beggar's sack.

Yosele doesn't let her talk.

MAKHLE. God our father, don't shame her.

MIRELE. Hmm, a windfall? I don't know. Understand me: business has been poor lately. But certainly, I won't let you leave my house empty handed. (*Pulls herself up out of her armchair and goes slowly to the children.*) Yosele, give me two hundred. I don't want people to know what's happening with us.

YOSELE. Don't say any more, Mama. (*Stretches out his hand to the money. Sheyndele covers it with her hand.*)

SHEYNDELE. Not necessary. Two hundred? Two hundred blows is what I'll give them.

DONYE. Throw money out on all these beggars?

MIRELE. Children, I beg you, don't shame me in front of strangers. You know I haven't asked for myself, and I never will. But now, for this— (*Trembles with agitation.*)

Yosele covers his face.

SHEYNDELE. Mother-in-law, listen to me, throw away your foolish conceit and childish pride. I'm telling you—

MIRELE. I do not want to hear what you are telling me. Out of here, all of you out.

Yosele gets up at once. Sheyndele doesn't let him go. Donye stays seated.

That is, I mean, if you have nothing more to do here, you can go. And if you want to stay, stay.

DONYE. Of course we'll stay here.

Mirele goes back to her armchair and practically falls into it. Makhle supports her.

MAKHLE. (*Quietly*) Mirele, don't get mad at me. You know I have put together six hundred and twenty rubles. What do I need money for, someone like me, old, without a husband? (*Pulls out a shawl bundle.*)

MIRELE. Yes, that's right. Give me your money, lend it to me. Nobody needs to know how I have fallen. (*Takes Makhle's money and sits down.*) Gentlemen, you must not hold it against me. A windfall is more than I can give. One hundred. (*Gives a hundred. A businessman puts it away in his pocket. Mirele remains thoughtful.*) No. Forgive me, give me back the money. I was committing the worst sin in the world. Makhle collected that money with bitter sweat and blood, and I wanted to be a philanthropist on her shoulders, because I was ashamed to tell the truth. No. My daughter-in-law is correct. One must throw off foolish conceit and childish pride.

SHEYNDELE. The days when they threw hundreds in the mud around here are finished.

MIRELE. (*Takes the money back.*) Yes, my friends, those days are over. Now Mirele Efros is very poor herself. It may be that I myself will be coming to you, and soon. I might come to beg for charity. Makhle, take back your money. One should not borrow when one does not know how one will ever repay.

All stand, amazed.

MAKHLE. Mirele, may I be sick if I can understand what kind of person you are.

SHALMEN. Understand me, gentlemen, Mirele Efros is making a joke. Ha, ha, ha. What do you mean, you have no money? I myself owe you so many hundreds.

MIRELE. You, Shalmen? What do you mean?

SHALMEN. Just stop playing tricks on us. Here's a hundred for Mirele Efros. Come, gentlemen, let's go. (*Quietly to Makhle.*) I'm coming right back immediately. (*Sharply*) Mirele, enjoy your day and be well.

As they leave, all ask: "What's this, Reb Shalmen? What was all that, ha?" Shalmen answers, "How should I know. Don't you know Mirele? Must be some joke or a whim. Come, let's go." Off.

SHEYNDELE. You feel bad, Mother-in-law, ha? Never mind, it will pass, and the hundreds will remain in our pockets. A lot healthier.

MIRELE. I have often wondered how there can be men so bad that they go so far as to hit their wives. Now I see that there are wives whom one can talk to only with a stick. (*Raps her stick.*) With you there is no other choice.

YOSELE. What are you saying, Mommy? Who could—God forbid—dare to raise a hand to my Sheyndele? She is my wife, she's my Shloymele's mother, she's the mistress of the house.

MIRELE. (*Sadly*) See how he remembers: she is mother, she is mistress. And what I am, everyone has forgotten. Let it go that I am not the mistress of this house—I myself made myself no longer mistress. But am I not a mother anymore either? Who made me no longer a mother? They say: we quickly forget those whom the earth has covered. Me, unfortunately, they have forgotten even before the earth has covered me.

Makhle weeps.

Makhle, I beg you, don't cry, because now it won't take much for me to cry like a child myself. (*Tears choke her.*) No. I will not reveal my wounded heart for strangers to see. (*Proudly*) Come, help me leave this place.

Makhle leads her off.

DONYE. Oh, how I love those old-lady dramas. Ugh. (*Exits.*)

SHEYNDELE. Just look how he hangs his head. How come the whole thing slides off your brother like a wall?

YOSELE. Her old gray head makes me so sad. Sheyndele, you know how dear you are to me, but when I see my mother suffering because of you, I hate myself for being so weak about you. I hate you for having such a nature. And I often think that I am your bitter enemy.

SHEYNDELE. (*Coquettish*) Oh really? You're my bitter enemy? Come, let's be good friends again. (*Embraces him and leads him out.*)

YOSELE. What devilish power women have. Who invented them to torment us? No, I mustn't think about it.

Both off.

MAKHLE. (*Opening door carefully.*) She leads him by the nose. She'll never be left without a husband, that one. Reb Shalmen will come soon. Wait till he sees they've made a Slutsk meat market out of Mirele's house.

Shalmen arrives. Later Sheyndele steals in and listens.

SHALMEN. Heavenly father, what's going on, Makhle? Why didn't you let me know sooner?

MAKHLE. She forbade me—in God's name—that anyone in the world should know, not even Shalmen. And today she went and told the world. Oh, Reb Shalmen, what our Mirele has to suffer here. They have stripped her from head to foot, robbed, stolen. Not a groshn left. You know how hard it is for her to bear that the house is dirty, always a mess. A fairground. She is used to eating at a set time, everyone together at the table. Now they eat sometimes at two o'clock, sometimes at three, sometimes at four, everyone separately. Always dirty dishes on the dining table. She has lost her appetite. She doesn't eat, she doesn't drink. She doesn't sleep whole nights. When I wake up, I hear her groaning, poor thing.

SHALMEN. Makhle, what are you saying here? I can't understand.

MAKHLE. Today was like every other day here. They insult her. They treat her worse than a servant. Every day yelling, curses, insults, fights. Shh. Today, with God's help, they made progress: they actually hit each other too. Oh, Reb Shalmen, I don't know how she'll survive.

SHALMEN. I knew she'd made over her property to the children. But that Mirele Efros suffers such sorrow and shame in her old age, that nobody could have guessed. (*Wrings his hands.*)

MAKHLE. The daughter-in-law, that wicked woman, sucks her blood every day. I don't know where Mirele draws so much patience. Her only comfort is her grandson Shloymele. She takes him on her lap, talks to him, presses him to her heart, and then she remains sitting deep in thought.

SHALMEN. And you were able to watch all this and keep silent? Makhle, may God not punish you for it. Makhle, I will not allow Mirele to suffer so terribly. And I will say this to you: Fool. Fool. Fool. (*Exits to Mirele.*)

MAKHLE. What do you think, was I really a fool for keeping silent?

SHEYNDELE. Start by keeping silent about me, you carcass, you gossip. Blabbing to the world what goes on in this house. You won't live to do it. I can't drive you out, I'm not going to divorce Yosele over you, but you'll get blows from me like a chopping block. Blows! You gossip. There, there. (*Hits Makhle.*)

MAKHLE. God be with you, Sheyndele, what are you doing, dear father in heaven? (*Gray hair falls out of her kerchief.*)

SHEYNDELE. There, now complain about me to Shalmen. Go complain about me. (*Hits her. Mirele appears.*)

MIRELE. (*Agitated, raps hard with stick.*) What are you doing? Whom are you hitting? Whom have you raised your insolent hand to? An elderly person, Makhle, my Makhle, my only friend in the world—hit her? Hit, actually hit, my God. Here in this house nobody, in the old days, used to even insult anyone with a disrespectful word, and you dare to hit Makhle?

SHEYNDELE. I'll hit her every day till I teach her who's the boss here. It's nobody's business to figure out where I come from. I want respect from everyone just as much as you do.

MIRELE. You hit her? You?

SHEYNDELE. Yes, me. If she doesn't like it here, she can leave.

MAKHLE. Dear Mirele, having even more troubles because of me isn't worth it. I'd better leave. You'll manage without me somehow. What can we do?

Yosele runs in.

YOSELE. What now? What a day this is, God in heaven.

MIRELE. Nothing. Now you have an aristocratic household. The husband has become modern, everything fancy, and the place is dirty, mud up to the throat, and they are beating the servants. That is how it is with our aristocrats.

SHEYNDELE. What's the matter, you're not pleased with the match? Well, have them harness the wagon and start the trip home.

MIRELE. True, I am not pleased with the match. Makhle, run, call Shalmen back fast.

Makhle off.

Yosele, we cannot live both together here in the house. It is impossible. I want you to divorce her right now, this minute. Give her a divorce paper. You hear? There is no other way. (*Raps the stick.*) A divorce. A divorce.

YOSELE. Mama, what are you saying? God be with you.

Sheyndele laughs.

MIRELE. You were frightened, ha? Ha, ha, ha. I was joking. I know it is easy to divorce an old mother but a young wife, especially a pretty one, you don't divorce so fast. I surrender the field.

Shalmen enters with Makhle.

Here is Shalmen. Good, I am making an end. Hear me out, Shalmen, I have a very great request of you. Thirty-five years you served me here in this house. Now permit me to serve you. I have no other choice. I don't want to die on the street. I will come be a servant in your house.

SHALMEN. Servant? What are you saying? Like a mother, like a child, you'll be in my house. We are plain people, but we can treasure a person. Serve? Oh my lord, don't you know the business that the firm of Mirele Efros and Shalmen could do if you said the word?

MIRELE. Mirele Efros won't compete against the firm of Yosele and Daniel Efros. No. I will be a servant. It is dreary for me without work; I go out of my mind. As long as I can still see out of these old eyes, I will keep the books. After that, Shalmen, I will do whatever you order.

SHALMEN. Order you? Oh, stop. (*Wipes his tears.*)

MIRELE. Enough. I do not want, I cannot, I do not need to suffer anymore. Mirele Efros has not fallen so low that she permits people to trample her underfoot. Love of children and maternal feelings have a limit too and a boundary. I am leaving at last. One minute. (*Exits rapidly.*)

SHEYNDELE. And she can do it, too, no question. Yosele, don't let her. It will be so embarrassing.

YOSELE. I'm afraid it's already too late. Sheyndele, what will become of us now?

MAKHLE. Every little corner of the house will weep and wail.

Mirele enters, carrying a little bundle of things.

MIRELE. You see, Shalmen, thirty-some years ago I came into this house with a lot of things, with a lot of sweet hopes, a lot of good expectations. Now I go away with only a little bit of linen and one dress, without hopes, without expectations. I came here to live, and I leave here to die. What did Job say: "Ha shem nosn ve ha shem lokakh" (God gave and God took away).

All weep. Sheyndele wipes away a tear.

SHEYNDELE. Mother-in-law dear, don't do it. I beg you, forgive me. Oh my lord, such a scandal. Yosele won't survive it.

YOSELE. Mama, don't go away from us. If not for our sakes, stay for the sake of our child. You know how you love our child.

MIRELE. No, it is too late. Mirele Efros does not stay once she has decided to leave. I cannot stay any longer. Yosele, give Shloymele a kiss for me, and if you want to be kind, you will send him to me once in a while. I am going. Let the whole world know the truth. Hide the scandal that has already taken place, deceive the world and tell lies? No. That was my mistake and my weakness. Shame exists only because we try to deny it. Shalmen, give me your hand. I would rather be a servant in a stranger's house than be a fool in yours. Well, Makhle, and what will be with you?

MAKHLE. What do I care? Mirele, Reb Shalmen will certainly permit me to come see you once in a while.

SHALMEN. Don't be silly, Makhle. What do you think, you won't earn your piece of bread in my house? Never mind, we're not aristocrats. Come, Mirele. Makhle, come with us. Old soldiers don't abandon their general in retreat.

Shalmen and Makhle lead Mirele.

MIRELE. Well, children, be well. I do not know if my foot will ever cross this threshold. I am leaving. (*As she goes.*) My old friends are leading me. Certainly, it would have been nicer and better if I had been carried out on my deathbed. It is a very great misfortune for a person to outlive himself. But when God does not send death, one must live. One comfort is left me: children lost, everything lost, but a few good friends have remained. (*At the door, turns and contemplates the whole house.*) Makhle, you know how familiar all this is to me. And now I feel I am seeing it all for the last time. Who could have believed that I—that the two of us—in our old age—Yosele, be well.

Exits with Makhle and Shalmen.

YOSELE. (*Falls onto a chair.*) Oh heaven help me. Mama, Mama.

Sheyndele weeps.

END OF ACT 3

Act 4, Scene 1

A room in Shalmen's house. Makhle dusts the furniture. She has aged greatly.

MAKHLE. (*Looking into mirror.*) If this mirror is honest, I must really not be a young all-alone wife anymore. God of the world, what is a person? He is exactly like a sack of sour milk with a heavy stone on top. The stone presses down, life pours out like cheese, and the sack is left empty. Lord, so many years dried out of me. How long ago was Yosele's wedding in Slutsk? I remember it like today. It rained, musicians played a wedding march, and I danced a wedding dance with Mirele. And now Yosele's son is a man. Today is Shloymele's bar mitsve, sweet father in heaven. More than ten years. It is indeed as they say: What is man and what is life? No less—

A noise.

Reb Shalmen.

Shalmen enters in overcoat.

SHALMEN. Shh. Makhle, is she there? What's she doing? How does she feel?

MAKHLE. Not good. Since she came from synagogue, she walks back and forth, thinking, sighing. Think of it. Her only grandchild, her beloved Shloymele, bar mitsve today, and for her, poor thing, there is no celebration. Reb Shalmen, what was the rabbi doing here?

SHALMEN. He came to make peace between them. The old rabbi tried it long and tried it wide, made every effort, poor thing, for nothing. Poured out a mountain of Torah. What can I say? His words stuck the way a chickpea sticks to the wall. You know yourself that when she says no, it's no. He left her a beaten man.

From the wings Mirele's voice calls Makhle.

MAKHLE. Coming. Right away. (*Exits.*)

SHALMEN. Not nice of me maybe, and God shouldn't punish me for saying it, but I'd prefer her not to make peace with them. These ten years that she's been here in my house, it's been like having a high priest or Elijah the Prophet himself as a boarder. Quiet, peaceful, everything with respect. My wife has forgotten all her curses. I'm clear out of the habit of yelling. Sit at the table like civilized people, and all the rooms are clean, tidy. Not that we're scared of her, we just feel her presence. Not to mention business with her in charge: new health, energy—terrific. Still the brain of a prime minister. No wonder the landowners call her Napoleon in a Dress.

Noise.

Who's this? Yosele. I'm afraid they'll make her sick before the day is over.

Yosele enters.

Welcome, Yosele.

YOSELE. Good day, Reb Shalmen. What do you think: will I be able to see Mama?

SHALMEN. Have to ask her. But I don't know whether it's worthwhile upsetting her.

YOSELE. Please, if you would. The rabbi had no success, so I'm going to ask her again myself.

SHALMEN. No, it didn't work for the rabbi. He told her what the holy Torah says: one can make peace when the heart commands.

YOSELE. Yes, I know everything. We all came together from synagogue, and we waited near there for an answer. That's how it is, Reb Shalmen, that's the way it is. Her heart is still full of hate.

SHALMEN. Hate? Oh, don't be a child. She doesn't want you to know, but I have to tell you: when you get coins from me once in a while, whose money is that? You don't know, right? It's hers. Mirele's got herself a nice few hundreds again. She doesn't complain, you know. Went off to the synagogue all by herself, without a word, to see Shloymele pray in phylacteries for the first time. (*Moved.*) You know? When they called him up to bless the Torah, she drenched her prayer book with tears. All the women wept looking at her; my wife came home from synagogue with her eyes swollen. Mirele doesn't talk about it, but what her heart feels—

YOSELE. Reb Shalmen, I'm begging you, would you take the trouble to tell her I want to see her? I can tell you: my Sheyndele is waiting for me out in the alleyway. It makes no sense to either of us that so many people are coming. You yourself, Reb Shalmen, probably you won't allow us to invite you?

SHALMEN. If Mirele has no objection, certainly. (*Puts on jacket.*) You know? For me she has remained the same Mirele Efros. And till today, when I need to go in to her, my heart pounds a little bit. (*Coughs, fastens all jacket buttons. Exits.*)

YOSELE. If not today, the day of her beloved Shloyme's bar mitsve, then this is how it will stay forever, God forbid. Terrible, terrible. Strangers forever.

SHALMEN. (*Returning.*) Yosele, forgive me. She says she's tired and can't see you now.

YOSELE. I beg you, Reb Shalmen, tell her: only one minute, only two words.

SHALMEN. Two words. You know how much health those two words will cost her? Oh, those words, those words, how dearly they cost. (*Exits.*)

YOSELE. I have to talk with her and see her. Can't I keep hoping? Can it be that she, with her noble heart, will never forgive?

SHALMEN. (*Returns.*) She's coming. I beg you—Shh.

He opens the door. Yosele stands up, Makhle leads in Mirele. She is very old and weak.

MIRELE. Yosele—a guest! Sit. What good news do you have to tell?

YOSELE. Mama, I've come again to beg you: have mercy on us. It's ten years that you haven't been to our house.

MIRELE. What, after ten years your old mother has suddenly become such a valuable bargain?

YOSELE. Not ten years. Every minute, every second, all along, it has stabbed me with knives that you aren't there with us, that in your old age you're alone in the world among strangers.

MIRELE. I am extremely sorry that it upsets you but talking about it is superfluous. Useless talk.

YOSELE. Mama come back to us.

MIRELE. What do you think, Yosele, I am playing puss-in-corner with you: dance here, dance back?

SHALMEN. But to go to them, just to sit an hour, on such an occasion. Why not?

MIRELE. Shalmen, you want to play the role of peacemaker and you come out looking like a fool.

YOSELE. I know when you say no, all talk is useless. I saw that when Donye got married. Not Donye's begging, not his bride's tears, not the intervention of the whole town could help. You said no and you didn't go to his wedding. And I, God forbid, I don't consider myself any better than Donye. Only Shloymele—you love him so much.

MIRELE. Yes, I love Shloymele, and I am not an enemy to any of you. But to go to your house— (*Raps with stick.*) Yosele, I will not go.

YOSELE. Every poor man, every workman, gets you at his celebrations, but not me. Shloymele will give a Torah speech.

MIRELE. You know that I care very little for such speeches. Shalmen, I put aside a telegram from Brisk. They're reporting that the commandant of the Brisk fortress— (*Takes out a paper.*)

MAKHLE. I know it's not right for me to mix in, but after all, may you be healthy—

MIRELE. Makhle, hand me my glasses.

Makhle brings her the glasses.

Yosele, go, be well, have a happy celebration. (*To Shalmen.*) This is a very big contract, Shalmen. We have to answer right away.

YOSELE. A good day, Mama. A good day, everyone. (*Goes sadly to the door.*)

MAKHLE. Poor thing.

MIRELE. Yosele, listen. I had something to say to you. Hm. What did I want to say to you? Yes, Shloymele's grandmother won't hear his speech, but she did not forget to buy him a watch and chain. (*Takes watch and chain out of her pocket.*) Here, you give it to him, may he use it in good health. Go, Yosele. God send you more joy from your child.

Yosele wants to say something, gestures with his hand and slowly exits.

MAKHLE. Gone, poor thing, with his heart broken. And it won't do Shloymele's health any good either. He's counting on his grandmother.

MIRELE. Makhle. (*Points with her stick to the door. Makhle off.*) Shalmen. (*Sighs deeply.*) The commandant needs five thousand barrels of gravel. We can make a good profit. Here are the figures. (*Reckons. Neither notices Sheyndele entering quietly and standing in the doorway.*) Breaking the stones and delivering them from Visoke will cost . . .

SHALMEN. Mirele, forgive me. That commandant is an enemy of the Jews, and I think—Ay, look!

Both notice Sheyndele.

SHEYNDELE. An unexpected guest, right? You can order them to throw me out of the house. I knew that could happen, but I came anyway.

Mirele takes off her glasses and remains seated.

SHALMEN. Naturally. Anyone who shouldn't be here certainly will be thrown out. Could be my own blood sister.

MIRELE. Shh. We don't have to throw people out. A person must understand for himself where it is not appropriate for him to be.

SHEYNDELE. Reb Shalmen, I think that if it's not appropriate for me to be here, then it's not appropriate for you either.

SHALMEN. In other words, you mean that I should throw myself out? Well, well. (*Off.*)

Pause. Both silent.

MIRELE. What is it? You have something to say? Please, do it quickly.

SHEYNDELE. Mother-in-law, I haven't spoken to you for ten years. I haven't even seen you from close up. And now I've come. If this was only about me, you can believe me for sure, if I was dying, I wouldn't go beg from anybody in the world. Nobody. My enemies shouldn't live to see it.

MIRELE. Your old tune. I haven't heard it for a long time.

SHEYNDELE. (*Doesn't hear.*) But it's Yosele. He feels so bad. Heartache. He is beside himself. And I don't want him believing that it's all my fault. Maybe I do have a bad character, but don't forget that even children who have been raised by a mother like Mirele Efros may also turn out not so ay-ay-ay, and my mother is nothing more than a Khane-Devoyre, and I grew up in Nokhemtse's house . . .

MIRELE. You said this was not about you. And who, God forbid, called you guilty, and who is arguing with you?

SHEYNDELE. That is exactly the misery: that you hate to argue. We plain people argue ourselves out, and then the anger is over. We fight very easily but making up is also easy for us. But you keep your silence, you're proud, and that's why it's hard for you to make an end to it. You'd be better off if you could yell and curse.

MIRELE. What do you mean: I would be better off? We would still be fighting every day.

SHEYNDELE. You think I wanted to do you harm for no reason. And I did want to spite you and your friends, because you considered me low and looked down at me like a nothing.

MIRELE. A person who is not a nothing is not afraid of how people look at him. And a person who has a good heart doesn't do harm for spite.

SHEYNDELE. How is it my fault if I don't have a good heart? And anyway, you think I had something to celebrate when I got rid of you out of the house? You can believe me if you want, and if you don't believe me, I don't care: when you left, it tore my heart. Mother-in-law, I can tell you, I haven't smiled happily in ten years. I haven't even opened the piano in all this time. I didn't have it in me to play, if you know what I mean.

MIRELE. (*Ironically*) What a sinner I have been to cause you such suffering. But what can one do? That's the kind of world it is. Everyone worries only about himself. I do not care about you, and you do not have to care about me.

SHEYNDELE. I don't understand. Are you—? You're laughing at me, and I came to you to make up.

MIRELE. I am amazed that someone so smart should try to do something so foolish.

SHEYNDELE. If it was a foolish quarrel, I wouldn't bother. It's a very hard and bitter thing to go to someone to apologize. But Yosele, your Yosele, believes that I drove his old mother out of the house, so I decided to go and bring his mother back to him.

MIRELE. You take too much on yourself. What does that mean: "you decided"? Well, and where am I? Don't I belong in there somewhere? You made a little mistake in your reckoning. I am Miriam Efros. Nobody brings me, and nobody drives me away. A thousand rabbis with intermediaries will not bring me there to you, so long as my heart does not command me to go. An entire regiment of heroic daughters-in-law would not have driven me out; ten plagues would not have had the smallest effect, if it were a matter of stubbornness. But, you understand me, here it was a matter of whose life would be broken, my life or Yosele's. (*Hands trembling.*) So I walked away from the battlefield. Because, you understand, I love Yosele.

SHEYNDELE. If you love Yosele, turn around. Have pity on him. On me, I know, nobody's ever going to have pity. But he is one of the good souls, after all, and he cries bitter tears.

MIRELE. What can one do? In this world, there are very few lucky people who never shed a tear. Who knows, maybe I have cried myself, once or twice.

SHEYNDELE. I envy the women who can cry easily. I can't. My heart closes up. Oh, if I could cry. But then, I'm here already, I'm ready to try anything, everything, even what I've never been able to do. How should I beg you? Should I fall at your feet? Should I kiss your hands? (*Wants to fall to Mirele's feet.*)

MIRELE. No, no. Whether you are play acting or you mean it with your whole heart—it's all the same. Your effort is useless. It was a great shame when I left the house. It would be a greater shame still, and stupid, if I came back. When your celebration is all over, when the dear old mother is again, God willing, worth less on the market, when the Sabbath mama becomes weekday again—and that will certainly happen very soon—what do you think: I will be in a position to pick myself up and leave? An experience like that one can survive only once. Don't make a fool of yourself—understand once and for all—my foot will not cross your threshold. The dead do not return from the grave, and I will not return from my exile. But enough. I beg you, you have opened all the old wounds of my heart. I have no more strength. Go in good health.

SHEYNDELE. That's your last word?

MIRELE. Yes, that is my last word. (*Raps with stick.*) Makhle.

SHEYNDELE. Well, if your judgment—

MIRELE. Exactly. Every person must do as he judges best and must judge what he does.

SHEYNDELE. Good day. (*Leaves quickly.*)

MIRELE. Shalmen. Makhle.

Both in.

Shalmen, a—What did I want to say? Oh, Makhle, it looks as if I have become a foolish old lady too.

END OF ACT 4, SCENE 1

Act 4, Scene 2

A room in Nokhemtse's house

NOKHEMTSE. (*Offstage.*) Come in here. It is written.

> *Nokhemtse enters with two chairs, followed by SHLOYMELE with a big paper in his hand.*

(*Nokhemtse wears old patched pants and a darned undershirt.*) The rabbi's granddaughter shut the room behind her and left, so we'll do our learning here at home. (*Sits down.*) Well, Shloymele, where do you stand with your speech, ha?

SHLOYMELE. Oh, grandfather, I stand way, way behind. (*Reading.*) "Before Passover, on the fourteenth day before dawn, search the house by candlelight for crumbs of leavened bread; they are impurities in the house." Grandpa, tell me, please, does every Jew have to become bar mitsve?

NOKHEMTSE. What a question. That's the difference between a Jew and a gentile. That is to say: bar mitsve and—and . . . and there must be some other difference too.

SHLOYMELE. Oh, Grandpa, bar mitsve is bad enough, but the speech is an eleventh plague that isn't even listed in the Torah. I'm only learning it for grandmother's sake. I mean that grandmother, the big one. Isn't it true that she isn't, I guess, so very tall but looks big anyway? (*Reading.*) "Light of the fourteenth—" Oh—

NOKHEMTSE. It's hard for you, poor thing? Listen, I'll go over the whole speech for you again. "'Or le-arbo osor bodkin es ha-khomets le-or ha-ner.' When it just begins to get light on the fourteenth day, that's when you check the house for crumbs of leavened bread, which are impurities during the Passover week, by candlelight. Sirs, bar mitsve is the day when thirteen years are over, and then comes the dawn of the fourteenth year of being Jewish. It's the day when a Jew is obligated to search himself by the light of Torah and scour out every bit of impurity from his soul." You understand? Every bit of impurity from his soul. Well, it's good?

SHLOYMELE. (*Has been sitting thinking and not listening.*) When I was coming here today, I hit a boy. I beat someone up. Not the first time.

Wherever I go, they run after me and sing a little song, "Shloymele fanny, Threw out his granny." I just got sick of it. Tell me, please, did we really throw her out?

NOKHEMTSE. God forbid. Nobody threw her out. Only, I don't know—as it is written.

SHLOYMELE. Grandpa, they say that when Grandmother was with us, we were very rich. Is that true?

NOKHEMTSE. "Truth everlasting, eternal and sure." Treasures of gold. Your uncle Daniel, before he got married and left for Moscow, set the fire that burned up the world. He made a ruin of half the property. And everybody gradually used up the rest. A little here, a little there. As it is written. Me, myself that you're looking at here, in those days I was the High Chief Director in Charge of You-Name-It. And now in my old age I give Talmud lessons. That is to say, I'm not a rebbe, I just teach little children.

SHLOYMELE. (*In melody used for discussing Talmud, imitates him.*) As it is written.

NOKHEMTSE. You clown, what's written here is really important. Well, well. Go over it by yourself. Practice hard, Shloymele. There's not much time left till the banquet. Go over it. (*Takes out pipe and smokes.*)

SHLOYMELE. (*Practicing.*) "Search by candlelight."

Noise.

Grandpa hide the pipe. Grandma's coming.

Khane-Devoyre enters with shawl on her head. She knits a sock as she walks. She has aged greatly.

KHANE-DEVOYRE. We should say the blessing over fragrant spices. You're smoking your pacifier again? Smoke him like a fish, Lord of the world. (*Coughs.*) Shloymele, do you know your talk yet?

Shloymele practices quietly.

NOKHEMTSE. (*Hides his pipe.*) Smoke? Spices? What do you imagine you smell? Never mind that, since when did you start locking the door?

KHANE-DEVOYRE. Since when, my wise man? The rooster isn't tied up under the bed, and who can I depend on? On you? Nokhemtse, pay attention to this instead: the old lady doesn't want to make peace. Sheyndele herself went to beg her to forgive. Talk to the wall! And we were counting on her.

SHLOYMELE. What? Grandmother isn't coming to us, even today? You know what? If grandmother won't be there, I don't need the whole speech. (*Throws away the paper.*)

KHANE-DEVOYRE. Are you crazy? Enemies of Israel! What are you doing? A paper with the name of God, and you throw it on the ground? (*Picks it up.*) Never mind, you can give your speech for me too. I myself, from my grandfather, may he rest in peace, I heard a few talks even a little better than this one. Here. (*Gives him the paper.*)

SHLOYMELE. (*Doesn't take it.*) I don't need any speech.

NOKHEMTSE. Shloymele, don't be stubborn. What do you mean? The rabbi—the whole town—knows I'm teaching you your Torah speech. Did I spend whole nights for nothing, scratching through the commentaries of the sages, may their memories be for a blessing?

SHLOYMELE. Yes, Grandpa, you spent whole nights scratching for nothing. I'm not giving any speech.

NOKHEMTSE. As it is written . . .

SHLOYMELE. Grandpa, I'm running home quick. I'll explain later. Meanwhile you practice the speech, because that is what's written. (*Exits.*)

KHANE-DEVOYRE. A spoiled only son—he's his other grandmother's grandchild. When he says no, you can hit your head against the wall.

NOKHEMTSE. As it is written.

KHANE-DEVOYRE. According to you, there's only what's written. Who needs a speech, just so long as there's a banquet with flowing wine—you should flow away in the river. Take the talk and come on to their house. (*Picks up a stool.*)

NOKHEMTSE. Come, give me my satin caftan.

KHANE-DEVOYRE. You can put on your Sabbath long johns too.

NOKHEMTSE. What am I, an aristocrat? (*Takes the other stool.*)

KHANE-DEVOYRE. Some aristocrat, little mothers! If all aristocrats were aristocrats like him!

NOKHEMTSE. Idiot. As it is written . . .

KHANE-DEVOYRE. Go on, go.

She pushes him out. Both off.

END OF ACT 4, SCENE 2

Act 4, Scene 3

Scene change back to Efros's house, much shabbier. Dark walls, old furniture. Mirele's armchair covered with a white sheet. In the background, a long table, all set. We hear a flute playing, then silence.

YOSELE. (*Alone, with the flute in his hand, contemplates the set table and goes over to his mother's armchair.*) No one has sat in her chair since she left. I hoped to see her today, the way it used to be, sitting there among us like an old queen among her servants. At my bar mitsve, this house was a better and happier place. But that was not destined for Shloymele.

Shloymele runs in.

SHLOYMELE. (*Out of breath.*) Daddy, I heard that grandmother Mirele won't come here even today. That can't be true, can it?

YOSELE. Yes, my child, she won't come here even today.

SHLOYMELE. Today? For my bar mitsve? What does she have against me? I don't understand. She lives with us in the same city and never comes to us. She isn't mad at me, and not at you either. It's Mommy's fault. She and her family made Grandmother angry.

YOSELE. Shh. Don't be unfair. (*Embraces him.*) Shloymele, today you have become a bar mitsve, you're becoming an adult already, and I can tell you the truth. Here, in Grandmother's own house, she was not treated by any of us as a mother should be treated by decent children. She sacrificed her life for us, and we broke her noble heart. Well, she suffered, and finally she left us. And happiness and good fortune left with her.

SHLOYMELE. And she'll never come back?

YOSELE. Till today I kept on hoping. But see how much she loves you. She sent you a watch with a chain. (*Gives it to him.*) "I will not hear his speech," she said, "but he must have a gift from me."

SHLOYMELE. Daddy, I'll go to her myself. I will say to her, "If you don't want to hear my talk, Granny, I don't want your watch." And I'll say a lot, a lot, of things to her.

YOSELE. Little silly, what good will that do? We've already said a lot of things to her.

SHLOYMELE. She'll come with me.

YOSELE. You're still a child. You don't understand that she is not one of those people who can change in a minute from no to yes.

SHLOYMELE. You'll see. She'll come with me.

YOSELE. Don't make yourself believe foolish things.

SHLOYMELE. She will come with me. You don't understand that I'm not one of those people who make themselves believe foolish things. When I tell you that I will bring her, I will bring her. (*Rushes off.*)

YOSELE. Proud, and strong-minded—takes after his grandmother. A child: how can he understand who Mirele Efros is? When she says no, it can thunder and lightning. (*Contemplates his flute.*) No, she won't come, and my only joy and only comfort will continue to be my old flute. (*Looks around.*) Nobody's here yet. In the meantime, let me talk out my bitter heart. (*Sits in a corner, plays the same sad melody as in the second act. Deep in thought.*)

Sheyndele enters.

SHEYNDELE. Well, what are you moping about now? You're not only a son, you're a father too, after all.

Noise.

Shh, here come the guests already. What can we do? We'll celebrate by ourselves, as best we can. Well, well, come on. Enough. (*She leads him by the hand.*)

Nokhemtse and Khane-Devoyre come toward them.

That's it? I thought we had guests.

KHANE-DEVOYRE. In your house, we're not exactly guests. All the same we will be polite and say, "May you both live to lead Shloymele to the wedding canopy."

NOKHEMTSE. And where is he, the rascal? I wanted to go over his talk with him one more time. Oh, a talk—a jewel.

YOSELE. Shloymele will be right here. Sit—you are very good guests and very dear guests in our house.

KHANE-DEVOYRE. How did we manage that? As they say, "Not all mamas have the same luck."

SHEYNDELE. And not all mamas have the same sense, "as they say."

YOSELE. "Every mama is a mama." Sheyndele, today there has to be peace here.

Noise.

Shh, who's there? Welcome in God's name.

Shalmen enters.

SHEYNDELE. Amazing! The mother-in-law actually permitted you to come?

SHALMEN. You're very wrong. She sent me here herself. Told me more than once that I should—for God's sake—be here. She is Mirele Efros.

YOSELE. More than once? Oh my, oh my. Maybe she'll come after all?

SHALMEN. No, not a chance of her. Better off not talking about that and not thinking about it. Hello, Reb Nokhemtse, how are you?

NOKHEMTSE. Eh, how should I be? You open your mouth and out come the words.

Noise.

KHANE-DEVOYRE. The rabbi is coming with people. Sheyndele, all the silver in the sideboard is out on the table?

RABBI, an old man, enters, followed by GUESTS, including adults and young people.

ALL. Good day. Good day. May it be for a blessing.

SHALMEN. Good day. How do you feel, Rabbi? Ha, ha. You danced with the bear. Don't forget, she is Mirele Efros. Yosele, where is the bar mitsve boy himself?

YOSELE. Shloymele will be right here. Sit down. Come in, everybody. To the table. I beg you, Rabbi. If you please, Reb Shalmen, Father-in-law.

All sit down, drink and eat.

KHANE-DEVOYRE. (*To Nokhemtse.*) I'm afraid your czar's palace of a speech will end up just a plain old attic with a wooden beam.

NOKHEMTSE. (*Drinks.*) So I built an attic with a beam. As it is written.

More adults and youngsters come. All sit at the table, drink, and eat.

YOSELE. Sheyndele, what in the world has happened to Shloymele? Drink, eat.

Both serve guests.

NOKHEMTSE. To life! Gentlemen, I heard a pretty commentary written on the verse "kerem hoyo le-shloyme" (King Solomon had a vineyard) and—ah—What's going on?

Makhle runs in, very agitated.

SHALMEN. What's the matter, Makhle? What happened?

ALL. What happened, God forbid?

YOSELE. Makhle.

MAKHLE. (*Can barely breathe.*) Yosele, everybody, I—I have the honor—I'm announcing—I ran.

YOSELE. What is it, Makhle? I'm scared.

MAKHLE. Why be scared? God be with you. She, Mirele, she's coming here. Shloymele is leading her straight to you. Oh, what a sage that is. If you heard how he talked to her. She couldn't hold out. She cried, he cried, I cried. Well, they're both coming here. As I live and breathe.

All stand up.

YOSELE. Mother is coming. Sheyndl, gentlemen, oh my. (*A sob tears itself out of him.*)

SHEYNDELE. (*Moved.*) Little silly, why are you crying? Now is when you shouldn't cry.

YOSELE. What are you saying, Makhle? Mother is coming here? Where is she going? What did you see? What are you telling me? (*Runs, opens the door.*)

Mirele appears, leaning on Shloymele.

SHLOYMELE. You already started the feast without us? You had no time to wait for us? You were in such a hurry? You know I told you I'd come with the big bad granny.

YOSELE. Mama, you came? You came to us?

MIRELE. (*Smiling.*) With your family connections, how could I resist? Your father was Shloymele. Your son is Shloymele. Sit, sit. Makhle, I think you have my eyeglasses.

All sit. Makhle hands her the glasses.

YOSELE. Mommy, I don't believe my own eyes. You are here? You came?

MIRELE. You see for yourself. One cannot be clever and escape when one carries inside oneself a mother's heart. A useless thing, really, but what's to be done when one simply cannot cut it out and throw it away? Rabbi, you know it's true. Tell us something the Torah says about such silly things as a mother's heart.

SHEYNDELE. (*Kisses Shloymele.*) My scholar, my jewel. Sit, Mother-in-law, here is your chair.

Moves out Mirele's chair. Makhle helps her.

MIRELE. No, thank you. I have recently learned to sit on every chair. (*Sits on a different chair, puts on glasses, and looks around.*) Look, Makhle, how old and changed everything has become. If we had been here all along, we would never have noticed the way that everything around us becomes old and passes. And it might not even have occurred to us that we are no mightier and no more solid than these wooden chairs, than the wallpaper. A human being believes he has something to pride himself on. (*Thoughtful.*) Changed, how changed, and yet how familiar every little corner, how dear every object. Shalmen, you know what I lived through here and how much I suffered. How many good hopes were born here, how many heavy sighs torn from my heart, how many quiet bitter tears poured out from my soul.

Makhle weeps.

Oh, my heart.

Faints. A tumult.

YOSELE. Mama, mama, God help us.

All surround her. She comes to herself.

SHEYNDELE. Water. Water. Mother-in-law, for you to let go like that—

MIRELE. Shalmen, we weak human beings must be stronger than iron to bear our sorrows.

SHALMEN. (*Tears choke him.*) Enough, Mirele, calm yourself, you'll have time later. Now is the celebration, and we still have to hear a speech. Well, Shloymele, you scholar, show off your Hebrew.

ALL. Yes, yes. The speech, the speech.

YOSELE. Mama, you sit in your place. (*Lifts her and sits her down in her armchair.*) You know, your chair waited for you. I used to talk to your chair when my heart ached, and I believed it listened and understood what I was saying. No, Reb Shalmen is right. Enough for now. You are here, you came. Why talk?

MIRELE. If your Sheyndl could come to me, I didn't show such great courage in coming to you. I will tell the truth, Sheyndl, you broke my heart today more than anybody. Ah, here are the in-laws.

KHANE-DEVOYRE. You should be healthy, Mirele, I knew that you would come. Already early in the morning I said, "Look, Nokhemtse, a guest is coming: The cat is washing itself backwards, you mark my words."

NOKHEMTSE. Now it's the cat. As it is written. The sages say: "Kol ha-dokhek es ha-sho, ha-sho dokhekaso" (He who strikes the hour, the hour strikes him). Whoever pushes time, the time goes, and it pushes him. All in good time.

ALL. The speech. The speech.

YOSELE. Well, Shloymele, let's hear.

SHLOYMELE. (*Quietly*) I'm going to hang like Haman. (*Clear voice.*) Light of the fourteenth searching for leavening by candlelight. When it comes—which—When—Oh, on my word, I've forgotten it. I mean, to tell the truth, I really didn't know it in the first place.

All laugh.

It's Grandmother's fault.

KHANE-DEVOYRE. Oh, Shloymele, I'm blushing.

MIRELE. It's not such a great misfortune. Everyone can give a speech, and eventually he will be able to do it too. You come here, Shloymele, come to me. It's my fault, ha, ha, ha. (*Takes him in her arms.*) Well, who needs wisdom when children are so darling and precious?

YOSELE. Shloymele, you're a rascal. But today I don't mind a bit. Your bar mitsve is not my highest holiday today. Jews, drink up. Sheyndele, look who is sitting here with us.

All drink, Nokhemtse more than anyone.

MIRELE. A celebration, ha? This is the proverb, precisely: "When does the pauper celebrate? When he finds what he lost." (*Knocks with stick.*) A foolish world. Wouldn't it be better if everyone could treasure his little bit of happiness before he loses it? Wouldn't it be healthier for ourselves, after all, if we didn't repay bad with good? We should not poison the springs from which we ourselves draw our life and our joy. But who stops and considers that till it is already late, till life is over?

SHALMEN. Mirele, you've forgotten?

YOSELE. Mama, do you want to upset yourself again?

MIRELE. No, no. Enough, I did not come to you—God forbid—to spoil the celebration. Give me a glass of wine too. Makhle, you take a little also. Shloymele's bar mitsve must be a celebration for everybody. To life, children. To life, friends.

All drink.

NOKHEMTSE. (*Drinks.*) I remember something that's written on the verse "Peace, peace, far and near."

YOSELE. Drown the commentary. You heard what Mirele Efros said? (*He drinks, runs around, kisses his mother, kisses Makhle.*)

People begin quietly to sing a merry tune.

SHALMEN. (*Goes over to Yosele with a glass in hand.*) I'll tell you the truth. When I recall that my house will now remain empty, naturally my feelings are dark and bitter. But children come first. A mama, brother, is no small thing. (*Wipes a tear.*) Eh, to life. Let's celebrate. (*Embraces Yosele.*) Jews, celebrate. Jews, be lively.

All sing a merry tune. Nokhemtse dances with two decanters in his hands.

SHEYNDELE. (*Runs to the piano, tears off the cover, and plays what they're singing.*) I haven't played for ten years. Ten years.

Mirele takes Shloymele in her arms, Makhle beside her. A merry song, loudly accompanied on piano.

The End

Notes

Theater J in Washington, DC, a program of the Edlavitch DCJCC in association with Georgetown University's program in Theater and Performance Studies, produced this translation in the spring of 2019. Theater J is normally reviewed by all the major Washington, DC, press, and *Mirele* earned praise—even from a local college newspaper. Artistic Director Adam Immerwahr, who had considered it something of a risk, was happily surprised when by the end of its six-week run it had exceeded its single ticket sales goal.

While actually speaking the lines in the course of rehearsal, director and actors could hear spots where the translation had made Gordin's words come out awkward or unclear. I am indebted to them for their many very helpful suggestions.

For that production, Immerwahr made some cuts—more than a quarter of the text! Gordin's four acts, the standard length of his times, is, after all, much longer than modern audiences are used to sitting through. It is worth noting that when a staged reading of my translation of Gordin's four-act *God, Man, and Devil* was performed at the HOTink Festival, not a line was cut, and Gordin came through, nineteenth-century rhythm and all. I didn't see anybody squirming impatiently, not even when the text alluded to unfamiliar religious practices. Still, in the end each director must use his or her own judgment, and Immerwahr's cuts were intelligent and worked well.

Act 1

I changed several characters' exclamation *oy* to "oh" or "ah"; *oy* has come to sound comical to American audiences. Also I changed *lekhayim* to "to life" or simply "a toast" and changed *mazl tov* to "congratulations" (though I confess I am less sure about eliminating *mazl tov*) because the sound of Yiddish has sentimental associations for some people, and that distracts from the reality of the play. Besides, it's only confusing to mix languages. However, if the director feels strongly about it, *lekhayim* and *mazl tov* can be put back in. Actors should not speak with a Yiddish accent, which evokes affectionate or comic associations that have nothing to do with the play—and besides makes no sense in a translation.

The suffixes *-l*, *-le*, and *-ele* are diminutives; *-tse* and *-ye*, too, transform a name into a nickname. Mirele's formal name is Miriam, Yosele's is Yoysef (Joseph), Shloymele's is Shloyme (Solomon), Sheyndele's is Sheyne (Belle), Nokhemtse's is Nokhem (Nahum), and Donye's is Daniel. Gordin's cast of characters lists them all by the nicknames by which they are familiarly known to one another.

Soliloquies, in which a character is understood to be thinking aloud, and asides, in which he is speaking directly to the audience, were familiar stage conventions before Shakespeare. Following the notes, Allen Rickman discusses the degree to which they have become unfamiliar and potentially off-putting to today's audiences. I disagree. The 2019 production at Theater J in Washington, DC began when Makhle came to the apron and addressed the audience with touching (and slightly humorous) effect. Later, Mirele's sad reflections worked well as soliloquies. Shakespeare's soliloquies and asides do fine, and voiceovers in various guises are common in movies.

The blessing referred to in Yiddish as *bentsh gomel* is recited by one who has recovered from serious illness, returned safely from a long journey, or survived danger. "Praised are You, Lord our God, King of the universe, who graciously bestows favor upon the undeserving, even as He has bestowed favor upon me." All translations from Hebrew are by Rabbi Jules Harlow, as they appear in the prayer book *Siddur Sim Shalom* (New York: The Rabbinical Assembly, 1985).

An *agune* is a woman whose husband has gone without giving her the legal divorce that would free her to remarry. He may have done this deliberately, or because he is captive or missing in action, or he may be dead; but the wife has no way of knowing or proving that she is a widow. (Nowadays, the plight of the *agune* is receiving active attention.)

Nokhemtse has studied Talmud; he is a teacher, though only of small boys, meaning he is not so great a scholar as he would like to think. The verbal tic Gordin gave him means, literally, "What's the difference?" But this question, which is Aramaic rather than Yiddish, is a familiar formula from Talmud study, used when logically analyzing some philosophical or ethical proposition. I chose "as it is written" in order to capture some of those associations, which suit his character. In the 2019 production of this translation that played at Theater J, "as it is written" did get most of the laughs that were intended, though I still hope to come up with a better translation someday. (Maybe, "That's what the rabbis said"?) Repeating a characteristic phrase was common in Yiddish comedy, as indeed it is to this day in television sitcoms; it is shorthand for the character himself. Gordin's actors must have added or subtracted a few repetitions, as a director is free to do today.

The noble Polish Potocki family (descendants of whom still exist) were famously wealthy and powerful. Someone who pretended to be rich or aristocratic might be called, mockingly, Count or Countess Potocki. In both Polish and Yiddish, the name is pronounced Pototsky.

"Who is like You, Lord, among all that are worshiped?" This is part of the Sabbath prayer service.

". . . like dancing bears, . . . with tears"—Notice "tears" should rhyme with "bears."

Chelm is a real Polish city, but in Yiddish folklore it is the name of a legendary town of fools.

The Jews had to cross the Red Sea to escape Pharaoh's army during their exodus from Egypt, but at first they were afraid to enter the water.

It is customary for the wedding ceremony to take place under a canopy big enough to shelter the couple, the rabbi or other officiant, and sometimes other participants as well. It is supported at its four corners by four poles, planted in the ground or held by relatives or friends. It may be a simple or an elaborate cloth, a prayer shawl, or even made of flowers. It is often taken to symbolize the couple's new home together.

It is the custom for bride and groom to fast the day of the wedding. Immediately after the ceremony, before joining their guests, they go off together to a small private room where they eat a small meal together.

Giving charity is an integral part of traditional Jewish practice. There are specific occasions when it is customary to give, such as the anniversary of a loved one's death and certain holidays, but in general giving charity to communal causes is considered an obligation. In act 2, Sheyndele protests Mirele's large gifts for Torah study, but that is yet another sign of her low character; to support scholars, individually or through an institution, is a duty, and Mirele's famous generosity is inseparable from her position in the community. Many Jewish communities, even small ones, were (and still are) organized into committees responsible for coordinating charitable giving and volunteer activities. In act 3, an ad hoc committee has formed to raise money for a Jewish hospital; today such committees are still likely to go directly to community members to ask for donations.

"To life": the familiar toast *lekhayim*.

"No evil eye": common superstitious formula.

"If I am not for myself, who will be for me? If I am only for myself, what am I?" Attributed to Rabbi Hillel, this familiar saying is from the book *Pirkei Avot* (*Ethics [or Sayings] of the Fathers*).

At the start of traditional weddings, the bride sits enthroned, surrounded by her mother and other women, until the groom approaches to cover her face with the wedding veil.

"El moley rakhamim." This Hebrew prayer is chanted, usually to a particularly haunting melody, on many occasions remembering the dead. The melody is simple and can be learned from a cantor or on YouTube. Here is Jules Harlow's translation:

> Exalted, compassionate God, grant perfect peace in Your sheltering Presence, among the holy and the pure who shine with the splendor of the firmament, to the soul of our dear [*name*], who has gone to his eternal home. Master of mercy, remember all his worthy deeds in the land of the living. May his soul be bound up in the bond of life. The Lord is his portion. May he rest in peace. And let us say: Amen.

Here and elsewhere, Yosele and Mirele translate or gloss bits as the Hebrew goes along, which means that the speaker is actually saying the same thing twice, once in the Hebrew original and then again in Yiddish, chanting the two alternating phrases to the same musical cadence. It is still common to interrupt Hebrew quotations this way, interpolating translations or glosses in Yiddish, English, or whatever the speaker's vernacular may be.

Note that the Hebrew is not pronounced as modern Hebrew is spoken in Israel, which is the Sephardik pronunciation. Hebrew pronounced in the Sephardik way will sound distractingly incongruous to anyone in the audience who knows Yiddish culture—imagine King Lear speaking like a Mississippi farmer, New York cabby, or Irish folk singer. I advise finding somebody to coach or some online recording. (See the appendix to this book, the guide to pronunciation.)

Act 2

Sabbath lasts from before sundown Friday night to after sundown Saturday night, when the customary greeting is "A good week." "God of Abraham" is a traditional song for the end of Sabbath.

Because it is forbidden to cook on the Sabbath, the Sabbath stew, called *tsholent*, traditionally bakes in the oven from Friday afternoon till Saturday lunch.

The book of Lamentations, an account of the sorrows of Jerusalem and the destruction of the Temple, is read annually on Tisha B'Av, the yearly commemoration of the event.

"European" is generally used to mean assimilated. Here it is a matter of modern rather than traditionally Jewish style: suit rather than gabardine, clean-shaven rather than beard and earlocks.

According to Jewish law, a married woman covers her hair with a hat, scarf, or wig. In some communities, she shaves her hair and then covers her head.

"Rebbe" here means respected teacher.

"Motzi" is the blessing over bread; "matzo" is unleavened bread eaten on Passover. Khane-Devoyre is too ignorant to have heard of Mozart. This is my version of Gordin's original, in which Mirele asks for a trio and Khane-Devoyre thinks she's talking about a *truah* (a note played on the shofar or ram's horn).

"Rubles for Talmud study": Mirele donates to support students and scholars.

It is customary, especially for women, to recite psalms in moments of extreme danger or sorrow. Mirele is reading Psalm 69. As explained previously, she translates as she goes along. Here are several fuller, less colloquial excerpts from the psalm, as translated in the *JPS Hebrew-English Tanakh* (Bible):

Deliver me, O God, for the waters have reached my neck; I am sinking into the slimy deep and find no foothold; I have come into the watery depths; the flood sweeps me away. I am weary with calling; my throat is dry; my eyes fail while I wait for God. More numerous than the hairs of my head are those who hate me without reason; many are those who would destroy me, my treacherous enemies. Must I restore what I have not stolen? . . . I am a stranger to my brothers, an alien to my kin. My zeal for Your house has been my undoing; the reproaches of those who revile You have fallen upon me. When I wept and fasted, I was reviled for it. I made sackcloth my garment; I became a byword among them. Those who sit in the gate talk about me; I am the taunt of drunkards . . ." (*JPS Hebrew-English Tanakh* [Philadelphia: Jewish Publication Society, 1999]).

Act 3

The Jews' wanderings in the desert are narrated in the Old Testament, book of Numbers, 33: 5–37 and 41–49. The chapter is read in synagogue every year. Here are the first few verses:

> And the children of Israel journeyed from Rameses and encamped in Succoth. And they journeyed from Succoth, and encamped in Etham . . . And they journeyed from Etham . . . and encamped before Migdol. And they journeyed from Pene-Hahirot and . . . encamped in Marah. And they journeyed from . . .

Nokhemtse actually mixes in a few place-names from the Torah in among the Polish towns he has just visited. Naturally Gordin's audiences recognized it, though they might not have been able to quote it from memory, and were amused by Nokhemtse's drunken semi-conscious parody.

"Eesha kley zayne aleha" (A woman comes with her own weapons). This phrase appears in a passage of Talmud Bavli, Avodah Zara 25b.

"God of Ages": a common phrase from prayers.

"To fast and remember Jerusalem": pious practice on Tisha B'Av.

Act 4, Scene 1

"Bar mitsve": When a boy turns thirteen, he takes on the ritual obligations of a man. The traditional bar mitsve ceremony consists simply of being "called up" to bless and read from the Torah, generally followed by a celebration at which the boy interprets a Torah passage. (In recent generations, there are also ceremonies for girls when they reach twelve or thirteen, especially in non-Orthodox communities; either the girl participates in the synagogue service or else she marks adulthood in some other way.)

"We would be fighting every day": Literally, she says they would still be dancing a *broygez* dance—a folk dance in which two dancers pantomime a fight.

Ten plagues: The plagues, enumerated in the Passover ceremony, that finally convinced Pharaoh to free the Jews from slavery in Egypt.

Act 4, Scene 2

Nokhemtse actually refers to his wife humorously by the honorific *rebetsin*, meaning "rabbi's wife." I substituted a different joke, referring to her pride in her grandfather.

A bar mitsve boy's talk is supposed to interpret a Talmudic passage. Shloymele's text happens to be a law referring to Passover. Before Passover, traditional households remove all traces of *khomets* (food forbidden on the holiday): leavened bread in particular, plus (in Ashkenazi communities) legumes and other substances. Just before the holiday, the house must be symbolically searched, with a candle, to check that all *khomets* is gone. Nokhemtse is coaching Shloymele—the quotation comes first and then the exegesis, which proposes an analogy between scouring the house for impure food and scouring one's own soul for impurity.

"Truth everlasting, eternal and sure": phrase from prayers.

There is a specific blessing to be said over fragrant spices, as well as specific blessings for other experiences and natural delights like sunsets.

Act 4, Scene 3

"May you live to lead Shloymele to the wedding canopy": This is a traditional formula of congratulations at a child's birth and his bar mitsve.

"Kerem hoyo le-shloyme" (King Solomon had a vineyard). It is common for pious people to converse about interpretations of Torah as social conversation. Nokhemtse, who loves wine, is naturally drawn to a text about vineyards.

"Kol ha-dokhek es ha-sho, ha-sho dokhekaso": Appears in Talmud Bavli, Eiruvin 13b.

Haman is the villain of the book of Esther, read on the holiday of Purim. In ancient Persia, he tried to kill all the Jews, but in the end he himself was hanged.

The High Holidays are Rosh HaShana and Yom Kippur, the New Year and the Day of Atonement, which fall in autumn and are the most solemn and holy days of the year.

The conclusion of this play can be a problem today when, as Allen Rickman points out, audiences may scoff at a happy ending that seems implausible and sentimental. But Adam Immerwahr of Theater J made a few cuts and shifts in the end of the scene that reduced the sentimentality and made the emotional satisfaction of the characters' reconciliation accessible to the audience. He cut Shalmen's last speech and ended with Mirele's lines from earlier in the scene, addressed to the audience:

> A foolish world. Wouldn't it be better if everyone could treasure his little bit of happiness before he loses it? We should not poison the springs from which we ourselves draw our life and our joy. But who stops and considers that till it is already late, till life is over?

In other words, he moved the focus from the personal to a larger idea and from forgiveness to the appreciation of human happiness, and this was a subtly effective solution.

Allen L. Rickman: Thoughts on Reviving *Mirele Efros*

Why revive *Mirele Efros*? *Mirele Efros* is compelling theater, with a rich collection of characters, a unique atmosphere, and an involving story whose underlying values do not date at all. But the strongest argument for a revival is the figure Gordin put at the play's center.

There was always a rich, juicy role for the star of a Gordin play, and it was usually a figure of some status who is struggling with a giant conflict. This was, of course, a necessity in the actor/manager era. And though Gordin wrote a number of plays with strong, intelligent female protagonists for the name-above-the-title actresses of his day (he was also, conveniently, a proto-feminist), Mirele herself is perhaps his outstanding achievement in character writing.

According to Yiddish theater historian Zalmen Zylbercweig, *Mirele Efros* took Gordin much longer to write than his other plays of the era; the actress Keni Liptzin, who had commissioned it, remembered seeing Gordin looking rather haggard while he was slaving away at the script. He must have gotten a little dozy because it feels like Mirele snatched Gordin's pen and ran away with it, forcing him to follow her rather than letting him squeeze her into one of his stage lectures. It's astonishing to realize that this lifelong, antireligious socialist wrote his best-regarded play about an Orthodox woman who is also a virtuous and successful capitalist.

Mirele is an admirable character, but she's no "goody-goody"; she's very strong-willed, very reserved emotionally, and can be very sharp-tongued at times. But her errors in judgment do not come from ego or spite but rather from unselfishness; even her greatest mistake—not letting Yosele find an educated city girl to marry, as he'd likely expected—was motivated by her idea of what was best for him. She's a perfect example of what E. M. Forster called a "round" character; that is, "a character who is capable of surprising in a convincing way." The action of the play hangs entirely on choices that Mirele makes, which are both well motivated and surprising. Unlike many Yiddish plays of its era, *Mirele Efros* is not a story with one-dimensional characters that exist to enable Big Stage Moments. No, this play is a mature character study along the lines of Gordin's models, Ibsen and Turgenev. About the fall of a great figure, it is almost a tragedy, except in the sense that Mirele's decisions that lead to her unhappiness are motivated admirably. The classic Tragic Hero is brought down by his flaws; Mirele is undone by her virtues.

It's also quite well built, at least for the first three acts. Particularly impressive from a storytelling standpoint is how Gordin manages to build up to a strong scene of dramatic conflict right in the first act, which is a very hard thing to do that early on. And he had a superb sense of theatricality. He knew how to "make things happen," how to direct the eye, how to create excitement without resorting to the melodramatic tropes so typical of his era. Mirele's banging her walking stick on the floor at certain moments—commanding all activity to stop and all eyes, both onstage and in the audience, to go to her—has the same kind of impact that that helicopter landing onstage had ninety years later: you're seeing an event, something important is happening right now in front of you.

Yes, *Mirele Efros* should be revived. But several problems will need to be addressed.

One that pops up right in the opening stage direction is the issue of supernumeraries. Present in most, perhaps all, of Gordin's plays, supernumeraries are not used in theater anymore because they cost money. In this case, however, at least a few are absolutely necessary for dramatic purposes.

At the top of the show, the bustle of Mirele's arrival in Slutsk, with porters rushing about with trunks, and so on, not only lends the beginning of the play an impressive theatricality but also tells the story of Mirele's status in the most vivid way possible. The bar mitsve guests in the last act make that scene into a climactic event that would dwindle to nothing without them. In the third act, the businessmen who accompany Shalmen when he calls on Mirele to ask for a donation are particularly important: without the chance of Mirele's straitened condition causing her embarrassment in front of strangers, the scene has almost no stakes. (Among other cuts, the 1994 Folksbiene production eliminated the "supernumerary businessmen," costing the play all of the impact of both one of its strongest scenes and a major turning point for the protagonist.)

Another issue is the question of "asides." Asides ring very odd to a modern audience at a naturalistic play. They strain the suspension of disbelief. In this play, Gordin uses asides extensively in two different ways. The first is in expository monologues. This is a convention that couldn't look clunkier today, but there are ways around it. One obvious choice is to put these monologues in a different reality than the rest of the play, via shifts in light, sound/music, and so forth. Another would be to cut them entirely, folding anything significant into dialogue in other scenes (e.g., Makhle's autobiography, the description of the trip from Grodno to Slutsk, etc.). Nokhemtse's monologue at the top of act 3, so awkward to a contemporary eye, could be made into something both useful and entertaining by the addition of a silent and disinterested servant whom Nokhemtse is trying to amuse. Probably some combination of these would be the best solution.

The second type of aside is more difficult to deal with. The play is full of moments where a character comments on the action directly to the audience, usually for comedic effect, or where a character speaks his or her inner thoughts aloud. This latter is particularly jarring, and the former is just dated. One solution is to cut the first, and to do with the second, where possible, the sort of thing I'd suggested with the expositional monologues, that is, put them into another reality through light and sound. Something must be done to make asides "play" to a contemporary audience, and it would certainly involve at least some cutting.

Which brings us to the question of adaptation/editing—namely, ought we to? Well, why not? I've done it myself for almost every Yiddish play I've directed. A theater is not a museum. (Moreover, presenting a play in translation, even in one as rigorously accurate as this one, is already not presenting it in its original form.) For example, Gordin has a technique of identifying characters by their use of individual catchphrases. It's a useful bit of dramatic shorthand and can be very effective when not overdone. Nokhemtse's "As it is written" might have worked in 1898, but not now. The play could also use some general cutting; a few ideas are a bit protracted, there's some unnecessary repetition, and so on. There is no reason not to thin these things.

But the biggest issue scriptwise is the play's four-act structure. Three acts make the perfect, instinctive structure for telling a story. In the case of *Mirele Efros* the necessity to present a fourth act led to the play's one great flaw (Spoiler Alert!): Sheyndele's having an utterly unconvincing change of heart, followed by Mirele's doing the exact same thing, setting up a "they lived happily ever after" ending that wouldn't convince a moose.

Contrary to what an uninformed reader might suspect, most of Gordin's plays end tragically. And the happy ending in *Mirele Efros* makes no sense on any level. It was not even a compromise made for box office reasons—Gordin's plays with tragic endings were very popular. The only possible justification for it I can come up with is that Gordin was flailing about, desperately trying to justify a fourth act.

My own recommendation would be to cut act 4 entirely, eliminating also Gordin's forced attempts late in act 3 to "plant" Sheyndele's transformation. But the act 3 curtain is not really an ending. So what is needed is a new coda of some kind that leaves the characters where they were at the end of act 3, but still provides a feeling of closure. Unfortunately, there is nothing helpful in Gordin's act 4, which revolves entirely around that forced happy ending. A creative and insightful adapter/director will be able to correct this.

❧

Allen Lewis Rickman is a director, writer, actor, translator, dialect coach, and an internationally produced playwright whose work has been presented in six languages. He has acted widely both on and off Broadway, in regional theater, and in Yiddish theater, as well as extensively in television and film: he is perhaps best known as Velvl, the shtetl husband, in the Yiddish-language prologue to the Coen brothers' Oscar-nominated *A Serious Man* (for which he also translated the Coens' dialogue into Yiddish).

Much of his directing and adapting work has been in Yiddish theater: for the Folksbiene he adapted and directed Leon Kobrin's *The Lady Next Door* and Avrom Goldfadn's *The Capricious Bride* (retitled *A Novel Romance*), as well as coadapting and directing Al Grand's Yiddish version of *The Pirates of Penzance*. For New Yiddish Rep he created and directed *The Essence: A Yiddish Theater Dim Sum*, and codeveloped and directed *The Big Bupkis: A Complete Gentile's Guide to Yiddish Vaudeville*. He developed and directed *Tevye Served Raw* for the Congress for Jewish Culture. For Target Margin he directed his own translation of Isadore Zolotarevsky's classic Yiddish melodrama *Money, Love, and Shame!* He regularly directs his own and other people's translations of Yiddish plays presented in workshop form for the YIVO Institute in New York. His English subtitles for nine classic Yiddish films were released in 2019 by Kino/Lorber.

Yankl the Blacksmith

DAVID PINSKI

Introduction

Yankl (Jake) the blacksmith is an inarticulate man struggling to re-create himself. He has depths he himself is dimly aware of but cannot develop. He wants his parents and community to respect him, and he wants to respect himself. It is clear to both him and Tamara that marital fidelity will be the measure of his personal achievement of virtue—the touchstone for his becoming the man he longs, and has it in him, to be. Adam Immerwahr, whose Theater J performed a staged reading of the play in 2019, calls it "a story about change: what does it mean for a human being to truly change? Is it even possible?" The drama lies in the psychological interaction of characters, confrontations spoken and unspoken, and Yankl's (to quote director Moshe Yassur) "heroic struggle" against his own weaknesses.

Yet in his director's notes in this volume, Yassur approaches the play as Rivke's story as much as Yankl's—indication of the century that has changed perceptions since the play appeared, as well as of the play's power as commentary on class structure and the position of women. Certainly, what in 1906 read as a happy, even humorous, ending, today is darkened by a new understanding of Rivke's situation. That can be a problem for directors who tackle the play; it can also be an opportunity to explore the female characters and, more generally, women's roles in the society in which the story is set. (I'll add that though I agree that Rivke is cruelly imprisoned in her marriage and is fighting to free herself for a better life, I find Tamara a more sympathetic, braver character than Yassur does, and Rivke more ruthless and manipulative.)

The star David Kessler, famous for his sensitivity, created the role of Yankl and often repeated it. Ester Rokhl Kaminska, "the Yiddish Duse," was a famous Tamara, and the beloved comedian Sigmund Mogulesko in the course of his career played both Rivke's husband and Yankl's father.

Pinski himself, with playwright Osip Dimov, turned the play into a screenplay, transforming it into light entertainment. The 1938 Yiddish film version entitled *The Singing Blacksmith*, with English subtitles, is still screened, starring popular singing star Moishe Oysher, sleeves rolled up to show off his biceps at the forge. When the National Yiddish Theatre–Folksbiene presented the play in 1998, Hy Wolfe played the role with strength. Caraid O'Brien adapted the play in English as *Jake the Mechanic* and workshopped it in 2001; excerpts were performed at the Association for Jewish Theaters Conference at Theater J in 2003.

Pinski was drawn to studies of intense people in extreme situations. Comparable in that way to *Yankl the Blacksmith* is his *Isaac Sheftel*, in which a creative but inarticulate workingman creates a mechanical invention but, frustrated in his attempts to develop it, finally goes mad with rage. On the other hand, many of Pinski's plays seem to dramatize ideas rather than psychology. *The Treasure*, his best-known work, is a harsh comedy about the effect on an impoverished community when gold coins are found in the cemetery. Pinski's socialist (and eventually Labor Zionist) convictions are discernible in that play and a number of others. Staged in German by Max Reinhardt and in English by the Theatre Guild, *The Treasure* is expressionist in its broad characterizations, crowd scenes, and occasionally almost choral dialogue.

Pinski was unusual among intellectual Yiddish dramatists in his depiction of frankly sexual relationships. Like their counterparts in all languages, popular Yiddish shows and revues certainly did make hay out of sex appeal and bawdy jokes. But Pinski presented passionate women drawn to powerful men, such as *Gavri and the Women* and *King David and His Wives*. He also wrote about men in thrall to women, such as *Professor Brenner* (an elderly professor desperately in love with a much younger woman) and *Each with His God* (an immigrant desperate for money to satisfy his wife). In that regard, *Yankl the Blacksmith* is not a typical serious Yiddish drama—except in the characters' energy and high temperament, terms of high praise among Yiddish audiences.

Pinski also wrote several plays of a type favored by audiences who preferred theater that made them think about philosophical and social issues. His play *The Tsvi Family* (*The Last Jew*) depicts a middle-class family in an Eastern European city, cowering in their apartment as a pogrom mob approaches and debating among themselves what to do. This play is thought to have been inspired by the 1903 Kishinev pogrom. It was controversial when it debuted in New York in 1905. Two years later, sewn into a coat lining, it was smuggled into Russia, where censors prevented Konstantin Stanislavski from staging it at the Moscow Art Theatre, but it was printed and circulated and even performed clandestinely. It received a staged reading at the National Yiddish Theatre–Folksbiene in 2003.

Sholem Aleichem, Sholem Asch, and others wrote plays set up like *The Tsvi Family*: invariably one family member is a socialist, one a Zionist, one traditionally pious, one desperately concentrating on making money, and one assimilated into the non-Jewish world where he knows he does not really belong. In Asch's play, there is also one who feels a passionate mystical love for the Polish soil; in Sholem Aleichem's, one is an artist. The issues—personal and national identity, anti-Semitism, conflicting loyalties and responsibilities—were basic to the Jewish community at the turn of the nineteenth century and indeed remain so. But this trope with its philosophical and political implications struck a chord not only with Jews but also with Russian intelligentsia, with the result that Asch's play *The Messianic Era* was a huge success in Russian even before it was produced in Yiddish.

Such allegories were popular with Yiddish audiences. Sometimes little more than staged discussions and always springboards for further debate, they were didactic in purpose and thus congenial to Yiddish culture. Some were more symbolist and poetic in tone than the rather harsh *Tsvi Family*. For example, Pinski's *The Dumb Messiah* and *The Eternal Jew* depict Jews confronting their communal destiny at moments of crisis. The former shows the remnants of a medieval Jewish community, exiled and in disarray; their rabbi's tongue was cut out, and his daughter kills herself because she is unable to take his place and lead them to Jerusalem. The latter takes place in Jerusalem immediately after the destruction of the Temple in 70 AD; the infant messiah has just been born, but a wind blew the baby away and the Jews must search for him over the world.

Pinski's upbringing was unusually privileged and cosmopolitan. He was born in 1872 and spent his early years in Moscow, where only the elite among Jewish families were allowed to live (though even those few were expelled when he was eighteen). He studied at universities in Moscow and Vienna and continued to pursue academic interests. When he was about to enter medical school, the great author I. L. Peretz, a mentor to many young writers, inspired him to devote himself to the development of the then-emerging modern Yiddish literature. Later, after he'd settled in New York, he took courses toward a doctorate in German literature at Columbia University—but dropped out to finish writing *The Tsvi Family*. He wrote not only plays but also novels and essays, including an insightful monograph analyzing the development of Yiddish drama. Many of his novels and some of his plays are available in English; his plays have also been published and performed in German, Russian, French, and Spanish.

Like his mentor Peretz, Pinski was generous to the next generation of Yiddish writers and opened his home as a salon to encourage them. He was a beloved figure in the Yiddish cultural world; he edited the long-running and highly respected literary journal *Der Tsukunft* (The Future) and during the last part of his life, when he lived in Israel, he served many years as president of the Yiddish section of PEN International. When he died in 1959, he was mourned as a "grand old man" of Yiddish letters.

Yankl the Blacksmith

DAVID PINSKI

1906

Characters

YANKL	A blacksmith, brawny, handsome, early thirties.
REB[1] SIMKHE	Yankl's father, a wagoner, ignorant and weak.
MARIOSHE	Yankl's mother, ignorant and querulous.
TAMARA	Strong-minded and intelligent young woman in her middle to late twenties.
FRUME	Tamara's aunt, cold.
REB ARON	Frume's husband, learned and pious.
RIVKE	Passionate, bitter, good-looking.
RAFAEL	Rivke's husband, pawnbroker, cringing and unpleasant.
KHAYE PESHE	Matchmaker and broker, always running to do business.
WAGONER	
VILLAGE GIRLS	

---

1. *Reb* is simply Mister, not Rabbi.

PLACE	The action takes place in a small Russian town.
TIME	Around 1900.
ACT 1	The parlor of the comfortable home of Frume, Reb Aron, and Tamara on Saturday evening at sundown as Sabbath is ending.
ACT 2	The modest home of Tamara and Yankl several months later.
ACT 3	Yankl's forge several months later.
ACT 4	The home of Tamara and Yankl the next day.

Act 1

A small town in Eastern Europe in the early twentieth century. Saturday, near sunset, as Sabbath ends, between afternoon and evening prayers, in Frume's old-fashioned, well-worn parlor. On the back wall are two windows with vases of flowers on the sills, between them a large, plush sofa flanked by a pair of armchairs. In the middle of the right wall is a doorway with a large cupboard of holy books behind it and a nice chair in front of it. Brown wallpaper on the walls. Over the sofa hang portraits of holy Jews, and over the book cupboard hangs a clock. In the middle of the ceiling, a chandelier. The floor is washed clean and covered with several carpet runners. FRUME sits at the window, stage left, in an armchair with a woman's bible in her hands and glasses on her nose, reading to herself quietly. Soon the matchmaker KHAYE PESHE enters.

KHAYE PESHE. Frume dear—

Frume gestures as if to say she'll just quickly finish the line.

The door is open and there's nobody else at home. Somebody could make off with everything in the house.

FRUME. (*Looks up, seems not to recognize her guest at first, but catches herself quickly.*) Oh, Khaye Peshe, good Sabbath, good week. I was so deep in reading that I didn't hear you come in. (*Takes off her glasses and puts them onto the bible, which she closes.*)

KHAYE PESHE. (*Sits in a chair near Frume.*) So how are you, Frume dear? I haven't seen you in a long time, really, an age, really.

FRUME. And now you probably have a match for my Yente Dvoshe? You can't stand that I've gone too long without servant problems?

KHAYE PESHE. Well, and if I did have something for her, that would be nothing to feel guilty about. What's the matter, isn't a servant a Jewish girl too? She is a Jewish girl; she ought to get married, and I'd find you another maid.

FRUME. Thanks for the favor. Never mind, she still has time. She's young. Nothing's burning.

KHAYE PESHE. And don't even the young ones want to get married? A girl, as soon she gets a little sense, she wants to get married.

FRUME. As you see me alive, I'm going to quarrel with you over this.

KHAYE PESHE. (*Laughing.*) You just stay healthy. Here's the story: I didn't come to you about Yente Dvoshe at all.

FRUME. Not about Yente Dvoshe?

KHAYE PESHE. I'll say what you said: Yente Dvoshe still has time. Used to be, no girl was too young. Today no girl is too old. Never mind, she can spend a few more years with you, if you want to hold on to her.

FRUME. So, if it isn't about Yente Dvoshe . . . ?

KHAYE PESHE. Can't I just pay a friendly visit? Does it absolutely have to be about finding a servant or finding the servant a match?

FRUME. I think . . . I thought . . . You're a welcome guest. But usually, when you come . . .

KHAYE PESHE. There's only the one bride here in your house?

FRUME. (*Looks at her amazed.*) Tamara? You mean my Tamara?

KHAYE PESHE. You're amazed. Imagine: Khaye Peshe, the servant girls' marriage broker, comes with a match for your niece. Some nerve, hm?

FRUME. Oh, to talk to you a person has to be—

KHAYE PESHE. Don't be embarrassed, you can say it, I won't be insulted. Because to tell the truth, it wouldn't have entered my mind to come propose a match for your niece. Why should I try to deny it: my merchandise is not for her, my merchandise is for a much cheaper kind of market. I know it very well, that what's good for Yente Dvoshe is not good for Reb Aron's Frume's niece, even if she is a poor orphan.

FRUME. And now you've got something for her?

KHAYE PESHE. If it was up to me, I wouldn't have anything, not even in a dream.

FRUME. But you say you're here with a match for her?

KHAYE PESHE. How can I tell you? It's not my match, it never occurred to me.

FRUME. Oh, my little crowns, look, what do I care who it occurred to?

KHAYE PESHE. Understand me, it's the first time in my life that this has happened to me. What can I tell you? I've had a lot of experiences in my life. If I got started telling you all my stories that I have experienced in my life, I'd have to live twice as long just to have time to tell you them all. But this kind of thing—it happened for the first time.

FRUME. My little crowns, my little hearts, they'll be coming from evening prayers any minute, and I still cannot get any sense from you at all.

KHAYE PESHE. What is there to make sense out of? They'll come from evening prayers, they'll put on the lights, and then we'll go on talking. Your niece isn't home?

FRUME. She's off promenading on the boulevard. Well, and are you saying that without her you won't tell me who, what, where?

KHAYE PESHE. Who says I won't? Of course I will, certainly I will.

FRUME. (*Angry*) Do you know what: go bother somebody else. You're driving me crazy. If you want to talk, go ahead and talk. If not, I don't care. You're giving me a headache.

KHAYE PESHE. Frume dear, anybody who wishes you a headache should get a headache herself that lasts her whole life. But you shouldn't be angry at me. If you knew the whole story, you wouldn't dare be angry at me for what you call driving you crazy. Here's the point: if you promise that you won't be angry at me, I'll speak openly.

FRUME. Why in the world should I get angry at you? If I don't like the match, I'll say no, and we won't do business. But talk.

KHAYE PESHE. Yes, but you ought to know first, though, that it wasn't me who thought it up. They came to me, you understand. I want you to know that. They came to me. By myself, it would never have occurred to me.

FRUME. Look how you're scared to say who the bridegroom is. You're not offering a match with an escaped convict?

KHAYE PESHE. God forbid. You think I deal in escaped convicts? My merchandise is inexpensive, maybe, but it isn't escaped convicts. Besides, it isn't even me that wants to talk to you. They sent me, so I came.

FRUME. Who sent you? Why are you driving me crazy, why?

KHAYE PESHE. Who could it be? That fine piece of goods, the blacksmith: Yankl the blacksmith.

FRUME. Who? Yankl the blacksmith? The . . . ?

KHAYE PESHE. Yes, yes, him, that's the one. That fine fellow. He came running to me all out of breath, I should go right over to you and propose the match. I wanted to spit in his face. "What do you mean?" I say to him. "Are you out of your mind? That's all you need? It has to be Reb Aron's niece, nobody else will do?" That's what I said to him, as you see me here alive. What, I should embarrass myself for his sake? "How could you come here like that?" I said to him. "You are this and that, you know it yourself what you are, and she is a kosher child, such a precious child, and a golden soul." He says to me, "Go. What do you care? If it's no, let them be the ones to say no, not you, that's not your business." I say to him, "What do you mean? I should go for them to throw me out of all the doors in the house? They'll do to me—I don't know what they'll do to me—and they'll be right." That's what I said to him. Plain and simple. Why should I be afraid of such a piece of nothing? He answers me, "You just go. I'll pay you good for everything. And if they bash your head in, I'm a blacksmith after all, I'll hammer it back into shape." So I get ready to pour out all my bad dreams on his head, and he doesn't answer back; he throws my shawl over my shoulders and pushes me out of the house and brings me practically all the way here. What do you say to that? He brought me to the little bridge, and I'm ready to bet he's standing there right now and waiting.

FRUME. Look, haven't they put the lights on in the study house?

KHAYE PESHE. Certainly Sabbath is over by now.

FRUME. So we should put them on too. (*Begins to recite the "God of Abraham" prayer for the end of Sabbath.*)

KHAYE PESHE. Oh my, if you haven't kicked me out of the house yet, that is already a kind of a miracle. Oh, I ought to say psalms now. (*Also recites "God of Abraham."*)

FRUME. (*Goes out, returns with a match, starts to light the chandelier.*) A good week.

KHAYE PESHE. (*Ending the prayer.*) A good week, a good year, it should only be a lucky week, a joyful week. Who knows, maybe—After all, you didn't kick me out, so . . . Who knows?

FRUME. (*Busying herself with the lamp, which for some reason doesn't light.*) I may not be such a good woman, but kick someone out—I've never kicked anyone out.

KHAYE PESHE. Let me tell you, my skin was shaking on me. If he hadn't dragged me here by force, I would never have come, absolutely.

FRUME. Why did he go crazy like that? Why did it have to be Tamara all of a sudden?

KHAYE PESHE. I have no idea. You think he told me? I asked him, too. Do you think he answered? I started to lay out for him various brides, girls of his own kind, I don't know: Yisroel the butcher's daughter, Efroyim the tailor's, Mikhel the shoemaker's. He says to me: those girls he can get by himself; he doesn't need me for those. "So go and get them." I say to him, "Why have you set your mind on Reb Aron's niece?" Did he answer? He dragged. He grabbed my hand so hard that if he didn't break it, it's a miracle from heaven.

FRUME. He's a good earner, probably?

KHAYE PESHE. Is he a good earner? If he wasn't such a lowlife, who could compare to him? He always has work thrown at him. If he were only a decent man, his wife would eat her fill of bread and more.

FRUME. And a fine fellow like that probably also wants a dowry?

KHAYE PESHE. From who? From your niece? Not a kopek. That's what he said: In the clothes she stands up in, that's how he'll take her. He doesn't even want a bridegroom gift. In fact, he'll buy for her—

FRUME. His father, it seems to me, is—Wait, if I'm not mistaken—

KHAYE PESHE. Who would his father be? He doesn't come from such a great family. His father is Simkhe the Wagoner.

FRUME. Nice family connection, can't deny it.

KHAYE PESHE. Listen, that is exactly the story. Why was I so scared to come to you? You know I'm not such a bashful person, after all, but one has to know where the mule is stabled.

FRUME. And what kind of a person is he?

KHAYE PESHE. What kind of a person? You must have heard. A drinker, a—but just look, Frume dear, you should be healthy and strong, you're asking questions exactly as if you actually—So look then, I beg you, in that case, let's actually talk facts—Should I—Do you want me to actually go ahead and propose the match to your niece?

FRUME. What do you mean: do I want? What does my wanting have to do with it? Is she my daughter, after all? Am I giving a dowry, after all? She is an orphan and her own boss, and she'll do what she wants to. And if I don't want, so what? She herself is no catch.

KHAYE PESHE. This is amazing. Would I ever have dreamed I would earn a fee from you?

FRUME. You're not going to earn a fee from me in any case. That's first of all. He's going to pay your fee.

KHAYE PESHE. I just mean—

FRUME. And second, better wait till you hear what she says.

KHAYE PESHE. What do you mean? She'd be a fool if she didn't grab him with both hands. You think grooms like that are wandering around in the street? Handsome he is, after all; you can hardly look him in the face; it's like looking at the sun. I don't need to describe him; you've probably seen him. Handsome and healthy, blood and milk, makes you healthy just to look at him. They all fall for him. And a good heart—you can travel the world. What he earns, he shares.

FRUME. So where does he get the money to drink?

KHAYE PESHE. Drink? You think he's a drunk? The amount of drunkenness between him and a real drunk, that's what should come to the chief of police, the villain. It's exactly the opposite. A good earner, with no wife and no children to support, so he has himself a good time. Once he gets married . . .

FRUME. Wait, didn't somebody come in the house? (*Goes to the door.*) Tamara, is that you?

TAMARA. (*Her voice is heard from the other room.*) Yes.

FRUME. Come in here a minute.

TAMARA. Right away. (*TAMARA enters, fixing her hair with her hand.*) A good week.

FRUME. Good year.

KHAYE PESHE. And here she is herself. A good week, a good year to you, Tamara dear.

TAMARA. What do you mean: "Here she is herself"?

KHAYE PESHE. Probably somebody was talking about you.

TAMARA. Saying something nice? Something bad?

KHAYE PESHE. Bad? They didn't leave a single bone unbroken. Weren't your ears ringing?

TAMARA. I wasn't listening in.

KHAYE PESHE. On the boulevard, eyes are so busy that you forget the ears. But if you knew what we were saying, you would have paid attention.

TAMARA. Maybe, maybe not.

FRUME. She came to propose a match for you. And do you know who?

KHAYE PESHE. You should just be healthy, Frume dear, you're no matchmaker. You leave that to me. We'll talk a little, and we'll talk it all through. You don't jump in feet first like a Greek into a synagogue. When you tell a girl, "I'm here about a match," she could just up and run away. Because what girl wants to get married? They're embarrassed to hear about such things.

TAMARA. Well, since I haven't run away, you're allowed to make it a little shorter.

KHAYE PESHE. Shorter! What does short have to do with it? We're not standing out in the cold. We'll do it the way it's done between us women, with plenty of conversation.

TAMARA. If I had known, I'd have stayed longer on the boulevard.

FRUME. Still longer? Not enough "promenade"? Your uncle is about to come from evening prayers, and we have to start the samovar. Yente Dvoshe also forgets she's supposed to come home.

TAMARA. I'll go start the samovar.

KHAYE PESHE. No, you hear me out. The samovar won't run away. And maybe, could be, a man is standing out there and waiting. Because you ought to know that somebody sent me here, took hold of me and dragged me here—that's how determined he is to have you as a bride.

FRUME. In short, it's Yankl the blacksmith.

TAMARA. Who?

FRUME. Yankl the blacksmith. Let's get this over with. You know him, you've probably heard about him, so if you like him, say yes and go start the samovar.

KHAYE PESHE. But Frume dear, darling, sweetheart, you can't ruin the whole match for me that way.

FRUME. I hate chatter for nothing. What's so complicated here? She's no child, she knows very well that Khayim Shimen's son won't propose a match with her, and Polyakov's either, and Rothschild for sure not, so there's nothing to talk about. An orphan without a dowry has no reason to act proud. And since his family connections don't bother me—

TAMARA. (*Standing all this time as if frozen, barely audible.*) Yes, you're the main thing, that we know.

FRUME. What does that mean: "I'm the main thing"? What do you know about it? You just tell me what will come of your staying here? What will be the practical result? What will you get by sitting and waiting? Do I have a way of supporting you?

TAMARA. I have no complaints about you.

FRUME. Thank you very much. As if you're entitled to have complaints against me. I won't ask again how long you'll keep living at my expense. But if somebody comes and wants to take you as you are, there is nothing to think over.

KHAYE PESHE. Just as you are, that's how he wants to take you, just as you are. And he promised gifts and whatever you want. It has taken hold of him so that he positively dragged me here, with violence, exactly as if you were waiting to welcome him. He led me up to the bridge, and he stood there to make sure I went into your house. He must be standing there still, waiting till I come back.

Tamara goes to window left and looks out at the street.

Well, you see him there? It's dark, otherwise you would probably see him there.

TAMARA. (*Turns from window.*) Go tell him that . . .

KHAYE PESHE. That—that—that—?

TAMARA. (*Quietly*) That . . . good.

KHAYE PESHE. (*Astonished, claps her hands.*) My God, my little fathers, just look, oh my, I don't believe my own ears. A—

FRUME. I think you should think about this seriously. I'm certainly not forcing you. You yourself certainly must know what kind of person he is.

TAMARA. What difference does it make, Aunt? What does a poor orphan have to think over?

FRUME. Just look, was I so wrong when I said that?

TAMARA. I have nothing against you, Aunt.

FRUME. And if you did have something against me, you think I care?

TAMARA. So then there's for sure nothing to talk about.

FRUME. The great wrongs I did you! Supporting you wasn't enough.

TAMARA. Whoever said anything to you at all?

KHAYE PESHE. Oh, little crowns, will you look at me, I'm somehow sitting here like an idiot. What am I sitting for, what? I have to run to him. So really, what should I tell him?

TAMARA. You heard what.

KHAYE PESHE. Oh, he'll crown me with a golden crown. So that means he can come, let's say, today, actually today, for the engagement contract?

FRUME. What's the hurry? No need to rush.

KHAYE PESHE. What's the point of postponing? If the answer is really yes, why put off the engagement? Oh, lord in heaven oh my, the things that can happen. Oh, I'm going to run to him as if spirits were chasing me, oh—In the meantime, a good week to you. (*Hurries out.*)

FRUME. Really, though, why such a hurry?

TAMARA. I'll go start the samovar.

FRUME. Why are you being so snooty with me? Exactly, really, as if I'd forced you somehow.

Tamara goes toward the door. REB ARON enters.

REB ARON. Good week. Why is it so dark in the dining room? And who was that running out of the house like a lunatic?

FRUME. Khaye Peshe the broker. (*To Tamara.*) Go bring in the things for the end-of-Sabbath blessings.

Tamara exits. Frume covers an edge of the table.

You can wish Tamara *mazl tov*. Khaye Peshe was here with a match for her. The groom sent her himself, and our girl has agreed.

REB ARON. Well, in a lucky hour. Who is the groom?

FRUME. Even if the groom is not such a catch, so what, so long as she wants him.

> *Tamara enters with the equipment for the ceremony that ends the Sabbath: a carafe of red wine, a goblet, a spice box, and a special braided candle.*

REB ARON. Who is it?

FRUME. First make the blessing.

REB ARON. Why are you afraid to name the groom to me?

TAMARA. Yankl the blacksmith.

REB ARON. Who? Who did you say? Yankl?

TAMARA. What frightened you so, Uncle? Maybe you don't approve of the family connection?

REB ARON. With that—? With him? But he is—You must be joking. (*Looks at Frume.*)

FRUME. (*Crossly*) No joke. No joke. Make the blessing, go on. How much longer do I have to wait?

REB ARON. (*Pours wine in the goblet.*) I won't believe you even if you—I don't know what.

TAMARA. You will believe it, Uncle, because he'll arrive here any minute. What's the matter, is it possible you don't like him? I like him very much, and so does Aunt.

REB ARON. But he—Oh well—But you could have asked me first, too. What was the big rush?

FRUME. Just make the blessing already. You can talk it all over later. Didn't I ask her what was the rush?

REB ARON. Well, ah—How can a person do such a thing? He's after all, he's—Oh my— (*Reb Aron starts the ceremony, makes the blessings, interrupting himself often with exclamations of unhappiness and bewilderment.*)

After the blessings, everyone wishes each other "Good week."

Ah. I mean—Ever hear of such a bridegroom? Yankl the blacksmith.

Tamara takes the ritual things and exits.

Now what is the true story? Is this really true?

FRUME. Who would lie to you, who?

REB ARON. So then what way is this to behave?

FRUME. What kind of way should it be? She got stubborn and that was that.

REB ARON. What does that mean: "She got stubborn"? How can we allow such a thing?

FRUME. What "allow"? Is she asking for your advice? She is an orphan and can make decisions for herself.

REB ARON. And if she decides to take a rope and hang herself, we allow that too? Ever hear of such a groom for her? Yankl the blacksmith. Such a contemptible person, such a piece of nothing, a—a—Forgive me for talking this way. Such a womanizer, such a drunk.

FRUME. Doesn't she know that? What do you have to yell about like a madman? Do you have any other groom for her? Can you give her a dowry? And he'll take her as she is.

REB ARON. And that's reason enough for us to hand her over to an I-don't-know-who, an outcast, a—

FRUME. Will you look at him: now we're handing her over. What does that mean, we're handing her over? She herself snapped him up. You don't know what you're talking about.

REB ARON. What does that mean: she "snapped him up"? How could she possibly have "snapped him up"?

FRUME. How could she have snapped him up? What do you think she is? A little girl? A charming little child, you think? She is already—no evil eye—getting on in years and understands that one is better than none. What is she waiting for, what? And besides, what are you making such a fuss for? Doesn't he make a good living? Doesn't he have money? So he's not such a saint—when she's his wife, she'll make him over. And she is such a piece of goods, don't you worry, she'll wind him around her finger, whatever he is.

REB ARON. That drunk, that womanizer, that . . .

FRUME. If he wants to get married, that's a sign that he wants to stop being what he was.

REB ARON. So according to you, in other words, it's a good match? So according to you, in other words—

FRUME. What, according to me, what? Why am I talking to you?

REB ARON. All right, she is your niece, after all; she's your brother's daughter. All I'm saying is, I'm saying, that if she hadn't had you for an aunt—

FRUME. Oh, here it comes back to me. Why come pick on me? If she made a grab, it's my fault? I'm forcing her? She should have taken the yeshiva boy when she still lived in her father's house; he was soaked through and through in the ritual bath.

REB ARON. Listen, what have you done? This is what I'm saying: that if she hadn't had you for an aunt and didn't have to come to you for favors, she would—I'm not talking about good family, I don't care that he's a blacksmith, I don't care about his father the wagon driver. I'll even say what you said: an orphan, without a dowry, a poor girl, what can you do? But speaking plainly, what is a fine and pious girl doing with such an outcast? How can she want him at all? When—when—when he isn't even a Jew. You want to convince me that she snapped him up of her own free will? When—No.

Tamara enters. Her eyes look as if she's been crying.

FRUME. What's happening with the tea?

TAMARA. Yente Dvoshe is here.

FRUME. What's the rainstorm in the eyes?

REB ARON. Ever hear of such a match? Yankl the blacksmith. But it's nothing; you have nothing to cry about. He came? So he'll go. I'd just like to know how the thought even came to his mind to think of a match with you. Such arrogance from such a contemptible creature.

TAMARA. Uncle, don't insult him, because he's going to be my bridegroom.

REB ARON. What kind of talk is that? Do you know what you're saying? What does that mean: he's going to be your bridegroom? He'll do it by force?

TAMARA. Not by force, but—

FRUME. So then what were you crying about?

REB ARON. (*Taking a prayer book from the bookcase to say evening prayers.*) You see, my daughter, I say it to your aunt to her face, she really is bad, but . . .

FRUME. You don't like me, so maybe you might divorce me? I'm so bad. All the bad things I've done to her! I didn't give her food to eat. I ate and drank bird of paradise, while the poor thing was hungry in my house.

REB ARON. (*To Tamara.*) But, you understand, I really want to say this to you: even so, it's still not so bad for you here that you should have to run away to Yankl the blacksmith.

TAMARA. I don't want to run away, and I didn't say that it is bad for me with you.

REB ARON. No, I really mean it. You understand, it's nothing. There's nothing to run away from, nothing to rush from like from a fire. You're not so old yet, you can live with us till your true predestined one comes, some decent person.

TAMARA. If Yankl doesn't bother me—

FRUME. See, is it worth talking to her?

REB ARON. What does that mean: "Yankl doesn't bother you"? Do you know what you're saying? Do you know what kind of a person he is? He is—Hm! He shouldn't be allowed into a Jewish home. Do you know that at least?

TAMARA. I know.

REB ARON. So then?

TAMARA. I know everything about Yankl. I know maybe more than you do. And all the same . . .

FRUME. (*Ironically*) He is so handsome, after all.

TAMARA. Well, Aunt, after all, that's not such a terrible flaw.

FRUME. (*To Reb Aron.*) You see? What more do you want?

REB ARON. His good looks are ruining him. That's why he is so debauched. I tell you, I can forgive what he was, but I'm afraid that he won't become better, that he will remain the same scoundrel after the wedding that he was before, that—that he is just somehow not a decent man.

TAMARA. (*Sighs.*) That's what I'm afraid of too. I'm not crying over what he has been up to till now, or that he is a blacksmith, that he doesn't come from a great family. He is a thousand times dearer to me than the yeshiva scholar wet from the ritual bath.

FRUME. (*To Reb Aron.*) Now you see?

TAMARA. Why should I deny it? I know that he has many good qualities. People love him the minute they meet him. But I wouldn't like to live to see him come home drunk, and there are a lot more things I wouldn't like to see.

REB ARON. So why should a healthy person crawl into a sick bed?

TAMARA. (*Sighs.*) Oh well, I'll risk it. After all every match is a gamble. (*Triumphantly*) But how do you like it that of all the girls, he chose me?

REB ARON. Is he a fool? He already knows what a girl is. And a girl like you—

FRUME. Just look at the old man. Soon his mouth will start to water.

TAMARA. So why should it trouble you so, Uncle? It will be fine. I'll—I will make a decent man of him. You'll see, Uncle.

FRUME. Shh, isn't someone opening the door?

We hear Khaye Peshe's voice and other voices.

Here they are.

Tamara becomes very agitated but controls herself and puts on a calm expression.

REB ARON. And look, I still haven't said my prayers.

Enter Khaye Peshe followed by YANKL, and after him REB SIMKHE with MARIOSHE. People greet each other: "Good week. Good week."

KHAYE PESHE. Here you have the groom and the in-laws. We made it fast.

FRUME. Sit down, have a seat.

Yankl sits down in an armchair down near the right wall, looks around at the room and throws side glances at Tamara. Marioshe sits with a sigh on a chair near the left wall and supports her head in her right hand. Reb Simkhe sits not far from Marioshe, making chewing motions with his toothless mouth and periodically emitting noises: "hm, hm, khe."

KHAYE PESHE. (*Sitting on a footstool in the background.*) You see that? Nobody like him: sat himself down like an aristocrat.

MARIOSHE. (*Sigh.*) Sure, an aristocrat. Let it be said of the enemies of Zion.

YANKL. (*Embarrassed laugh.*) Some good reference.

REB ARON. So then, Reb Simkhe, you want to become my in-law.

REB SIMKHE. (*Emitting noises.*) Hm, hm, khe. "I want." What does that have to do with it? What he wants, he does.

MARIOSHE. He rushed in like he was poisoned. Like a man that was poisoned. We should come here with him. I thought he was talking crazy—enemies of Israel! If Khaye Peshe wasn't with him and didn't tell us, I'd have let loose all my nightmares on his head and wouldn't have budged. I'd have taken it for one of his jokes and tricks. And I'll tell you the truth: we still don't believe him.

FRUME. Oh yes, when you're poor, everybody's family is equal.

MARIOSHE. I always wondered where he'd find somebody who'd take him.

Tamara laughs nervously.

KHAYE PESHE. Shh, you'll ruin the match for me.

REB SIMKHE. Shh, shh. Opened her mouth. (*To Marioshe.*) Cow, horse.

KHAYE PESHE. Well, and you sat yourself down, nice and quiet like a bridegroom.

YANKL. That's what I am.

MARIOSHE. All of a sudden he got bashful.

KHAYE PESHE. You know what, let's let the bride and groom be by themselves to talk things over.

FRUME. Come into the dining room and let them talk things over.

REB ARON. Why do they have to be alone? They can sit there, and we'll sit here. Or we can all go into the dining room. They'll talk about their things and we'll talk about ours. I still have to say evening prayers.

KHAYE PESHE. Look at that, may I be healthy, Reb Aron is scared to leave them alone.

REB ARON. I'm scared? What do you mean I'm scared?

MARIOSHE. He's right, too, upon my faith.

FRUME. Never mind, let's not make him out to be such an I-don't-know-what. What was, was. Now he'll be a bridegroom, he'll get married and become a better man.

MARIOSHE. A better man. Look who'll become a better man.

KHAYE PESHE. Come, come. (*To Marioshe.*) Listen, you should have stayed home.

REB SIMKHE. (*To Marioshe.*) Shut up, you. Shut up. Cow. Horse. Go home.

REB ARON. (*Groans.*) Ah, ah, well, well. (*Exits, reciting prayers.*)

MARIOSH. (*Groaning.*) "Shut up," "shut up," and that's all. (*Exits.*)

REB SIMKHE. Cow, cow, horse, horse. (*Exits.*)

KHAYE PESHE. Ever heard a person's own mother talk like that?

Khaye Peshe exits. Frume exits last, leaving the door open. Khaye Peshe comes back and shuts it. Yankl is embarrassed, doesn't know what to do with his hands, takes off his hat, turns it around a while, and smiles with an embarrassed smile when his eye catches Tamara's. She is altogether calm. She sits on the sofa stubbornly, meets his glances steadfastly, and waits for him to say something.

YANKL. (*Smiles.*) Ah, can I smoke a cigarette? Maybe I'll find my tongue. (*Without waiting for an answer, takes out a tobacco case and starts to roll a cigarette.*)

TAMARA. (*Another short pause.*) I had no idea that you're the shy type.

YANKL. (*Licking the cigarette paper with his tongue.*) Yes, that's right, you say something too.

TAMARA. I don't need a cigarette to do it.

Just behind the door we hear Reb Aron singing end-of-Sabbath songs.

YANKL. (*Strikes a match on his pants and smokes.*) Your uncle is really listening in to what we're saying.

TAMARA. Not much for him to hear. (*Yankl laughs. Smokes. They are silent.*)

YANKL. You—you—Soon you'll believe I can't count to two.

TAMARA. And can you?

YANKL. Even higher than two. The—the devil, I don't know, my tongue is somehow not working.

TAMARA. The cigarette didn't help either?

Yankl and Tamara are silent.

(*With a penetrating look, calmly*) Tell me, what put it into your head to send the matchmaker to me, and even to push Khaye Peshe to rush so?

YANKL. That's it, that's the way. Now I'll be able to talk. (*Puts out the cigarette, stands up, throws it into the spittoon near the door, and begins to talk in excitement, with a lot of hand gestures.*) Listen, Tamara, I—How should I tell you? Ha, I won't be able to get myself out of this. A plague, I somehow don't know how to talk so it comes out right. But you'll understand me all right. So listen. You tell me: why have I gotten rid of all my nasty ways lately?

TAMARA. I had no idea that you have gotten rid of them.

YANKL. As I am a Jew, as you see me here, I have thrown them away.

TAMARA. Probably you found that you'd had enough of behaving as you used to behave.

YANKL. No, not that. I—I—How should I tell you? I was—I was—I was longing for you.

TAMARA. Longing for me? How did that happen?

YANKL. You see, then, you know it, you know it from since I met you at Leah the seamstress's, from then and ever since then, it's—how can I tell you?—you're somehow, like, baked into my heart. You believe me, right? As I stand here, your voice is in my ears. I bang with my hammer and hear your voice. Will you believe me?

TAMARA. I didn't know that my voice is so loud.

YANKL. No, exactly because you have such a quiet, somehow such a quiet and happy voice. Somehow it got inside in—in—. A misery when a person can't talk! How will I tell you: it made me so warm in my heart. You must know, Tamara, that I know about girls, that—I've already gotten to know a lot of girls. You must know it. I don't have to tell you the story, then. And I haven't felt for any girl what I feel for you. Every girl was a toy to me, a plaything, a sort of game. How should I say it to you? I am a person full of fire, a—a—person full of gunpowder, and every girl was a match. The gunpowder used to catch, explode—and nothing left. That's why I never got married yet, although I am, to tell you the secret, almost thirty-two. You have affected me somehow altogether differently—altogether—differently. I've become somehow extinguished, as I stand here. I somehow feel so strange. How can I tell you? Somehow as if somebody poured ointment on my heart, somehow soft as butter, so soothing somehow. Why go on and on: since I met you, I've started to be ashamed of my own self.

TAMARA. That was the best thing you could have done. And you got rid of your old "good deeds"?

YANKL. Threw them away. As I live. I said to myself: "you drag yourself around with her in your head"—I meant: with you—"so stop being a pig." And done, finished, as if I never carried on at all.

TAMARA. That is very good.

YANKL. "Good" is nothing. You don't know how good it is. I feel I'm an altogether new person. And you'll laugh, right? I haven't stopped thinking about you. This whole time, never stopped. You followed me like a shadow. And today, when I saw you going around like that on the boulevard, like a queen, your face was shining and your eyes looked around so full of life—

TAMARA. Look what compliments you know how to make.

YANKL. No, it's not compliments. Compliments you figure out beforehand. But this I saw and I felt. I looked at you and felt. I looked at you and—and my heart hammered. So I said to myself this way: "Ah, what will be will be—I'm going to go and send Khaye Peshe to her." And from thought to deed. Oh, who could have imagined that you wouldn't kick her out of the house, and you even—oh, oh—I can't get it into my head. (*Suddenly, with doubt*) It is the truth? Khaye Peshe didn't fool me, right?

TAMARA. Of course not. Otherwise you wouldn't be here now talking with me.

YANKL. You don't know how—how——how should I tell you?—how happy I am. Oh Tamara, you will never regret it.

TAMARA. Let's hope not.

YANKL. Never mind, you'll see. Ah, but I can't get it into my head how quickly it went. You must have known what kind of a piece of goods I was: really, how come you didn't kick Khaye Peshe out the door?

TAMARA. You want to know?

YANKL. I guess. (*Embarrassed little laugh.*)

TAMARA. You are handsome, smart, and good. I knew that. I thought it over: it's not impossible that if you fell into the right hands, your good qualities would conquer the bad. Well, and I live with an aunt—

YANKL. Oho.

TAMARA. Settling myself was impossible, because for a year and a half I had to run the household for my sick father.

YANKL. Yes, I understand, I understand.

TAMARA. And life with my aunt is not so sweet.

YANKL. Yes, I know that. In fact, I guessed that.

TAMARA. And you guessed right.

YANKL. (*Heatedly*) You'll see; you won't regret it. Tamara, you don't know me yet. You've always heard that I'm a bum and an I-don't-know-what. I don't deny anything. That's what I was. Something like a demon sat inside me, I was possessed, and it pushed me and made me act like a bum. But when the demon let me be, I became a totally different person. When the demon let me be, I used to even go in the study house to hear a chapter of Talmud, or Ethics, or Proverbs, or take a holy book in my hand.

TAMARA. I didn't know that.

YANKL. You see, I told you that you don't know me yet.

TAMARA. But the demon didn't let you be very often, did he?

YANKL. (*Laughs.*) Unfortunately, no. Rarely, rarely. But in the last weeks, I've driven him out entirely.

TAMARA. What if he comes back?

YANKL. God forbid. His place has been taken by an—angel. (*Embarrassed.*) I mean you.

TAMARA. A demon is stronger than an angel.

YANKL. (*Heatedly*) No, never. Even in Torah, even in Ethics and Proverbs, an angel is stronger.

TAMARA. But really, only in Ethics and Proverbs.

YANKL. No, don't say that; don't talk like that. I want to be a different person, and I will be. There's no devil inside me anymore. You'll be my kosher mezuzah, my Sabbath song, and all the devils, all the evil angels, they'll run away from me. (*Embarrassed laugh.*)

TAMARA. I will do my best.

YANKL. You won't need to.

TAMARA. All the better.

YANKL. So, a deal?

TAMARA. (*Looks at him sharply a while.*) A deal.

YANKL. So—shake on it?

TAMARA. (*Giving him her hand.*) Shake.

YANKL. (*Shakes her hand strongly.*) Oh, this is good.

TAMARA. (*Laughing.*) Just don't squeeze it so hard.

YANKL. Oh Tamara, you don't know what I feel. Ahh. Listen, I want to tell you something. You just shouldn't be offended, you hear. Once the gunpowder went up with a match. (*Embarrassed laugh.*) I mean once I went with a girl, one of the girls from that time of my life. We went in the woods. You can already understand. (*Embarrassed laugh.*)

Tamara shudders.

She was a pretty girl and what they call a nice girl, and for a long time she didn't want to go walking in the woods with me. That excited me terribly, and whenever I met up with her, I used to feel like a wild animal. Until finally she let go of her stubbornness and set off with me to the woods. The whole way, the blood cooked in me so strangely, and when we arrived in the woods, something struck me a blow on the head, and I lifted her up in my arms and gobbled at her dress with my teeth, and yelled and snorted like a wild boar and ran into the wood.

TAMARA. (*Shivering with her whole body.*) Feh, feh. Why are you telling me this? Why are you telling me this?

YANKL. Why am I telling you this? (*His breath catches.*) Why am I telling you this? Because I feel I could lift you up now and yell—Oh, I could yell.

TAMARA. What? What?

YANKL. Because I feel that I have now become a different person. Oh, understand: now I could yell exactly—exactly as if I had somehow thrown off a whole burden off my back, a thing that pressed me down somehow. Oh, Tamara, if you knew—

REB ARON. (*Opens the door.*) What, you still haven't talked it over?

YANKL. Talked it over, talked it over.

REB ARON. (*To the others.*) Well, you can all come in. (*To Tamara.*) In the meantime, we have more guests.

Khaye Peshe, Marioshe, Reb Simkhe, Frume, RIVKE, and RAFAEL enter.

RIVKE. A good week and *mazl tov*.

REB ARON. Wait, first we'll perform the betrothal, the way Jews are supposed to do it, and after that we'll tell them *mazl tov* and drink a toast. (*To Frume.*) Where is my red kerchief?

Frume goes out for the kerchief and Reb Aron follows.

KHAYE PESHE. Well, what do you say to that? Did I dream that today I'd attend a betrothal, and I'd be the matchmaker, and where it would be, and who?

REB SIMKHE. (*To Yankl.*) You—you—Put on a hat. A gentile! Head uncovered altogether.

MARIOSHE. You never caught him in a greater sin than that?

Yankl goes back to his seat, picks up his hat, and puts it on with an embarrassed smile.

RIVKE. (*To Yankl.*) So, you're really going to be a bridegroom?

YANKL. You see for yourself.

RAFAEL. (*Positions himself between Yankl and Rivke.*) That's the way it happens, hm, Mr. Yankl—it's Mr. Yankl now, right?—Now you'll be a big shot. (*Giggles at every line. This is his characteristic speech mannerism throughout the play.*)

RIVKE. Nobody's asking you what he'll be.

MARIOSHE. Some big shot. (*Rivke laughs.*)

REB SIMKHE. Quiet, quiet. Cow, horse. He will be, why shouldn't he? You have to talk.

RIVKE. (*To Rafael.*) Why have you pushed yourself in the middle, with your beard like a goat and your laugh like a horse? Get away from me.

Yankl wants to go over to Tamara but Rivke gets in the way.

(*To Yankl.*) So sudden somehow, out of the clear blue sky. Why so sudden?

YANKL. My predestined one suddenly appeared.

RAFAEL. (*Again, positions himself between Rivke and Yankl.*) The predestined one. No use complaining. All the girls, all the young women—pushed to one side and—that's that.

Yankl goes over to Tamara.

RIVKE. (*To Rafael.*) Will you get out of my sight?

Reb Aron enters from stage right with a red kerchief in his hand.

REB ARON. Now they will be betrothed, and then we will give them a proper *mazl tov* and a toast and refreshments, and may it really be with good fortune and according to God's will. (*Winds the kerchief around his hand, leaving two opposite corners.*)

Yankl takes hold of one corner and Tamara the other.

Let it be known that you are now bride and groom before God and man, and may it be with good fortune and happiness.

ALL. (*All congratulate each other.*) Congratulations. In a lucky hour.

REB SIMKHE. (*To Yankl.*) Now you're a bridegroom, a bridegroom. (*Tearfully*) Be a decent man, my son. Do your best. Do your best. Throw away your tricks, throw them away. Otherwise it will be a bitter pity for her. You've had no pity on your parents, you wanted to bury your parents, be rid of your parents. And what could I do about it? But for her it's a pity. Throw away your tricks, throw them away, you hear? She's a dear girl. I'll tear you out of me. When it comes to her, I won't keep quiet. I won't keep quiet.

MARIOSHE. Why give a sermon? Gives him a sermon. (*Weeps.*) He's bound to—

REB SIMKHE. Quiet. Quiet. Cow.

YANKL. (*Moved*) It'll be good, Dad. It'll be good.

KHAYE PESHE. Now he'll put on the yoke, he'll do without his little games.

REB SIMKHE. (*To Tamara.*) You are a kosher child, my daughter. I'm on your side, always.

Frume appears in the doorway.

FRUME. Come, in-laws, come.

Marioshe, Khaye Peshe, and Reb Simkhe leave. Rafael goes to the door too, but seeing that Rivke isn't coming, he remains too.

RAFAEL. (*To Rivke.*) Well, come on, then. What are you standing there for, Rivke? Maybe the bride and groom want to be alone.

RIVKE. What do you say to this extremely pious idiot? (*Laughs.*)

RAFAEL. But you see they want to be alone.

RIVKE. (*Laughing.*) You know what, Tamara? Let's swap.

RAFAEL. Ah, silly, she's just talking nonsense. She wouldn't trade me for ten sacks of onions.

RIVKE. Wouldn't I just. I'd even give you away free, just to be rid of you.

RAFAEL. Ah, get out of here, you don't want to be rid of me at all. We're going to grow old together.

RIVKE. That remains to be seen. You with your adorable little giggle and your romantic little earlocks and cute little beard.

RAFAEL. (*Earnestly*) You shouldn't talk that way about my earlocks. What are you, a gentile?

RIVKE. Wait, you'll drive me to convert yet.

RAFAEL. What kind of a joke is that? May God not punish you for talking like that.

FRUME. (*In doorway.*) Well, why don't you come?

RIVKE. (*Goes to door.*) So, what do you say, Tamara? Want to swap? (*Exits laughing.*)

RAFAEL. (*Following.*) The things she can say. (*Exits.*)

YANKL. (*Has stood impatiently throughout.*) I see that you were frightened by what I told you before. Maybe it was stupid of me. I shouldn't have said it. I won't do it anymore, really.

TAMARA. (*With pain.*) Really, I beg you, don't tell me about those things. I don't want to know anything. I don't want to hear it. I can't hear it.

YANKL. (*Warmly*) No more. You'll never have to hear about my old doings, never again.

TAMARA. That's good. I really beg you very much.

YANKL. —And certainly never see such things. I feel that now I am an entirely different person.

TAMARA. That is certainly good. It's all I want.

YANKL. You're not angry anymore?

TAMARA. I wasn't angry. It just made me . . .

YANKL. (*Takes her hand.*) Then give me a smile.

TAMARA. (*Happily*) A laugh, even.

KHAYE PESHE. (*From outside the door.*) Bride and groom, bride and groom.

YANKL. We're coming, we're coming.

TAMARA. (*Joyfully*) Open the door. Make way.

KHAYE PESHE. (*Khaye Peshe opens the door, begins clapping her hands and dancing to the rhythm.*) Make way! A lucky hour. Make way! A lucky hour. (*She dances into the room and to the rhythm of the words, she triumphantly escorts Tamara and Yankl out to where the others wait.*) Make way! A lucky hour.

END OF ACT I

Act 2

About one year later.

The dining room of Yankl's house. Upstage, a door leads to the street, the kitchen, and the empty room. Stage left, a door to the bedroom. Stage right, two windows with flowerpots. Between the windows, a cane-seat sofa; standing before it, a round occasional table covered with a cloth. Chairs on both sides of the sofa and table. Right of the exit door, a glass-fronted cupboard; behind its glass door hang curtains, behind which can be seen glassware on the top shelves and books and holy books on the lower shelves. Left of the same exit door is a large wall clock. Left, near the upstage wall, is a large hearth for cooking. On the same wall, a dresser, covered with a cloth, with a mirror hanging above it. On the dresser lies a book and two standing, decorated brass candlesticks. Over the table hangs a nice porcelain lamp. Great cleanliness and order reign in the room. The furniture is brand new. The floor is freshly washed. A bright summer day shines in at the windows.

Tamara lies on the sofa sleeping. Yankl, his work apron around him, opens the door carefully and enters. His grimy face shines with a happy smile. He stands a while and gazes very lovingly at the sleeper, making faces as if kissing her. Then he tiptoes to the dresser, takes the book lying there, returns to the sofa, lowers himself to the floor near Tamara's head and reads. Tamara stretches out her hand and strokes his hair.

YANKL. (*Jumps up onto one knee.*) Sweetheart, you're not asleep?

TAMARA. You woke me.

YANKL. I'm such a bear. I thought I was being so quiet.

TAMARA. When you got down on the ground, I felt you.

YANKL. You understand, there's no work at all, so I'm allowed to come in to my little wife.

TAMARA. Was I asleep long?

YANKL. An hour and a half. It's three o'clock already.

TAMARA. I slept so long!

YANKL. You deserve it—you're sleeping for two, after all: for yourself and for the little soul who's right in there.

Tamara shows her pregnant belly.

Soon enough he'll come out and say, "Kaa, kaa, kaa." (*Imitates baby's cries.*)

TAMARA. (*Yawns.*) I'm still sleepy.

YANKL. So what will it be, a boy or a girl?

TAMARA. Whatever comes will be a welcome guest.

YANKL. Welcome guest, a precious guest. But I'd just like to know.

TAMARA. You'll know soon enough.

YANKL. You understand, naturally, whatever comes will be a precious guest. But all the same I can't help wanting—a boy. Somehow, you understand, a boy is a whole other thing.

TAMARA. I know, I know. I know all about it.

YANKL. Somehow a boy—a strapping boy, you understand. A girl is also not second-rate merchandise, God forbid. But a boy is altogether something else. Somehow a rascal, a kid, a tough guy— (*Laughs, embarrassed.*)

TAMARA. Was Khaye Peshe here?

YANKL. No, she hasn't come yet.

TAMARA. She is supposed to bring me a good servant girl.

YANKL. In your hands, every servant becomes good.

TAMARA. (*Caressingly*) You're pretty pleased with your wife, aren't you?

YANKL. And who isn't pleased with my wife? You could travel the world.

TAMARA. You're going to make me conceited.

YANKL. That is just fine.

TAMARA. And if I want a dish from heaven?

YANKL. Then I'll forge a great big ladder from the ground to the sky and go up and get you your dish.

> *Tamara strokes his head then bends over him and kisses him on the lips. Yankl grabs her around with both hands and kisses her hard and painfully.*

TAMARA. (*Lies back down and gazes at him a while. Caressingly*) You know, I could really enjoy something warm to drink.

YANKL. (*Jumps up.*) Well, why didn't you say so? One, two, three and there it is. (*Goes to the door.*)

> *Marioshe enters, knitting a sock.*

And here's Mama too. She sniffed that I was going to put on the samovar.

MARIOSHE. (*Offended, sarcastic*) Sure, I sniffed it. I can't do without your tea.

YANKL. Tamara sweetness, can you tell me when Mama is going to stop scowling?

MARIOSHE. Go. Go put on the samovar.

YANKL. (*Laughs.*) Oh, Mama is mad. (*Exits.*)

MARIOSHE. (*Sits on a chair facing Tamara.*) What are you doing?

TAMARA. I'm busy feeling proud of my husband.

MARIOSHE. Proud of him? Of him and his father too, some lot to be proud of.

TAMARA. Can't you ever forgive them, Mother-in-law?

MARIOSHE. People like that. Are they human beings? The father would give his soul away to anybody in the whole world, but for his wife all he can do is be a big shot and yell. And the son—

TAMARA. What about the son?

MARIOSHE. (*Waves it away with her hand.*) Oh well, nothing to talk about.

TAMARA. Now what do you hold against your son?

MARIOSHE. What do I hold against him? It's simply a pity for you.

TAMARA. That is not nice of you, Mother-in-law. A mother who can't forgive her own son for what he used to be once upon a time!

MARIOSHE. Not worth talking about.

TAMARA. It's not nice. His own mother.

MARIOSHE. So his own mother, so what? I know my own troubles. He takes after his father. This way today, and that way tomorrow, and the day after tomorrow this way again.

TAMARA. Almost a year since our engagement and eight months since our wedding, and what bad have you seen from him?

MARIOSHE. Oh well, let's hope you're right.

TAMARA. No, I really mean it.

MARIOSHE. I know my troubles, I told you. What happened with him before the engagement? A crazy fit used to come on him, all of a sudden he used to become a saint in a hat and go off to the study house, and after that the crazy fit came and turned him around again, and again a disgrace among disgraces.

TAMARA. Are you trying to say that—

MARIOSHE. I'm not trying to say anything at all.

TAMARA. (*Sits up.*) Then I want to tell you, Mother-in-law, that you may calm down. You may drive all such thoughts out of your head. You wait, you'll have a lot of pleasure from your son yet. He'll pay you back yet for all the worries and anxieties that he gave you.

MARIOSHE. (*Groans with a frown.*) Yes, yes, he'll pay me back.

TAMARA. If I'm not scared, then you for sure shouldn't be scared.

MARIOSHE. I'm scared? What do I have to be scared about? I'm only sorry for you.

TAMARA. Oh, go on, Mother-in-law, you're so gloomy; you really ought to cure yourself. What kind of silly things are you saying? (*Embarrassed.*) You'll be a grandmother soon; you should look more cheerful somehow, livelier.

MARIOSHE. Well, I'll probably look like this till I die.

TAMARA. Just trust me. Your Yankl is already not what he was and never will be. I guarantee it.

MARIOSHE. (*Again, scratches her head with a knitting needle.*) We'll see. Let's hope you're right and I'm a liar.

TAMARA. Ah, what are you talking about?

YANKL. (*Enters with the samovar.*) Make way. Make way. I gave the samovar an order, it should make it snappy because Tamara wants tea. So in one minute pif-paf-sssss, —and here you have it.

TAMARA. See, Mother-in-law, even the samovar is afraid of me.

YANKL. (*Takes out the teapot, brews tea.*) And how. In one minute—pif-paf finished.

Tamara wants to take the glasses from the shelves.

Now then, you, Tamaruk, don't help me, please don't. Sit like a princess and allow yourself to be served.

TAMARA. (*She sits in a commanding pose.*) My dear Sir Servingman, just don't break the glasses.

YANKL. (*In the manner of a waiter, pours out three glasses of tea and places them on three sides of the table. To Tamara.*) Well, is my tea so bad? (*To Marioshe.*) Come, Mrs. Fancy Lady. (*Imitates her expression.*) Why are you sitting like that?

MARIOSHE. (*Pulls herself up and goes to the table. Groans.*) Aaach—

YANKL. You'll see what'll happen. When the little cutie-pie is born, I won't let you near him looking like that. His little tummy could start to ache from sheer fright.

TAMARA. Don't talk foolishness and let your mother alone. A forehead that's been wrinkled for decades can't smooth out in a year.

MARIOSHE. Aaach, it'll never be smooth. When you have a husband like that and a son like that . . .

YANKL. (*Agitated.*) A son like what?

TAMARA. Shh, shh, no shouting. A quiet face, that's just right.

Reb Simkhe enters in the clothes he wears as a wagon driver.

And here's the father-in-law too.

MARIOSHE. Here he is. Just what we needed.

YANKL. Another one smelled the tea. Come sit down. I'm giving tea away today. (*Jumps up for another glass.*)

REB SIMKHE. (*Takes two oranges out of his breast pocket and gives them to Tamara.*) There, daughter. Two oranges for you.

TAMARA. Thank you very much, Father-in-law.

REB SIMKHE. Eat and be healthy. Today I was driving oranges.

YANKL. So you did some unloading. Only two?

REB SIMKHE. Horse! Horse! "Unloading"! A thief, right? A thief? Horse! Oh!

TAMARA. For shame, Yankl, don't you know your own father?

REB SIMKHE. They gave them to me themselves. As you see me here alive. As you see me here alive, gave me them themselves. "Unloading"! Horse. I told them: for my daughter-in-law.

MARIOSHE. "For my daughter-in-law." That's how it is. Forget they even have a wife.

REB SIMKHE. Cow.

MARIOSHE. That's how it is. Me he can only call "Cow."

YANKL. Mama is peppering up.

TAMARA. What do you care, Mother-in-law. We'll share. One for you and one for me.

REB SIMKHE. What? No. Brought 'em for you. Both of them for you. Don't be a fool.

MARIOSHE. Do I need an orange? If he had brought any for me, I'd have given them to you myself. I'm only talking. He doesn't pay a hair of attention to his wife.

YANKL. Well, after all he is my father. And we don't pay attention to old ladies.

TAMARA. Yankl, I hate that kind of smart talk.

MARIOSHE. There you have him. And welcome.

REB SIMKHE. Horse. Horse.

YANKL. (*Strikes himself ritually on the breast.*) I have sinned, I have sinned, I have sinned. Once in a while it slips out. Oh, may my tongue wither.

MARIOSHE. What do the peasants say? You can't hide a tack in a sack; it's bound to creep out. Ah, ah, ah.

All drink tea in silence.

YANKL. (*To Tamara.*) Another glass?

TAMARA. No, thank you.

YANKL. Are you mad, Tamaruk?

TAMARA. Mad? At what?

YANKL. You know my tongue.

TAMARA. I've already forgotten what you said.

MARIOSHE. He doesn't pay attention to old ladies, he doesn't pay attention to his mother, but young girls though, young girls, ahhhhh—

TAMARA. Mother-in-law! You don't have to repeat it. He didn't mean anything by it.

REB SIMKHE. She talks. She talks. God knows what she's saying. Cow.

YANKL. Tamaruk, you are golden. Father, may I give her a kiss? (*Wants to hug Tamara. She pushes him away laughing.*)

Marioshe groans. Khaye Peshe enters.

KHAYE PESHE. Now this is a couple. They'd spend all their time kissing. But the other couple—God forbid. A good day to all.

All answer her "A good year."

YANKL. (*Jumps up.*) You get a glass of tea immediately. I'm the tea pourer today. But who's the other couple?

KHAYE PESHE. (*Takes a chair and sits down at the table.*) Who do you think? Rafael the moneylender and his Rivke.

MARIOSHE. What's the matter now?

KHAYE PESHE. (*Pours her tea out into the saucer and blows on it.*) Now? When did it ever stop? But today it went so far that I felt I had to go there to their house and—what should I tell you? What I saw there shouldn't happen in a Jewish house.

TAMARA. She hit him again?

KHAYE PESHE. What do you mean "hit"? Hit and "hit" are not the same. If he got out of her hands alive, he must be stronger than iron. They had to come in and rescue him. She threw him down on the ground and stepped on him with her feet and—and—and what didn't she do with him?

YANKL. (*Laughs.*) A little lady and a tough guy.

KHAYE PESHE. "Come to the rabbi and give me a divorce," she screamed. And he—nothing. Somehow possessed. Anybody else would give her ten divorces just to be rid of her, and he acts like he doesn't know a thing. Takes the slaps, wipes his lips, and as if nothing happened, as if it had nothing to do with him.

REB SIMKHE. A donkey. A donkey.

KHAYE PESHE. And the end will be that she'll get her hands on him again.

TAMARA. And she isn't ashamed?

YANKL. She's not the shameable kind.

KHAYE PESHE. Oh my, is she a piece of work.

MARIOSHE. And—What's the problem? A husband can hit a wife? So never mind if once in a while maybe a wife hits a husband. If only all wives had her sense.

TAMARA. Mother-in-law!

REB SIMKHE. Shut up. Shut up. Cow. Opens up her mouth. Little Marioshe opened her mouth.

YANKL. Well, well, let's talk about happier things.

MARIOSHE. Right, what's the news about a servant?

KHAYE PESHE. Look at that, little crowns, the most important thing is what I forgot. He got hit on the head, and I got dizzy. And I don't have time to waste. I sat myself down to chat exactly as if nothing at all. So listen, Tamara dear, I've come to you empty-handed. No servant and no tenant and—and—and— (*Stands up.*) Well, thank you, thank you for the tea and be happy and I've still got to get to Nahum Gutke's and the Rabbi Hasye's and—and—and I've got to get to and get to—so Khaye Peshe, get going.

TAMARA. So then what's it going to be?

KHAYE PESHE. It'll be, it'll be. Good day everybody. (*Exits.*)

MARIOSHE. Somehow you can't depend on her at all anymore. No servant, no tenant. Think how long she's been promising you a tenant, and you're depending on her entirely, and meanwhile the room is empty.

TAMARA. I don't really mind.

MARIOSHE. Meanwhile the couple of rubles aren't lying around in the street.

REB SIMKHE. A sin, absolutely a sin.

MARIOSHE. You could go to another broker. I'm telling you, I know for a fact that Devoyre is—

Rivke enters.

RIVKE. Good morning.

MARIOSHE. (*Surprised.*) Will you look at that, here she is herself.

RIVKE. What do you mean, "here she is herself"?

YANKL. We just heard that you've been waging some kind of war. (*Laughs.*)

RIVKE. You heard already? Ha, well, what do you have to say about it? (*Screams.*) Oh I can't stand it anymore; I can't bear it.

MARIOSHE. There you go; she can't stand it anymore.

RIVKE. What do you know about what I go through? I can't find a place for myself because of him. I just have to look at him and I feel like I'm dying. And it's impossible to get rid of him.

TAMARA. Is it necessary to behave like that?

RIVKE. Oh, when the disgust comes over me, do I know what I'm doing? I feel as if I could kill myself or him.

YANKL. Him first, naturally.

RIVKE. I can't control myself. I feel my mind is going.

TAMARA. All the same.

RIVKE. "All the same." Easy for you to say. But now—over! Over! I don't want to lay eyes on his face. Let him refuse the divorce: I won't live with him anymore.

YANKL. So you'll live on your own, in other words. A wife on her own.

RIVKE. Call it on my own, call it whatever you want. I don't have any more strength left for him.

YANKL. Worn out from hitting, right?

RIVKE. I'll rent myself an apartment and live separately. We'll see how it will all end, we'll see. I think he'll divorce me in the end.

TAMARA. You seriously mean it——this "on your own"?

RIVKE. Of course I seriously mean it. What—I should go back to him? I'd sooner see him underground than go back to him. I don't want to know him anymore; I'm not his wife anymore.

TAMARA. So how will you manage?

RIVKE. I'll rent myself a room somewhere separately. And that in fact is why I've come to you.

TAMARA. To us?

RIVKE. You have a room. I want to rent it.

REB SIMKHE. (*Blurts angrily*) There is no room, none.

RIVKE. (*To Tamara.*) You've already rented your room?

REB SIMKHE. Not necessary. Do all right without that kind of tenant. "On her own."

RIVKE. What's eating you, Reb Simkhe? If I can't live with my husband, nobody should rent me a room? Do I have to wander in the streets, or jump in the river?

REB SIMKHE. "On her own." You don't leave a husband that way.

RIVKE. "You don't leave"—Whoever doesn't leave, doesn't leave, and whoever has to leave, does. I'm not the first and not the last. It depends what kind of husband you have.

MARIOSHE. So since you are so determined to go away on your own, it would be better to go to your parents in the village.

YANKL. Really. Mama is right. She'll be a prime minister someday. Really, why shouldn't you go to the village?

RIVKE. Everybody does what he judges best. If I don't go, that means I don't want to, or maybe I can't. I got myself out of the village once, and there's no chance I'll live there again.

TAMARA. But it would be the easiest thing.

RIVKE. Why are you so scared of renting me the room? I don't want it for free after all.

TAMARA. Scared?

YANKL. (*Forced laugh.*) Scared? What do you mean "scared"?

MARIOSHE. And if they're scared, so what? You don't wave a red handkerchief in front of a bull. All he needs is a tenant very, very nearby.

TAMARA. (*Laughs.*) What can enter my mother-in-law's head.

RIVKE. (*Laughs too.*) Is that how it is? What do you say, Yankl? (*Gives him a "non-kosher" look.*)

YANKL. (*Embarrassed.*) But Mama, ahh, what are you . . . what are you talking about?

REB SIMKHE. Right. Right. Mama is right. Not necessary.

MARIOSHE. "Scared" is a good thing. We know what we know.

TAMARA. But Mother-in-law, what are you talking about?

YANKL. (*Angrily*) You'd better stop talking, you hear? I don't want to hear it, you understand me?

REB SIMKHE. What are you yelling about? Who are you yelling at? Yell till your teeth break. Yelling at his Mama.

MARIOSHE. I need your permission to talk? Why didn't you snap her up, this precious bargain?

RIVKE. Will you look at this?

MARIOSHE. Because you yourself are scared, because you yourself know perfectly well what kind of devil is sitting inside you. And why didn't she snap it up?

TAMARA. But Mother-in-law, what is there here to snap up or not snap?

MARIOSHE. You're looking for a tenant, that's what.

TAMARA. Oh well, Khaye Peshe—

MARIOSHE. Never mind Khaye Peshe. Khaye Peshe hasn't brought you any tenant. You're just plain scared. And you're right. Now is when you really should be scared; then you won't have any regrets later.

RIVKE. Feh, it's a scandal, it's disgusting. What are you scared of, that I'll lead Yankl astray?

YANKL. I don't want anybody to talk about me like that. And basta. What kind of a way is that to talk about me? What do you think I am, anyway?

RIVKE. And what do you think I am, anyway?

YANKL. Have you got any complaints about me, Tamara? Can you accuse me of something? What do you want from me?

TAMARA. You don't have to yell like that and eat your heart out. You know perfectly well what I think about you. And your mother herself should say exactly what I was saying to her earlier. She can't have forgotten it all.

YANKL. So then there's nothing to talk about. And nothing to be scared of about me. The Evil Impulse itself can come move in here.

TAMARA. So good. (*To Rivke.*) So come take a look at the room.

YANKL. (*Cooled down and embarrassed.*) But if you don't want to, if you're scared, maybe, I don't know—You can also decide not to rent.

TAMARA. I'm not scared of anybody or anything. Just don't you be scared of your own self.

REB SIMKHE. (*With a blow on the table.*) And me, I say don't rent the room to her, that's what I say.

MARIOSHE. I'm not scared of the Evil Impulse; I'm scared of Mrs. Evil Impulse.

RIVKE. And what do you think, I'm going to listen to everything you say and not say a word?

TAMARA. Ah, never mind what they say. Better come take a look at the room. (*Pulls Rivke toward the exit door.*)

RIVKE. What do you think I am anyway? Am I some kind of prostitute? What am I that you can talk about me like that? (*Rivke is pulled out by Tamara, who shuts the door behind them.*)

REB SIMKHE. (*Jumps up.*) You want to rent her the room just to spite your parents? Fine, rent it to her. I won't set foot here. We'll just see what'll happen here. Disgrace, gentile, cow. Just what he needs. She'll live here without her husband, on her own. Some piece of work. Went a long time without trouble from you. Not going to set foot. Tfoo. Disgrace. Hm—

MARIOSHE. Well, and isn't he right?

YANKL. Just exactly because you're so scared, that's why. I can't stand it anymore: the way you're scared about me. It makes me sick. When will it finally be enough? I used to be—I used to be everything bad in the world. But not anymore. What do you want from me? My own parents—my worst enemies. Everybody else seems to have forgotten what I used to be, only not you. It is just unbearable. My own parents.

MARIOSHE. Own parents. And you yourself, have you forgotten what you used to be? Didn't I see how you yourself didn't want her? You invited her pretty please, did you?

YANKL. So what? I'm allowed to be scared myself, but not you. I'm allowed but you're not. Nobody is, you understand me. If a stranger said it to me, I'd smash his face. And I don't want to hear it from you either. I'm allowed, you aren't. And anyway, I'm not scared. The Evil Impulse and his missus can live there both together. Naked.

REB SIMKHE. Words. Words. Easy to say. I won't set foot.

YANKL. So don't. Don't come. You'll get over it. Never mind.

REB SIMKHE. Nice. Good. "Don't come," he says. "Don't come." You should die like an animal . . . Idiot. If I had my whip with me,

I'd—You'll see, wait, you'll see. I won't set foot here. (*Goes out slamming door.*)

YANKL. Don't worry, we'll make up.

MARIOSHE. "Don't worry, we'll make up." Get rid of your parents just to have her for a tenant. Drive us out: you'll drive yourself soon enough. But this I tell you: in the end, you'll start to play your old tricks and Tamara will start crying for her lost life.

YANKL. You better be quiet, you hear. I don't want to hear it. Leave me alone. Don't drive me crazy.

TAMARA. (*Hurries in.*) What's this yelling? What's going on? Where is Father-in-law?

MARIOSHE. Let him yell till his teeth break. He can't stand to hear the truth.

TAMARA. Father-in-law left? He's the one that slammed the door so hard?

MARIOSHE. What do you expect? He'll never set foot here again, that's what he said.

TAMARA. Oh my, what a thing to say.

MARIOSHE. Isn't he right, though? You'll see what happens with that piece there.

YANKL. Let it go, I told you, let it go.

MARIOSHE. What is good this way? That your father-in-law won't set foot here?

TAMARA. No—God forbid—not that, not that. But—it is good this way, that it turned out this way.

MARIOSHE. Daughter dear, I tell you, you shouldn't have her here.

TAMARA. She's already gone for her things.

MARIOSHE. She can take them back again.

TAMARA. That won't work, Mother-in-law.

MARIOSHE. Well, in that case, let me at least not be here in the house when that piece of misfortune moves in.

YANKL. It's enough to drive you crazy. What have they got into their heads? Lunatics, cattle, what have you gotten into your heads?

MARIOSHE. (*Putting her bag together.*) That's right, just call your parents lunatics and cattle, that's the way. We'll have respect from you, wait, we'll have it yet.

TAMARA. Mother-in-law, honestly, this is childish. What has gotten into you?

MARIOSHE. Let it go, let it go.

TAMARA. You shouldn't run away like this.

MARIOSHE. You should run away like from a fire. I know what this is, I know. Good day.

TAMARA. But Mother-in-law.

Marioshe hurries out.

YANKL. Crazy. They really can drive a person crazy. They burn a person alive.

TAMARA. You scared them for a lot of years.

YANKL. But it's got to come to an end someday. God forbid I might actually manage to forget what I used to be: they won't stop reminding me. As if for spite. As if for spite.

TAMARA. What do you care? So long as you're not what you used to be, so long as you know that you are another person.

YANKL. So long as I know—don't you know?

TAMARA. You know what I know. Calm down.

YANKL. They make my blood boil. I feel that I could I-don't-know-what. I could yell the house down—Go bang the hammer on the anvil. Something. (*Gestures as if banging with the hammer.*)

TAMARA. (*Strokes him.*) Calm yourself, Yankele, calm yourself. Come, I'll lie on the divan and you sit down next to me and tell me something. (*She sits.*)

YANKL. (*Agitated, he sits down next to her.*) They don't know you, that's the whole problem. And they don't know me. They think they know me. They don't begin to know me.

TAMARA. And you know yourself?

YANKL. I—what? Do I know myself? What kind of a question is that? Who doesn't know himself? Of course I know myself.

TAMARA. So then fine, if you think so.

YANKL. What does that mean: "if I think so"? And you don't think so?

TAMARA. I think that a person knows himself as little as other people know him. And maybe less.

YANKL. That's some kind of Torah that I didn't learn from the rebbe in the study house.

TAMARA. But that's how it is. That's why no one can draw his own boundaries.

YANKL. (*Jumps up, insulted.*) Do you mean to say that I can't stick to what I've taken on? That's what you mean?

TAMARA. Who's talking about you, silly? You've shown that you can accomplish whatever you want. The main thing is one needs to know what he wants, and you were able to do that. Come sit down again next to me.

Yankl walks around agitated.

You don't want to come to me?

YANKL. (*Roaming.*) Wait. You said, before, that it's good this way, that she'll live with us. What did you mean by that? Why is it good?

TAMARA. (*Carefully*) What did I mean by that? Well, of course it's good. Now they tremble over you all the time, it's so terribly dangerous for you to catch a glimpse of a girl's skirt. So now they'll see that it's not so dangerous. Isn't that so?

YANKL. I suspected something else.

TAMARA. What could you have suspected, little one, hm?

YANKL. (*Sits down next to her.*) Nothing at all. I mean, I thought you meant that you yourself wanted to test me.

TAMARA. The things that can come into your mind.

YANKL. Did I hit it, ha?

TAMARA. Oh, go on.

YANKL. If that's the way it was, you would have insulted me seriously.

TAMARA. So then you shouldn't think that way. I—

YANKL. If you didn't mean it that way, I won't think that way. But why did you get so red?

TAMARA. Oh, now look, Yankl, there's just no dealing with you now.

YANKL. I'm a plain guy. In the mind, out the mouth.

TAMARA. Go on, you're being bad, you're scaring me.

YANKL. If not, no, no—then, shh, just give me a good kiss. That's the way. And all gone. No more talking. I regret the whole business now. What if we really just don't rent to her after all?

TAMARA. She went for her things.

YANKL. Why do we need her here after all? A wife out on her own. I hate a wife on her own.

TAMARA. It's too late now. We can't shame her in public like that.

YANKL. Some public. That's nothing.

TAMARA. You tell her, if you want. I won't be able to.

YANKL. You don't think I'm scared of her living with us?

TAMARA. Don't start.

YANKL. But my parents will think that you were scared and sent her away.

TAMARA. You'll be the one sending her away.

YANKL. I mean that they'll think that we really were scared and that they're right not to feel sure about me.

TAMARA. What do you care? They'll be happy; let them think whatever they want.

YANKL. I don't want anybody to think about me as the bum I used to be.

TAMARA. So what do you want to do?

YANKL. Let things stand as before, ha? What about it? Let her live in there with us. What's it to us where she is? We'll probably have some tenant. What do we care who's living in there? Right? Don't you think so?

TAMARA. Obviously.

YANKL. Why are you talking to me so shortly, exactly—exactly as if you're thinking something else?

TAMARA. You are a funny man. It's nothing to me. If you want to send her away, send her. If you want her to stay, let her stay.

YANKL. No, something about the way you're talking.

TAMARA. You want plain speaking?

YANKL. Of course plain speaking, only plain speaking.

TAMARA. Then let's not have her. If because of her, your father won't come, then definitely not.

YANKL. Is that an excuse?

TAMARA. A what?

YANKL. I mean are you scared?

TAMARA. Enough. I'm not talking about this anymore. She's coming; let her stay.

YANKL. You don't have to get offended.

TAMARA. Enough talk. You yourself are scared about yourself, and you're searching around and don't know what you want.

YANKL. I'm not scared about myself, Tamara, but I want for all of you not to be scared.

TAMARA. We've heard all this already.

YANKL. So it's settled?

TAMARA. It's fine, it's fine. I think somebody's coming.

Rafael enters, face beaten up.

RAFAEL. Good day.

YANKL and TAMARA. Good day.

RAFAEL. Was Rivke here?

TAMARA. She was here.

RAFAEL. (*Sits down.*) I had a feeling. About your room, right?

TAMARA. Yes.

RAFAEL. Living on her own, away from me, that's what she wants.

YANKL. She seems to have broken your bones too, right? She gave you that black eye?

RAFAEL. All by herself.

YANKL. Oh, Reb Rafael, you are just not a man at all.

TAMARA. How can a man let himself be stepped on like that?

RAFAEL. If you love your wife, you let her step on you.

YANKL. You're a great fool, excuse me. Rather than suffering from a wife like that, you go and read her the morning prayer and send her to the devil. Anyway, Jews have a thing called a divorce. Why not divorce her? What do you get out of her?

RAFAEL. So then, in other words, she wants to come move in with you as a tenant?

YANKL. Why shouldn't we let her? Because you don't want to divorce her?

TAMARA. It's a pity for her too. She really doesn't want to live with you.

RAFAEL. It's a pity for her that you married Reb Yankl. Because she already had her eye on him.

YANKL. What are you talking about now?

RAFAEL. You remember she wanted to swap.

TAMARA. She didn't mean it seriously.

YANKL. (*Angry.*) You don't make that kind of joke. For that kind of joke you can still get it from me.

RAFAEL. What did I say? I didn't say a thing. Did I say you had an eye on her?

YANKL. What eye? What?

RAFAEL. Both eyes. She had both eyes on you. The minute she got to know you, that's when she began to make me miserable, as you see me alive. From the very first word you said to her.

YANKL. Don't talk foolishness.

RAFAEL. That is exactly when she started to scream I should divorce her. From that minute on, she wanted to get rid of me and get hold of you.

YANKL. You know what I feel like doing now?

RAFAEL. How should I know what you feel like doing?

YANKL. I feel like smashing your face.

TAMARA. Yankl, shame on you.

RAFAEL. (*Jumps up.*) What? What did I say so bad?

YANKL. Go to the devil with your wife together. Go tell her she shouldn't dare come here. Go fast, she's gone for her things. Tell her I'll throw her out with her things together.

TAMARA. But Yankl—

RAFAEL. I'll tell her, certainly I'll tell her, and how I'll tell her. I'm running, and how I am running. She already went for her things? (*Exits.*)

TAMARA. But Yankl, how could you—

YANKL. A miracle he got out in one piece. I felt like—

TAMARA. What do you have against him, poor thing?

YANKL. Such nastiness. I'll drive her out of the house if she dares to come. Do you understand a woman behaving like that?

TAMARA. I understand very well. I understood from the start.

YANKL. You understood? What did you understand?

TAMARA. That it's not for nothing that she wants to settle in right here with us.

YANKL. And you wanted to let her in?

TAMARA. I'm not afraid of her. Nobody's going to take you away from me.

YANKL. That's what you say now. At the start you were scared.

TAMARA. Was I?

YANKL. And how. My mama is smart. She read your prayer book pretty fast.

TAMARA. You were scared too.

YANKL. But you shouldn't have been scared.

TAMARA. And in fact, I'm not scared.

YANKL. Because now you know that she isn't going to live here.

TAMARA. I didn't tell you not to let her in.

YANKL. Oh well, you are right.

TAMARA. Yankl, what I mainly want is for you not to talk to me that way.

YANKL. So I'll keep quiet. I'm going to the forge.

TAMARA. You won't go away from me like that. Give me your hand and—

Frume and Reb Aron enter.

FRUME and REB ARON. Good day.

TAMARA. Look at that, Uncle and Aunt, in the middle of a Wednesday. Good day to you. What happened: both of you out of the store?

FRUME. A person's not allowed to take a holiday once in a while?

TAMARA. Really, what's going on?

FRUME. Just look, you see? We're not allowed just to come and see you?

TAMARA. You are welcome guests. Yankl, back to the samovar.

REB ARON. No, we don't want any tea, we came just for a minute.

TAMARA. In other words, some very important errand.

REB ARON. You're right. We want to talk something over with you. Your father-in-law came to see us at the store. (*Yankl breaks out in a laugh.*)

TAMARA. Well, now we know what this is all about.

FRUME. How could it have entered your minds to let such a nasty creature into your house?

TAMARA. And that is important enough to drag you away from the store?

FRUME. Important or not, the loss is not so big in any case, and the business isn't burning, and your father-in-law insisted that we both come, so we came.

REB ARON. And in fact, it really is important, too. I'll tell you the truth, I started shaking all over when I heard that you were turning a room over to her. Because considering what Rafael told me that—

TAMARA. Oh, what's the difference what that imbecile says?

FRUME. In his business, he's far from an imbecile.

REB ARON. And if he were an imbecile twenty times over, he's not a liar.

TAMARA. And who cares what plans she was hatching there?

REB ARON. What do you mean? What are you talking about, child? A woman like that under one roof with you—God knows what it can lead to.

YANKL. What can it lead to? To what?

REB ARON. To what? Do I have to tell you?

YANKL. To nothing. It can lead to nothing.

FRUME. (*Sarcastic.*) A new saint all dressed for the Sabbath!

TAMARA. You don't have to think of him that way.

REB ARON. If you're that sure, it makes me very happy, but plain and simple is best. The rabbis said, "Distance yourself from whatever may lead to sin."

YANKL. As you see me alive, as—as—Before you arrived, I reached the decision not to let her into my house. Rafael was here, and I kicked him out and told him so. And now, as you see me alive, you are irritating me right into renting her the room after all.

REB ARON. We irritate you? What do you mean, we irritate you?

FRUME. There you have it. We irritate him. How did we offend you so badly? What is it? We don't dare have doubts about you, God forbid? When did you get to be such a saint that the Evil Impulse can't possibly get a hold of you? (*Yankl grunts angrily.*)

TAMARA. (*Angry.*) Imagine that, Aunt; he actually is such a saint.

FRUME. How nice for you, if you believe him.

TAMARA. I believe him. I believe him.

FRUME. You don't have to yell at me like that.

REB ARON. It's true, you don't have to yell like that. What is our intention, after all? Our intention was only your good.

FRUME. But my heart told me we shouldn't come and shouldn't mix in and let them do what they want. If she's such a fool and wants to play with fire, let her bang her own head against the wall.

REB ARON. Shh, no cursing, no cursing, better to talk it over nicely.

Rivke enters, pushing before her Rafael, who carries a big pack of clothing tied up in a blanket.

RAFAEL. Here she is herself. You tell her what you told me to say. She doesn't believe me.

RIVKE. My clever one figured out a smart idea so I wouldn't come here. He picked the wrong one to fool. So in the end he had to drag my pack.

RAFAEL. I dragged it here, and I'll drag it back.

FRUME. And the sooner the better.

REB ARON. She's not going to live here, so you can take the pack home again.

RAFAEL. You see, ha? (*Picks up the pack.*)

RIVKE. (*Tears the pack away from him.*) Wait, I have time. So many landlords here. (*Goes to Yankl and Tamara.*) What do you have to say, hm?

REB ARON. First of all, what kind of way is that to behave, to run away from a husband, going away on your own? Where did you ever see that? Did your mother behave like that?

FRUME. You want to give her a sermon, with her bold face.

RIVKE. (*To Frume.*) And I myself don't want any sermons from anybody. I can manage without sermons. If you tried living with such a miserable pest—

(*Rafael laughs.*)

—you would know why a person runs away to live on her own, you'd know everything. You'd wonder why a person doesn't throw herself in the river.

FRUME. The best place for you.

REB ARON. Shh. And second, if you do want to go on your own, then take eighty black years and go; but why do you need to rent a room nowhere but right here? You shameless thing, it hurts you that they live here in peace? You want to commit adultery? Is that what you want?

RIVKE. How? What?

YANKL. (*Again grunts angrily.*) Huh! (*To Rivke.*) You rented a room from me? So take your pack and get in there. Go. Fast! Fast! (*Pushes the pack toward the empty room with his foot.*)

RIVKE. What is this? What's going on here? You think I'll stand for this?

YANKL. (*Beside himself.*) Go! Go! You can complain later. Go. (*Pushes Rivke toward the room.*) Go. If not, I'll throw you out entirely. Go. (*Pushes her with her pack into the room.*)

RAFAEL. What's this? What's this? What are you trying to do?

YANKL. (*Grabs Rafael too.*) And you too. And you too. You can go to her. Or go in the grave. Get out of my sight. (*Yankl pushes Rafael out of the house and closes the door with a bang.*)

Rafael is yelling something on the other side of the door.

TAMARA. But, Yankl! But Yankl, come to yourself.

FRUME. He's gone absolutely crazy.

REB ARON. Woe is me; woe is me. Hell will open right here.

YANKL. Not your granny's problem.

TAMARA. Shh, calm down, calm down.

FRUME. (*To Reb Aron.*) I told you we shouldn't come, we shouldn't mix in. I knew who we're dealing with here. (*Takes Reb Aron by the hand.*) Now come before they throw us out too. (*Leads Reb Aron to the door.*)

REB ARON. God help us, this is hell.

YANKL. Not your granny's problem.

Tamara covers his mouth with her hand. Yankl takes her hand away from his mouth and yells after them as they leave.

I'm as much a saint as you are.

TAMARA. Calm down. Calm down. You did right. (*Hysterically*) This is good.

From behind the door, the noise of voices.

END OF ACT 2

Act 3

A month later.

Yankl's smithy. Downstage left, a gate leads to the street. Stage right, a door to the courtyard of Yankl's home. Upstage, two little windows whose panes allow very little light to shine through. The forge stands in the middle, slightly upstage. The bellows, anvil, and hammers are in front of the fire. In a corner, stage left, stand a big whetstone and a tub of water. Pieces of iron are strewn about the floor. Old cart shafts, broken axles, and so on, lie near the walls. Old wheels stand propped against the walls, and on the walls hang various tools. The smithy is half in darkness. Singing is heard from the courtyard; people are singing a merry Jewish tune.

WAGONER. (*Stands impatiently in the doorway a while, looking out through the gate, then yells out to the courtyard.*) Well, is he ever going to come? How long am I supposed to wait?

RIVKE. (*Her voice heard from the courtyard.*) He's coming. He's coming.

WAGONER. The circumcision's over, and the dinner is over, so what's keeping him now?

RIVKE. (*From the courtyard.*) He'll be right there; he'll be right there.

WAGONER. "Right there"! I've been waiting for him an hour already. (*Runs to the gate and yells out.*) Get away from the wagon! Get away! I'm going for my whip. (*Runs out. We hear him yelling.*) Plague take you. Swarming like locusts.

We hear the laughter of children scattering. Wagoner comes back in.

Still not. (*He looks through the door.*) Well, here he comes, the big shot.

YANKL. (*His voice heard from courtyard.*) You, why can't you get it through your head? No work today. (*Yankl enters from the courtyard, dressed up, very excited and a bit drunk, humming the merry tune we hear from the courtyard.*)

WAGONER. I'll show you no work. My axle broke.

YANKL. Well, so it broke. Come inside instead, we'll drink a toast. Fix the axle tomorrow.

WAGONER. Tomorrow? I'll give you tomorrow. (*Indicates the street.*) You see what's going on there? A wagon full of apples. Maybe I'm supposed to leave it there on the street overnight and stand guard?

YANKL. Today in my place nobody works. I gave everybody the day off. It's a big celebration here, you understand. A circumcision. You understand, a circumcision. A big boy. So no work. We'll drag the wagon into the courtyard. I'll guarantee your apples.

WAGONER. Don't give me that; I have to deliver the apples today. The circumcision's over and the dinner is over, so what more do you want?

YANKL. No work today and basta. We'll drag the wagon into the courtyard, then you'll come in with me to the house and we'll drink a toast.

WAGONER. Impossible, can't do it. I have to deliver the apples to the boat today; the boat leaves tonight.

YANKL. The devil with it; why didn't you go to Borukh in the next village? Today is my holiday.

WAGONER. The axle broke here; I'm supposed to drag it all the way to Borukh? How do you think I could get there?

YANKL. I can't help it. No work. Think of it as Sabbath.

WAGONER. Smart guy, Sabbath would have been all right. Sabbath, the wagon would have been home in my own courtyard.

YANKL. (*Irritated.*) So what do you want from me? Should I ruin my celebration for your sake?

WAGONER. On account of your celebration, should I go and choke on my apples?

YANKL. Tell your granny. Not my problem.

WAGONER. But you're a man with a heart, have some feeling.

YANKL. (*Cooling down.*) If not for that, I wouldn't think of work. Today, you understand me, I'm making enough noise to last every day for a year.

WAGONER. You told me already.

YANKL. Anyway, how can I do anything without my helper Rakhmiel here?

WAGONER. You'll figure something out.

YANKL. You go to hell. What is it you broke?

WAGONER. You heard me. The axle.

YANKL. Right. A nice piece of work. Right. Go lighten the load. I'll go take off my celebration (*he means his good clothes*) and start up the fire again. Comes in like that and ruins a celebration. (*He goes out into the courtyard.*)

Wagoner goes out to street. Long pause.

RIVKE. (*Rivke's voice is heard from the courtyard.*) Done. Now you'll see what I can do. (*Rivke enters. She comes in covered by a big apron and starts blowing up a fire, singing quietly to herself.*)

Yankl enters in a while, having changed into his work clothes, a bottle of brandy in his hand.

YANKL. Really, why do you need to get involved? It's not work for you, and you already worked hard today.

RIVKE. Some hard work: served a little dinner.

YANKL. But you'll make yourself all black.

RIVKE. Then I'll be a dark beauty. Red cheeks with black spots—how pretty. (*Squeezes the bellows and sings.*)

YANKL. Meanwhile I'll go to that pest out there, help him unload the wagon and take off the axle. (*Exits to street.*)

In the next speeches, we hear Yankl's and Wagoner's voices from the street.

All right, you misery, how are you doing?

WAGONER. You see for yourself. Come help, it'll be faster with two.

YANKL. Doesn't care he's ruining a celebration. At least let's drink a toast first.

We hear Yankl and Wagoner toasting each other, "Life." Rafael enters in the doorway, pulls back and then reappears. He remains standing there with his head in the doorway.

RAFAEL. You're going to be a blacksmith?

RIVKE. (*Startled by his voice.*) Tfoo. All bad dreams on your head. What are you doing here? Why did you come? Go away nicely, or I'll give it to you in the head with an iron.

RAFAEL. You get angry so fast. I just came to take a look at how you work. I'm not allowed to take a look?

RIVKE. And now you can leave. You have no business coming to look at me.

RAFAEL. (*Enters the forge.*) Today I am Yankl's guest. Today I'm a guest at his celebration, so I'm allowed to be wherever I want. That includes the forge. All the more so when my own little wifey is in there.

RIVKE. Your little wifey? I am not your little wife. You haven't heard?

RAFAEL. Not my little wife? Over and done with, hm? Just because you're on your own, that means you're not my wife? Child, who told you that? Till I give you a divorce, you are still my little wife.

RIVKE. Better leave without a fuss.

RAFAEL. Why yell like that, little silly? It's not your forge, after all. All right, you don't let me into your room, well—in your own room, you turn the lock and finished. But the forge does not belong to you.

RIVKE. Listen, if I wanted now—

RAFAEL. Oh, Rivke, Rivke, you don't have God in your heart at all. How can a person so not have God in her heart?

RIVKE. Aren't you leaving?

RAFAEL. Shh. Well—If—Listen, you know the pearls that Malke pawned with me? This week was the due date and she didn't pay them off, so I thought to myself that if my little wife were home, she'd have a pearl necklace now.

RIVKE. Choke on them. Give them to your second wife.

RAFAEL. My second wife? I'm going to grow old together with you.

> *We hear Yankl and Wagoner outdoors heaving the wagon, grunting with effort.*

YANKL. (*From outside.*) Up a little—A little higher—That's it. Ah—oof.

RAFAEL. (*Giggles.*) Maybe you want to take a look at the pearls?

RIVKE. (*Throws herself at him with her fists.*) Get out of here. You get out now.

RAFAEL. (*Exiting.*) I'm going, I'm going. Just be nice.

RIVKE. I don't want a smell of you left! (*Returns to bellows.*)

YANKL. (*Yankl's voice is heard from the outside.*) And now another toast. A toast—To life! That's the way.

> *Yankl enters immediately, carrying the axle, immediately followed by the Wagoner, who remains standing in the gateway.*

WAGONER. Just make it fast, Yankl, make it fast.

YANKL. I'll make it fast all right.

WAGONER. Meanwhile I'll grab a little nap on the apples. (*Exits.*)

YANKL. I feel like working the way I feel like—

RIVKE. Like dancing.

YANKL. Dancing—I wouldn't mind dancing. My feet are itching. Oh, could I dance. (*Starts singing the merry tune and dancing.*)

> *Rivke presses the bellows, joins in the tune, and dances in place.*

Comes in and ruins the whole celebration. (*Lays an iron in the fire.*)

RIVKE. You'll get the work done, and then we'll dance our dance.

YANKL. And how! And make another toast, like this—and why not right now? (*Drinks.*)

RIVKE. You've drunk enough already today.

YANKL. Never mind. Today is my day. How do you like my little son, ha? (*Takes an axe and chops at the axle.*)

RIVKE. The image of his father, head to toe.

YANKL. What a kid, hunh? (*Yankl keeps breaking into laughter through all speeches, for the rest of the scene.*) What a guy, hunh? He should be healthy, all over, inside and out. How he yelled, poor thing. Some pair of lungs he's got. I'll kiss him all over, hands and feet. Ah, putshe mutshe dutshe— (*Talks baby talk, sings and dances.*)

Reb Simkhe enters from the courtyard in his best clothes.

REB SIMKHE. So that's how you're working? Of all things: dancing.

YANKL. Papa, my feet just keep flying up. If you didn't dance today, you'd be worse than I-don't-know-what. Did you expect a grandson like that? Admit it. Such a kid, such a big guy, such— (*Blows out his cheeks.*) Such a . . . So come on and let's dance. (*Puts his hands on his father's shoulders and sings.*)

REB SIMKHE. (*Removes Yankl's hands.*) Work and come inside. Dance inside the house.

YANKL. In the house, in the forge—Today I'm dancing everywhere. You're just . . . But you see, I told you, you'd make up. I knew who was coming. All of a sudden you go and get angry at me. Oh, Papa, now, even now, when such a guest has arrived at our house, you have to go and get mad.

REB SIMKHE. Better just be quiet. Quiet, quiet, ox.

YANKL. Just admit for once that you got it wrong. Why did you get so mad all of a sudden? What were you so scared about? "The Evil Impulse in the house." In the house a month—and so what? So there she is. Who even looks at her? (*Speaks the last few words as if he had caught himself and ends by muttering them.*)

RIVKE. Reb Yankl, the irons are already as red as fire.

YANKL. Let them sit a while longer. See, Daddy? Went and got mad.

REB SIMKHE. Why talk? Why talk? Work. Work.

YANKL. (*Again picks up the axe.*) I am working.

REB SIMKHE. Finish and come inside.

YANKL. That's what I'm trying to do. Why did you come out?

REB SIMKHE. (*With an angry glance toward Rivke.*) I missed you.

YANKL. (*Remains standing at his work and looks at his father fixedly.*) Ah, you were afraid to leave me alone with her? You were scared. In that case, you go inside this minute, but this minute. (*Pushes him to the door.*)

REB SIMKHE. You, you. No pushing, you horse. I'll go in if I want to, I'll stay if I want to.

YANKL. Go, get out fast. Or wait, I have an errand for you. Go call Rakhmiel for me; I need him. I can't finish this by myself. Go, go. Go right away.

REB SIMKHE. Don't you send me, I'm not your father's servant.

YANKL. Go, go, do me a favor, or I'll never be finished. (*Impatiently*) Go on, there's nothing to be scared of.

REB SIMKHE. This is who's going to say prayers in my memory. Boor. Horse. (*Exits reluctantly, looking at them suspiciously.*)

> Rivke squeezes the bellows slowly with one hand; she looks earnestly at the fire with an enflamed face. Yankl angrily lets down the axe on the anvil and groans angrily.

YANKL. Curse it, useless!

RIVKE. Keep blowing? The irons are so red.

YANKL. (*Gives a deep blow.*) Fui.

RIVKE. Why did you have to get so upset? You let everything upset you. So they'll be scared, and then they'll stop. I'll probably go to the village soon anyway.

YANKL. (*Dismissing her words angrily.*) Ha.

RIVKE. You must need to take out the irons by now.

YANKL. (*Comes over to the fire.*) No, keep blowing. (*He places his hand over hers and helps her press the bellows.*)

RIVKE. (*She places her other hand over his and presses, leaning in with the weight of her whole body.*) Are you still mad, hm?

YANKL. (*He laughs good-humoredly and tipsily.*) They're scared. Scared.

RIVKE. What do you care? Just so you're not scared yourself.

YANKL. (*He laughs.*) And who says I'm not scared?

RIVKE. What do you mean, "who says"? What—you are scared?

YANKL. (*He pats at her cheek with his other hand.*) Oh, what a woman you are. (*He immediately catches himself, pulls away his hand and moves away from her.*)

RIVKE. What happened—you burned your hand?

YANKL. (*Handles something.*) Where's Rakhmiel? My father left long ago.

RIVKE. Rakhmiel lives far away. You need a guard here? I can call Rafael.

YANKL. (*Embarrassed.*) No, it's time to take the irons out. You're planning to leave for the village soon?

RIVKE. I don't know, I guess . . . Why, you'd like to be rid of me?

YANKL. (*Embarrassed.*) Just asking. Why should I?

RIVKE. I don't know, just not to have the Evil Impulse around the house.

YANKL. The Evil Impulse, that's you all right.

RIVKE. Me? Really? The things you say! You never even look in my direction.

YANKL. If only it was true.

RIVKE. No? You do glance in my direction once in a while? And here I never knew.

YANKL. You are a Lilith, no question. They shouldn't let you into a Jewish house. Lilith. Move out, move back to the village, the sooner the better. And now you can go in the house. Go on.

RIVKE. What is this, all of a sudden? You're kicking me out?

YANKL. It's healthier not to see you, not to have you around. It . . . If—I'm still not altogether cured.

RIVKE. Poor Yankl. Not altogether cured? And here I didn't even know you were sick. Was it serious?

YANKL. You understand perfectly, don't pretend you don't understand.

RIVKE. Understand what? I have no idea what you mean.

YANKL. You understand perfectly and get yourself out of here.

RIVKE. I don't understand a thing, and I have nowhere to get myself to.

YANKL. (*Agitated.*) Understand me, I have unkosher blood in me; that's what it is. I thought it was gone, that I was clean, but it was a lie. I was wrong. It was a lie. My old ways are still boiling inside me. If I could only bleed them out of my body.

RIVKE. I wish I understood any of this.

YANKL. Why do you keep pretending you don't understand—why? The old Yankl is still crouched inside me, the old dog, that's what. My mother knew it, my father knew it, only Tamara and I didn't know it. Now I know it—and how! The old dog is still crouched inside me, the girl-chaser.

RIVKE. (*As if astonished.*) No! I would have sworn on the holy Torah that you don't even think about such things.

YANKL. I didn't know myself that such a dirty wild animal is inside me. Such an ugly animal. You understand me, I've seen you a few times, you know, when you were a little bit . . . not quite . . . not altogether dressed, like your feet bare, or your naked arm, or—

RIVKE. (*Innocently*) Living in the same house, it happens sometimes. And this last week, with the baby, I had to be around Tamara so much, day and night.

YANKL. I could take the axe to my own head.

RIVKE. Shh, in any case you shouldn't take it all to heart so much.

YANKL. Unkosher blood. Some kind of demon, a devil, sits there inside me. And today I've been drinking, too.

RIVKE. Well, such an occasion, after all.

YANKL. Not just the celebration. I wanted to get drunk. You understand me, I wanted it. The devil in me—you understand me—I wanted to drown him.

RIVKE. My, it's warm. So close to the fire. (*She unbuttons the top buttons of her blouse, revealing part of her breast.*)

YANKL. Just what I needed: use kerosene to put out a fire. (*He laughs.*) Oh, am I . . . Over the head with an axe——let the dirty blood run right out.

RIVKE. Should I keep blowing?

YANKL. (*Goes to fire.*) No. Enough.

RIVKE. (*Coquettish*) Well, and am I a good worker?

> *Yankl raises his eyes and looks at her. They stand a while looking at each other. Suddenly he grabs her, lifts her high in the air, and plants his lips on her uncovered breast, making crazy sounds.*

WAGONER. (*Voice heard from the outside.*) Look, he's still not done.

RIVKE. The wagoner is coming. (*Yankl lets go of her and remains standing as if drunk and dizzy.*)

WAGONER. (*In the doorway.*) How can you not be finished?

RIVKE. The irons are still in the fire.

WAGONER. Where's your head? Why are you standing there as if you're possessed? Finish and let me go.

YANKL. (*As if waking up.*) I told you that I can't work today.

WAGONER. What's the matter, they took your hands off for the day? Such a big deal—a son.

YANKL. (*Wildly*) A son, a son. I'm all alone, my worker isn't here.

WAGONER. What am I supposed to do, stay the night?

RIVKE. You know what? I'll be your apprentice.

YANKL. He'll help me. (*To Wagoner.*) You'll hold the tongs for me.

WAGONER. Who's going to watch my load of apples?

RIVKE. What do you care? I can do it as well as he can. (*Lifts the big hammer easily.*)

YANKL. He'll hold the tongs.

RIVKE. No. I'll take the hammer. I'll hammer. You think I don't have the strength? (*Rolls up her sleeves, spits on her hands, takes up the hammer, and starts hammering on the anvil.*) See? One. And again. And again.

WAGONER. Those kids are at my apples again. Hurry up! (*Rushes off shouting.*) Get away from there! Plague! (*Yankl picks up a bottle of schnapps and drinks deeply.*)

RIVKE. Hey, hey, now you're drinking too much.

> *Yankl takes irons from the fire with the tongs and lays them on the anvil. Rivke hammers.*

H-ah! H-ah! (*She sings a Russian song in rhythm with the blows.*)

YANKL. You'll burn your hand.

RIVKE. No danger.

YANKL. Better roll your sleeves down.

RIVKE. (*Rivke hammers and sings.*) What's the matter, scared to look at my naked arm?

YANKL. I—I—

> *Rivke keeps singing.*

YANKL. Schnapps in my head, a devil in my heart.

RIVKE. And Lilith by your side.

YANKL. That is the plain truth.

RIVKE. (*She keeps hammering.*) H-ah! H-ah!

> *Holding the tongs with his right hand, Yankl takes the bottle in his other hand and drinks.*

RIVKE. Don't drink. Don't drink.

YANKL. (*He drinks again, puts down the bottle, and points to a spot on his mouth.*) I want a kiss right here on the spot where the bottle touched me.

RIVKE. I'm in no rush. You've already got somebody to kiss you.

YANKL. (*Vulgar.*) Yes, and she's pretty good too.

Rivke hammers and sings.

Quit playing around. Hurry up. Just exactly right here, a big kiss.

RIVKE. Watch out, you'll get it with the hammer. (*Yankl lunges for Rivke's lips, but she pushes him away.*) Besides, the door to the street is wide open.

YANKL. (*He takes up a position with the tongs again.*) You'll kiss me yet. Just you wait.

RIVKE. We'll see.

With his free hand Yankl drinks again. Rivke hammers and sings. A GIRL appears in the courtyard and looks on.)

GIRL. Look! Come and look. Rivke's working at the forge with a hammer.

We hear laughter. A few girls come in, with much giggling and shrieking.

How do you like the new blacksmith? Just look—look how she lifts the hammer.

More laughter.

YANKL. (*He lays down the first piece of iron and goes to the fire. He is unsteady on his feet. He glances happily at the girls.*) Hey! Women!

GIRL. Look, he's drunk, he really is.

YANKL. (*Takes the other piece of iron out of the fire and lays it on the anvil.*) Yes, I'm drunk. I am drunk. I want a kiss. I want a girl to kiss me. Come here, girls.

Rivke hammers and sings.

ANOTHER GIRL. I'll send your wife. She'll give you a kiss.

YANKL. Not a wife. No. You come here. (*Suddenly lets go of the tongs and charges at a girl, grabs her, then goes after another one with a yell.*) Women! Women!

The girls run around the smithy, laughing. Some run back out into the courtyard.

RIVKE. Yankl, the work! The work!

YANKL. Ah, what about work? I don't want to work. No more work. I just want to get drunk and—and: yes, but now I'm happy. Now I want to dance. Hey! Hey! Hey! Hey! Hey!

He dances a Russian dance.

RIVKE. Well, if you're not going to work, there's nothing more for me to do here. I'm going. (*Rolls down her sleeves and buttons up her blouse.*)

YANKL. (*Staring at Rivke hard, he waves his hands in the air and dances by himself. When she gets to the door, he calls to her.*) Rivke!

RIVKE. What?

YANKL. Nothing.

RIVKE. That's all?

YANKL. I'll tell you some other time.

RIVKE. If I feel like listening.

YANKL. You will, you will.

Rivke starts out.

Rivke!

RIVKE. Go in the house and sleep it off.

YANKL. (*Yankl goes to Rivke and grabs her hand.*) Come on, dance with me.

RIVKE. (*Sarcastically*) That's all I'm dying to do is dance with you.

YANKL. Come on, dance with me.

RIVKE. Don't squeeze my hand like that. You'll break it.

YANKL. Come on, dance with me.

Yankl dances alone. Rivke stands in front of him arms akimbo, shaking her shoulders and bosom, Russian style, to the music. He dances around her. She dances toward the door, dances out, and escapes, laughing.

Yankl grabs another girl and dances with her, singing and squeezing her. She pulls herself away, laughing and squealing. The other girls sing and laugh.

Enter Marioshe. Behind her, Rafael and the girls who ran away earlier.

MARIOSHE. Oh, a curse on my years. He really is drunk.

Yankl lets go of the girl.

YANKL. Drunk, Mama, drunk. Is it my fault you had a drunken son?

MARIOSHE. And your father just sits there. (*Looks around.*)

RAFAEL. Look, Reb Simkhe isn't here at all.

YANKL. Aha. Reb Rafael. Come dance a little dance, Reb Rafael, come on. Reb Simkhe isn't here, no Reb Simkhe here; I sent him away, the witness, and I was here alone with her—no witness—behind closed doors and windows.

MARIOSHE. It's the devil in him.

YANKL. The devil.

RAFAEL. You're lying, Reb Yankl, you didn't close anything. I already looked.

YANKL. (*Yankl grabs Rafael by the lapels and shakes him.*) Why are you such a nasty little pest, ha? Why aren't you any kind of a man, ha? Why did your wife have to run away from you and hang on to me, ha?

RAFAEL. (*Quivering.*) Let go of me, just be nice and let go of me.

Marioshe tries to tear Yankl off Rafael.

MARIOSHE. Are you going to let go of him or not?

YANKL. (*Not letting go.*) Why couldn't you keep your wife next to you, ha?

Tamara, dressed in white, enters on the last words.

TAMARA. Yankl!

Yankl releases Rafael.

YANKL. (*Helplessly*) Tamara.

The girls move to the side and stay silent throughout.

RAFAEL. Like nothing, took hold of me and shook me. Exactly as if it was me that made him rent her a room.

Yankl laughs. Marioshe signals to Rafael to leave.

Like nothing, he shakes me. They should shake him. Wait, he'll get shaken, the lustful animal. Just let him start seducing her.

Yankl starts toward him. Rafael leaves.

MARIOSHE. Tamara! Naughty girl. How did you get here? Just out of bed today.

TAMARA. (*Battling tears.*) I wanted to see for myself how happy my husband is.

YANKL. Yes, happy. Don't make a son every day, right? Maybe you want to dance, Tamara? Come dance a little dance.

MARIOSHE. What do you say to a man like that?

TAMARA. If I only could, I would dance. Don't I have something to celebrate?

YANKL. You do.

TAMARA. But now it would be good for you to go into the house and lie down and sleep.

YANKL. What's the matter, you think I'm drunk? It's true I've drunk a lot, but— (*Dances.*) You see I still can dance. Come, we'll both dance. Don't we have a precious little son? A tough guy. A big fellow. (*Imitates a baby's cry.*)

MARIOSHE. Go sleep it off. Go before I pour my bitter heart out on top of your head.

Tamara goes to Yankl and puts her arms around him.

TAMARA. Don't be angry, Mother-in-law. He'll come now. When he feels he ought to go, he'll go.

YANKL. You're good, Tamara, smart and good. I'll come. Is that one in the house? Is she in there? Ha? You—you—Why don't you curse me? Ha? I'm a dog, Tamara, I'm a big dog. You don't dare live with me. I'm a nothing, I'm—I'm not worth the bottom of your shoe, not even worth—Everything inside me. Too late for me, Tamara, I'm a pig, a swine.

TAMARA. Shame, Yankl, don't talk like that.

YANKL. No, I know what I'm saying. You can't make a rebbe's hat from a pig's tail, and you can't make a decent man out of me.

MARIOSHE. Didn't I know that all along?

TAMARA. Ah, you didn't know anything and you don't know anything, Mother-in-law.

MARIOSHE. What have I been telling you all along?

YANKL. Mama was right, Tamara. You understand, I'm talking to you here and I know that the dog is in me, the demon is in me. It pulls me, you understand. It pulls me toward the-devil-knows-what. I'm drunk, you see, but I know—I know—

TAMARA. Oh, whatever you say, let it alone.

YANKL. You're smart. You're good. You're barely holding yourself back from crying. You—

Tamara breaks down in hysterical tears but still holds herself back.

MARIOSHE. There, this is your doing. There. A plague on you. You should have leaked out and drained away before I gave birth to you.

TAMARA. (*Hysterically*) Don't curse, Mother-in-law, do me that favor, don't curse.

MARIOSHE. So what should I do with him? (*Weeps.*) I'm going into the house and throw the bitch out so she breaks her head.

TAMARA. No, no, Mother-in-law, don't make a scene.

YANKL. Throw me out. I'm the one to throw out. Me—me—I'm the dog.

TAMARA. Come in the house. You'll sleep it off, you'll calm down.

YANKL. Yes, come in the house. Ha! Looks like you'll have to lead me.

TAMARA. Well, so what, so we'll lead you. Me on one side, your mother on the other side. It happens once in a while; a person is only human.

YANKL. No, I know myself already.

TAMARA. You don't know yourself at all. Come. Come. (*She puts her arm around him.*)

YANKL. (*Suddenly lets himself down on the anvil.*) A fire burns in me. A whole inferno. Tamara, why aren't you ten women? Why aren't you all the women in the world all put together?

TAMARA. (*Hysterically*) Don't talk. Don't talk like that.

MARIOSHE. I'm going to smack his face. Should have died of cholera as a child.

TAMARA. You'd do better to beat those thoughts out of your head.

YANKL. You see, that's why I drank. I'll tell you everything, you'll know everything.

TAMARA. Yes, yes, but now come. (*Helps him up from the anvil.*)

YANKL. (*Stands up.*) Yes, now into the house, to the sonny boy. And you, no crying. You fell in the trap, now it's too late.

MARIOSHE. I'll give you "fell in"—Wait.

YANKL. Just don't get to be a funeral wailer like she is, like my old lady.

MARIOSHE. From you a person can get to be everything, both old and a funeral wailer.

TAMARA. Come, come, you'll have nothing to wail about from me.

YANKL. Yes, you are a pal. Be happy! Come see the sonny boy. Ah, ah, ah, ah, ah, ah . . . The way the peasant dances! (*Dancing.*) Dance, Tamara. You want to see how that one started dancing?

Marioshe pushes Yankl out the door.

MARIOSHE. I'll show you something. You stop talking about that one, you disgrace. (*Goes out after Yankl.*)

Tamara remains standing, wrings her hands, puts them on her head and pulls her hair, presses her breast, and covers her mouth as she exits, emitting held-back, heartbreaking, hysterical sounds.

WAGONER. (*From the outside.*) Will there ever be an axle?

Tamara barely drags herself off.

END OF ACT 3

Act 4

Early next morning, in Yankl's dining room. Now it holds a cradle. On the table stands a boiling samovar. We hear hammering from the smithy.

TAMARA. (*Stands at the back window and calls out.*) Yankl, the tea is already poured. (*The hammering doesn't stop.*) Yankl, come in now. The tea will get cold. The work won't run away. Yankl, I can't yell, I'll wake the child.

The hammering stops. Tamara leaves the window. She looks much paler, with circles under her eyes, as from sleepless nights. She goes over to the table, where she remains standing a while, sunk in thoughts. Yankl enters. He is entirely done in.

(*As if awakened.*) Yankl, come sit down and drink your tea. (*Sits down and looks at him searchingly.*)

Yankl sits too, not looking at her at all and avoiding her eyes.

How come you started work so early? I didn't hear you get up.

YANKL. (*Mumbles.*) You were sound asleep.

TAMARA. I did go to sleep late. Itsikl was so restless. (*Silence.*) You said your morning prayers already?

YANKL. Yes.

TAMARA. (*Carefully*) Does your head hurt?

YANKL. No. Why?

TAMARA. Just asking. Maybe you'd like a schnapps? (*Yankl doesn't answer.*) Yankl, don't be so . . . Take a schnapps, you'll feel better.

YANKL. Like all drunks, right?

TAMARA. I didn't mean it that way at all, Yankl, but you did drink yesterday, so a schnapps would help today. Do you want?

YANKL. I don't want anything. (*He finishes his tea.*)

TAMARA. (*Pours him another glass.*) When did you get home from morning prayers? You must have gotten up very early. When did you get up?

YANKL. What do you care? I didn't skip morning prayers.

TAMARA. And if you did skip them, I wouldn't take it to heart. But I'm afraid that you skipped something else.

YANKL. I don't know what.

TAMARA. (*Imitates him.*) "I don't know what." Tell the truth, did you kiss me?

YANKL. (*Slowly*) No.

TAMARA. See, hah! So do it now. (*Tamara gives him her cheek.*)

Yankl barely moves his lips toward her.

Oh, how cold.

Yankl jumps up and goes to the door.

Why are you running away?

Yankl exits. Tamara goes to the window and looks after him and then leans the back of her head against the wall and stands there frozen in thought. She dries a tear. Soon she goes over to the cradle, bends over the child, looks at it, touches it, and suddenly breaks out wailing.

My little child, my little son, what's going to be? What's going to be? What'll happen to us now? (*She weeps bitterly, giving way to her heart, freeing herself of the tears that she has held inside. But soon she strengthens herself and again holds herself in.*) No, no crying, little one. Your mommy won't cry. She mustn't poison your milk. You have to be a healthy boy. You have to be mommy's little comfort. (*Dries her eyes, bites her shawl, pulling in the tears.*) No, no crying, no crying. Ooof. (*She takes a deep breath and goes over to the open window to get a bit of air.*)

Marioshe enters quickly.

MARIOSHE. Good morning. Well, you see?

TAMARA. (*Broken.*) Good day, Mother-in-law. See what?

MARIOSHE. I just saw him coming out of Khayke's tavern.

TAMARA. (*Screams.*) From the tavern?

MARIOSHE. From the tavern, of course from the tavern. With my own eyes I saw him. Lord of the world, here come the good times starting up all over again.

TAMARA. (*Groans.*) Oh. (*Puts her fist in her mouth to bite on and breathes with difficulty and loudly.*)

MARIOSHE. (*Scared.*) Oh, I shouldn't have told you. I should never have told you. Oh, dear lord. What can we do? What in the world can we do now?

TAMARA. (*With strangled tears.*) Now he's been in the tavern. (*Holds herself.*) Well, then, we'll wait and see, we'll wait and see.

MARIOSHE. Dear lord, what we'll see. Dear lord, dear lord. What are we going to do? Have you at least told that one, that piece of garbage, that she's got to get out?

TAMARA. I haven't seen her at all since yesterday afternoon. She went out somewhere and came home late. And what's the use? How would that help?

MARIOSHE. What do you mean: how would it help?

TAMARA. If the good times are getting started, as you say yourself, then what difference does it make whether she is in the house or she isn't in the house? In fact, what difference does it make whether it's her or another one? The main thing is that the old Yankl is back. (*Starts walking around the room, hands on her shoulders, eyes downcast on the floor, very agitated.*) Something has to happen; something has to happen.

MARIOSHE. What should happen?

TAMARA. That I don't know . . . That I don't know.

MARIOSHE. If, according to you, even throwing her out won't work—

TAMARA. Something has to happen that will make him . . .

MARIOSHE. What "make him"?

TAMARA. I can't explain it, but I feel it, I feel, my heart tells me . . . Something that will return him to himself, that will support him somehow, somehow cure him from his bad ways forever.

MARIOSHE. Death. Death will cure him.

TAMARA. (*Shudders.*) Dear lord.

MARIOSHE. I know my misfortune. You see yourself, just when he becomes a father, just exactly when he ought to throw away his old tricks—

TAMARA. I'll end up killing myself.

MARIOSHE. What? Bite your tongue. Tfoo. A mama talks like that.

TAMARA. (*Breaks into tears, covers her face.*) My little son, my little child.

MARIOSHE. First you throw her out, and then you deal with him, you understand? She is the first thing. And if you don't get rid of her, I'll do it for you. You'll see. Shh, here comes your father-in-law.

TAMARA. (*Quickly dries her eyes.*) Mother-in-law, don't say anything to him about the tavern.

MARIOSHE. Some hope of hiding it!

TAMARA. (*Pleading.*) That doesn't matter, don't tell him, don't tell him.

REB SIMKHE. (*Entering.*) Good morning. Well?

MARIOSHE. What "well"? Can you budge her? She wants to keep her.

REB SIMKHE. (*Furious.*) What does that mean, "keep her"? What does that mean? What does that mean? Not enough troubles?

TAMARA. I don't know anything. I don't know anything. I need to think it all through, and my head is . . . You're coming from prayers? Will you make a blessing, Father-in-law? Will you make a blessing? Do you want, should we all have breakfast, ha? (*She sets out wine and cake.*)

A noise in the front room as if somebody has been thrown down. Rivke speaks in a low voice from the front room.

RIVKE. Disappear, you hear?

Rafael, sleepy, dirty clothes, face bloodied, falls in at the door and rolls into the room.

TAMARA. (*Frightened.*) Oh, dear lord, what is it?

Rivke, in nightclothes, appears at the door.

RIVKE. Get away from me.

TAMARA, MARIOSHE, and REB SIMKHE. What is this? What is this?

RIVKE. Get away from me right now.

TAMARA. What happened? Where did he come from so early?

RIVKE. You know where he was? He was lying above the oven. I jump up, my eyes are barely open, I take a look, a hand is hanging down from the oven. I was shaking, I was scared to death, I thought God knows what. I took a closer look—it was him.

MARIOSHE. He was on the oven? Little crowns.

RIVKE. All my nightmares. What could have happened to me should go to him, to his head. I threw him down so hard, he must have needed to pick up all his teeth.

Rafael dries the blood off his face with his pocket handkerchief and scratches his back and feet and feels his head.

What's the matter, it hurts, ha? You get out of here right away, you.

TAMARA. Let him pull himself together.

MARIOSHE. What way was that to behave, to creep up onto the oven?

REB SIMKHE. In my whole life . . . In my whole life . . .

RAFAEL. Why don't you understand?

RIVKE. What should they understand, what? Better to leave without a fuss.

TAMARA. Shh, you're going to wake the child. (*Goes to cradle, bends down to take out the child.*)

MARIOSHE. It could drive you crazy.

RAFAEL. Was I supposed to let her stay here alone all night?

Rivke bursts into laughter.

TAMARA. (*Straightens up from over the cradle and looks at him sternly.*) Fui, you should be ashamed.

RIVKE. (*Laughing.*) What do you say to that, ha? He was protecting me.

TAMARA. (*To Rafael.*) That is very low of you.

RAFAEL. How can you say that? May God guard and protect against what could happen here.

TAMARA. Be good enough to stop talking that way.

MARIOSHE. Oh, he is right. Oh, it really could have . . .

REB SIMKHE. Some pious Jew . . . Some pious Jew . . .

RAFAEL. She is my wife, you understand.

RIVKE. Get out, you hear me, get out of here.

RAFAEL. She is my wife, and if God forbid something happened here . . .

RIVKE. (*Throws herself to the table.*) Oh, give me a knife. Oh I'm going to grab a knife. This is what's going to protect me.

TAMARA. (*In desperation.*) Both of you out of here right now. Don't set foot here. I don't want to see either of you. Out. Out.

RIVKE. Look, if the sacrificial ox thinks up the-devil-knows-what, is that my fault?

RAFAEL. Why throw me out? Throw her out. She's the one you should throw out. She has a home—let her live in her own home where she's supposed to live, not carrying on with a strange man. Why in the world throw me out? Did I threaten your husband? I was only protecting . . .

TAMARA. Leave me in peace. L-e-a-v-e m-e i-n p-e-a-c-e! I don't want to hear it. Go and be well.

MARIOSHE. (*To Rivke.*) Really yes, do it, pack up your things and take yourself off.

REB SIMKHE. Shameless, brazen. Out, out.

MARIOSHE. Boldfaced. He thought up the-devil-knows-what about her. Get out of here right now and never arrive there and never come back and never remain in the middle.

RIVKE. Just look, just look, how everybody is against me. They honestly believe that I would . . . I'll leave if I want; if I don't want, I won't. Just look at them. Tfoo. (*Exits, and bangs the door loudly.*)

MARIOSHE. Bangs the door—Let her bang her head on the wall, lord in heaven. She might have waked up the child.

RAFAEL. Just throw her out.

MARIOSHE. She will, she will.

RAFAEL. Just let her not be with you, that's all I ask. I don't mind if we're good friends from a distance. Me, you absolutely do not need to throw out. I won't come even if you want me to. Because for me it will be the greatest holiday to know I don't have to meet Yankl.

TAMARA. So go. So go.

RAFAEL. I'm going. I'd like to do the ritual morning wash. But I have no idea whether I actually slept. The whole night I lay there on the oven like a dog. She stayed till late with Shaye's wife Elke, so I got myself into her room, hauled myself up onto the oven, and lay there hunched up like a dog and didn't close an eye. All night I was sure that any minute he would come in.

TAMARA. Don't talk. Go. I can't look at you. I can't listen to you.

REB SIMKHE. Go, go. (*Pushes Rafael to the door.*)

RAFAEL. Why is she mad at me? What did I do wrong?

Rafael is easily pushed out.

MARIOSHE. Thank the lord for deliverance. You see what could have happened? He knows his merchandise.

REB SIMKHE. Such a . . . such a . . . A . . . Feh . . . Keeping her in the house . . . In the house—

MARIOSHE. And now see to it that she gets out today.

MARIOSHE and REB SIMKHE. Today. Today.

MARIOSHE. We'll have to smoke out the house after her.

REB SIMKHE. Should have obeyed long ago, Daughter dear, long ago. Oh well, just so long as . . .

MARIOSHE. She was stubborn.

REB SIMKHE. Good, good.

MARIOSHE. And if he starts a fuss about why you kicked her out, remember we're still around.

REB SIMKHE. Just let him try, just let him try. (*Places himself over the cradle, stands a while, looks in a while and soon starts to talk to the child in baby talk syllables.*) Sleep . . . he he heh.

MARIOSHE. (*At the cradle.*) Look how he's covered up the whole cradle. You have somewhere to go. (*Pushes Reb Simkhe out of the way.*)

REB SIMKHE. (*Happy expression on his face.*) Heh, hmm, hmm . . . asleep.

MARIOSHE. My life for his little head, he shines like the sun. (*Kisses the coverlet covering the child and wipes a tear.*) He's going to have troubles in life from a daddy like that.

REB SIMKHE. Quiet . . . Quiet . . . Horse. Cow. Needs to talk. She needs to talk. Go, you need to go to the market.

MARIOSHE. (*Groans.*) Yes, yes.

REB SIMKHE. Well, good day to you, Daughter dear. Never mind, never mind, just be calm. (*Exits.*)

MARIOSHE. (*Quietly to Tamara.*) If he should come home, you know how, don't be a fool. Give it to him dark and bitter. Ah, ah, ah, a good day to you. (*Exits.*)

TAMARA. (*Has been agitated all this while, too restless to settle in one place. Starts to roam around the room again. Wrings her hands and groans.*) Oh dear lord, dear lord. (*Rivke enters.*)

RIVKE. Listen, did you seriously mean it before, that I should get out of the room?

TAMARA. And if I did, then what?

RIVKE. I paid three months' rent.

TAMARA. I'll give it all back.

RIVKE. I don't need your charity, and regret doesn't count in business. I paid for three months, so I'll stay three months. A deal is a deal.

TAMARA. With Rafael you had a betrothal and a wedding, and all the same you left.

RIVKE. I wanted to leave him. Here I don't want to leave.

TAMARA. Is that so? Then you'll be made to leave.

RIVKE. Made? Who's going to make me?

TAMARA. You'll find out. And I request that you leave me alone right away.

RIVKE. Shh, shh. Don't get so excited. You don't scare me at all. It's not clear yet who is moving out.

TAMARA. What do you mean by that? What are you trying to say?

RIVKE. I mean that Yankl is the head of the house.

TAMARA. He is. Yes, he is. So?

RIVKE. So whoever he wants, that's the one that will stay.

TAMARA. So he wants you, in other words? You're going to stay here?

RIVKE. Maybe. Who knows? After his kisses yesterday.

TAMARA. After his kisses yesterday?

RIVKE. He certainly did kiss me yesterday. And how.

TAMARA. Oh, oh, oh—

RIVKE. And since he kissed me yesterday, I don't figure today he'll kick me out.

TAMARA. You're right. You're going to stay. I'll move out. (*Screams.*) It's gone that far already.

RIVKE. And if I'd wanted, it would have gone further still.

TAMARA. Oh, oh. Get out, you bitch. Get out, you whore. Out of here. Oh, oh, oh. No, stay, stay. You're the lady of the house. (*Tears her hair.*) I can't stay anymore. I'm taking my child and running away. Oh, oh, oh.

> *Yankl is seen in the doorway and remains standing there astonished. Tamara doesn't see him. She snatches the child out of the cradle and goes with him into the other room.*

> I can't stay here. Oh, dear lord, dear lord. (*Goes into the other room.*)

YANKL. What's going on here? What was she yelling?

RIVKE. Do I know? Nothing much.

YANKL. What did she mean that she can't stay here? Why was she tearing her hair?

RIVKE. How should I know? She's crazy, hysterical.

> *Yankl starts to go to other room, turns and stares at Rivke. Rivke cannot sustain his gaze, unbuttons her blouse in front and fans herself with her pocket handkerchief.*

YANKL. (*Goes over to her.*) Did you say something to her? What did you say?

RIVKE. I didn't say anything to her. What should I have said? She said plenty to me. She called me bitch and whore.

YANKL. What did you say to her? That's what I want to know.

RIVKE. What do you want from me? Why make such a murderous face? Yesterday, I seem to remember, that's not how you looked at me.

YANKL. Did you say something to her about yesterday?

RIVKE. What did I say? Rafael spent the whole night lying over the oven—though when and how he got himself up there . . . and kept watch so you wouldn't—God forbid—wander in to my room, ha, ha, ha.

> *Yankl groans wildly.*

I gave it to him so hard that he'll have something to remember, so I guess Tamara couldn't stand it and she began to kick me out. So then we exchanged words. What do you think: I should let myself be called names like that?

YANKL. What did you say to her about yesterday?

RIVKE. And if I said something, so what? I certainly didn't tell any lies. I figure that if you kissed me, you did it for a reason. So I was allowed to say that she shouldn't be so sure of herself; we don't know yet who's going to be the lady of the house here.

YANKL. That's what you said to her? You said that? Bitch. Bitch. Get out. Out!

> *Tamara, all dressed in street clothes, the child on her arm, hurries into the room. Rivke grabs herself on the heart, leans against the breakfront of glassware, and becomes hysterical.*

YANKL. (*Yankl stands over Rivke with balled up fists and hisses harshly.*) Out. Out.

TAMARA. (*Lays the child in the cradle, speaking as if to herself.*) It did happen. It happened. (*Hurries over to Yankl and pushes him off Rivke.*) Don't be so wild.

YANKL. Take her away. I don't want to look at her.

Rafael sticks his head in the door.

RAFAEL. Is Rivke here? Oh my lord! What's the matter with her? What are you doing to her? Oh, Rivke dear, what's the matter with you? Look how he stands with fists. Oh, my lord. Oh, where is a little water? Help, a bit of water. (*Grabs a little wine.*) Oh, help. Help! I'm going to call people. I'm going to call the whole street. (*Straightens her kerchief on her head.*) Rivke dear, what's the matter with you? What does he want from you?

RIVKE. (*Groans.*) He wanted me to . . . He wanted me to . . .

RAFAEL. What did he want? He wanted, did he? What did he want?

YANKL. Get her out. I can't promise much longer.

TAMARA. (*Holds him back.*) Calm yourself, get hold of yourself.

YANKL. Take her away fast. The bitch.

RAFAEL. We're gone. I'm taking her. Right away. You'll see. I'll have you thrown in jail. Oh, what did he want?

RIVKE. (*Groans.*) He wanted to hit me. Yesterday he grabbed me and kissed me; today he wanted to hit me.

YANKL. Get her out of here.

RAFAEL. She's going. Womanizer. Unkosher creature. Kiss her, will you? Kiss my wife?

Yankl struggles to get at him. Tamara holds him back.

TAMARA. You stay just calm and take what you deserve. (*To Rafael.*) And you get yourself out but fast. But fast, you hear.

RAFAEL. We're going, we're going. Wait, you'll see. Such a womanizer. Such an unkosher animal. You'll see, you wait. How do you feel,

Rivke dear? Will you come home with me? Yes? Imagine, I actually brought a pair of horses to carry your things, he, he, he. As if my heart told me what to expect. You see, ha, the best thing is one's own home and own husband. Can you walk? Such a bum. Such an unkosher creature. Such a murderer. But it serves you right. You ran away from me, and that's what happens.

Rivke drinks from the wine that he gives her.

Drink another little bit. Another little bit. How do you feel? You feel a little better? Can you walk? Will you come with me? Will you come home? Yes? He, he, he . . . Now you see that there is a God in the world. Otherwise, anybody could do whatever he feels like. Wait, you'll see. He'll have his downfall too. Such a murderer. Such a criminal. If you come out of here in one piece, we both have to say a blessing. (*Leads her to the door.*) He, he, he . . . Home. Home, Rivke dear. Back to your husband . . . he, he, he, he. As soon as you get home, you'll put on Malke's pearls. He, he, he. (*They exit.*)

Tamara has held Yankl back all this time and not allowed him even to talk.

YANKL. (*Groans deeply.*) Ahhhh. Rid of them. (*Lets himself fall weakly onto a chair.*)

Tamara goes and locks the door after Rivke and Rafael. She turns and looks at Yankl hard. He can't look her directly in the eye. He can barely get the words out.

And you, you wanted to leave?

TAMARA. Yes.

YANKL. Oh, my God. Oh, my God.

TAMARA. Actually, to tell you the truth, going away felt like the wrongest thing in the world. But when she told me that you kissed her, something came over me somehow, such disgust, that I wanted to run away.

YANKL. But you're not going to leave now.

TAMARA. Now? I have to think it over very carefully. Yesterday you kissed her. Today you were in the tavern.

YANKL. How do you know that I was in the tavern?

TAMARA. Your mother saw you coming out.

YANKL. She did? Maybe, but she didn't see what I was doing in the tavern or whether I drank or not. So if you want, then hear me out. But first take off your coat—or no, wait, you'll see for yourself. You'll see for yourself . . . Tamara dear, you know what happened to me today? You're smart, but you didn't see.

TAMARA. Probably I'm not smart enough.

YANKL. You know what happened to me right here, that I slept off and sobered up. You understand that I myself believed that I was an entirely new man, you understand, I figured that I was once and for all healed from all my troubles, flaws, vices, and every weakness. And suddenly—all gone, everything disappeared, here's the old Yankl back again. I was ashamed to look you in the eye. It pressed on me right here like with tongs, as if my heart lay on the anvil and somebody was hammering it with a great hammer, you understand? I wanted to wake you up and cry myself out to you, that's how I felt. I don't have to tell you, you know it yourself, I love you as my life.

TAMARA. That's what I used to believe.

YANKL. And you can go on believing it. You can know it. That's why I took it so to heart. "You lowlife, you. You outcast, you." That's what I said to myself, as you see me alive. "You lowlife, you unkosher man, have you gone wild again?" And I wanted to cry myself out to you and beg your forgiveness but my heart told me that what . . . that how can I cry and beg forgiveness—that I'm just going stay a womanizer and an outcast forever. And you should know that today I prayed with such heart and such intention like Yom Kippur, no less. I somehow wanted God to help me, as you see me alive. And I went off to work in the forge. Because when I work, I can think better. And I wanted somehow to be clear inside myself. You understand.

TAMARA. Why didn't you tell me this before, at tea? (*She takes off her hat, goes to the cradle, and starts to undress the child from his outer clothing that she dressed him in.*)

YANKL. That's just it; I wanted to be clear inside myself. Am I an outcast, and will I remain an outcast, or—I don't know—what happened? You understand?

TAMARA. (*Going to him.*) And if you told me this before, I would have said to you: "Yankl, here is my hand that you are a kosher Jew."

YANKL. (*Yells out liberated, grabbing her hand.*) Ah! (*Begins to move around the room very excited and animated and gesticulating largely.*) But I wanted inside myself, and you know, I got the feeling that nothing . . . nothing will become of me. And the old Yankl began to rise in me, the drunk, the wild man. And you should know that when you put out your cheek for a kiss, I felt that I'd get drunk for heartache, that I have to get drunk. How do you like that, huh?

TAMARA. If I had known that my cheek could call forth such feelings . . .

YANKL. And I went off to the tavern, you hear? I went off to the tavern; I ordered them to serve me a big one, I poured out a glass and . . . and . . . and when I wanted to bring it to my mouth, I put the glass back down and I left the tavern. Ha? Well?

TAMARA. (*Taking him by both cheeks, excited.*) You did that? You did that truly?

YANKL. As you see me alive, I'm not lying to you. You can ask Khayke.

TAMARA. I believe you, Yankele. I believe you more than all the Khaykes. (*Embraces him and presses herself to him strongly.*)

YANKL. No, you listen some more. I left the tavern to go to the bathhouse, so as to refresh myself somehow, to be able to think about it all better.

TAMARA. Look, I'm just now noticing that in fact your hair is wet and your face is shining.

YANKL. And there, for a moment, suddenly it came to me that I should just drown myself.

TAMARA. (*Frightened.*) Oh dear lord.

YANKL. No, listen, just for a moment. When I thought that, I missed you so badly and our little son, and it grabbed my heart so much that I got out of the water fast, got dressed fast, and ran home.

TAMARA. (*Embraces him.*) And now you're here. (*Kisses him on the mouth.*) Mine, mine, mine.

A pleasant male voice is heard from the forge, singing quietly.

YANKL. He, he, heh . . . So now you know everything. So now what do you think about me?

TAMARA. The best and the handsomest.

YANKL. The be—?

TAMARA. The best and the handsomest. I think that a husband like mine is very rare.

YANKL. You really mean it? You're not laughing?

TAMARA. I'll repeat it before God and man.

YANKL. You don't think it could happen over again with me? That—you know . . .

TAMARA. No, no, no.

YANKL. It hammers in my brain. I'm scared. A month ago I wasn't scared a bit, but now I'm scared. The devil knows me. You know, let's not take in any more boarders.

TAMARA. Silliness. Don't talk like that, don't think like that. Throw it all out of your head.

YANKL. You know, I'll pray every day the way I prayed today and also every day I'll say fifty—thirty—psalms.

TAMARA. Or you'll sit with me, when you have free time, enjoying ourselves, together with me and our little son.

YANKL. That's for sure.

The singing from the forge breaks off.

VOICES FROM THE FORGE. Reb Yankl, hurry up, come to work. The work is waiting.

The singing starts up again.

YANKL. I'm coming right away. (*Rolls up his sleeves.*) That's the way. Ah, will I work now. From today on and on. I'll work. With all my strength, I'll work— (*Embraces her and whispers as if a secret*)—and I'll love you—love with all my strength.

TAMARA. (*In his arms.*) Yes, love, strongly love.

The singing swells. The curtain falls slowly.

The End

Notes

Act 1

Sabbath lasts from before sundown Friday evening till after sundown Saturday evening. On Sabbath it is prohibited to work or kindle lights or ovens. The end of Sabbath is marked by a ceremony called *havdala*, which literally means "distinguishing"—between Sabbath and the rest of the week, the holy and the not holy, light and darkness. The ceremony takes only a few minutes; it entails blessings over wine, over fragrant spices representing the sweetness of Sabbath, and over the shadow cast by one's hand, representing the distinction between light and darkness. On Sabbath, the customary greeting is "good Sabbath"; after *havdala*, one says, "good week." "Good year" is an ordinary polite response.

The matchmaker, male or female, was a stock character in early Yiddish literature and theater, especially comedy. The male matchmaker even had specific associated stage conventions, such as carrying an umbrella.

The behavior of a Greek in a synagogue or *sukka* (temporary hut built for the holiday of Sukkot) is a common image of somebody who does not know how to behave in an unfamiliar setting.

A *yeshiva* is a Jewish educational institution that focuses on religious texts, primarily Torah and Talmud. In Pinsky's time only men attended yeshivas.

The local bathhouse made it possible for people without modern plumbing to be clean. However, for traditional Jews, then and still today, more than physical cleanliness is at stake. Jewish law and custom demands ritual immersion in flowing water for men and women on a number of specified occasions. Although many towns had a ritual bath, bathing in fresh flowing water was and is ritually acceptable. Frume is being ironic, however, in imagining someone "soaked through and through."

A *mezuza* is a small decorative case, most often between two and six inches, fixed on the doorway of a Jewish home, and sometimes on the doorway of every room inside the house as well. Inside the case is a parchment with the Hebrew prayer known as the *Shma*, beginning, "Hear O Israel . . . the Lord is one." It immediately identifies a home as Jewish.

There is a huge repertory of songs, lively or melodic, sung around the table at Sabbath meals.

Jewish men keep their heads covered and therefore wear a hat, at least a skullcap, at all times.

The toast *lekhayim* literally means "to life."

Having the couple grasp opposite ends of a kerchief is one of various old-time betrothal customs. Another has the two mothers together breaking a dinner plate.

Kosher is often used to mean "honest, virtuous, decent."

Yankl's parents have always been presented as comic roles. Reb Simkhe repeats his catchphrases in a style typical of (but not unique to) comic characters in Yiddish domestic dramas. (See the introduction to *Mirele Efros*.) These repetitions are a technical matter and can, to some extent, be cut. I think a greater difficulty for modern directors lies in the parents' insistence on Yankl's flaws. However, audiences seem to be able to accept this seemingly unnatural behavior, remembering that, as Tamara reminds Yankl, he scared them for many years.

Act 2

On Yom Kippur, the Day of Atonement, Jews fast from sundown to sundown and pray. Striking oneself on the breast while publicly listing one's own and the community's sins in the preceding year is a part of the Yom Kippur service.

From Psalm 137: 5–6: "If I forget you, O Jerusalem, let my right hand wither! Let my tongue cling to the roof of my mouth if I do not remember you."

At the time of this story, there were still, in some rural communities, women who contributed to the intensity of funerals and burials by wailing. The custom was common to other societies in Eastern Europe and elsewhere.

The universal struggle between evil and virtuous behavior is commonly semi-personified as two competing forces, the Evil Impulse and the Good Impulse.

Perceptions of Rivke and of her marital situation have changed since Pinski's time. As discussed in Moshe Yassur's comments on this play, and mine, this can be a problem—or possibly an opportunity—for a new production. However, I believe that basically changing the thrust of the play for ideological or political purposes, making Rivke the heroine and Tamara an antiheroine, distorts the play, which is essentially about Yankl; the play rests on Tamara as a good woman doing her best in the world she knows, and Rivke as an unfortunate woman who is willing to destroy other people's happiness for the sake of her own.

Act 3

Jewish circumcision takes place on the baby's eighth day, which is the optimum age for the baby's health, unless there is some health reason to postpone. It is the occasion for celebration. The Hebrew word for the event is *brit* (in Yiddish: *bris*), which means "covenant." The child participates in the collective Jewish commitment to God.

Lilith is a mythological character in Jewish folklore, a beautiful, seductive female demon. Sometimes described as Adam's first wife, she is especially dangerous to babies.

Basta is the word in the original.

Act 4

Itsikl is the Yiddish diminutive of Yitskhok (Isaac).

It is virtuous for a man, even if he is not a scholar, to regularly spend at least some time studying Talmud.

Moshe Yassur: Director's Thoughts

From the very beginning, the Jewish tradition grappled with the problem of good and evil. If the Almighty created a perfect world, where does evil come from? Of course, there are as many answers as there are human beings in the world. The non-Jewish world solved the problem simply by declaring that the world is good, and the Almighty is perfect, and evil comes from the devil. The Jews however, in striving for unity, could not accept a dualistic world and kept the belief that good and evil come from the same source. And in the good old Jewish style: perhaps good is not so good and evil is not so evil. Good and evil are, of course, acknowledged as *yetser tov* and *yetser hara*, or the "good impulse" and the "bad impulse," and both have room in one and the same human being. The tension between the two is eternal but it is in human hands to bring them under control. Why, after all, has the idea of free will come into the picture? All this is oil to the machine driving religious writings, secular literature, and, most of all, drama and theater. Our sages are not strangers to the foibles of this world, they cut a little leeway to the *yetser hara*. Perhaps the Evil Impulse is not so evil after all. They gave us a marvelous parable about the rabbis who caught the Evil Impulse and locked him up. The Good Impulse reigned alone in the world for twenty-four hours. The next morning, they couldn't find a newly laid egg. It is in this spirit that one is to consider David Pinski's hero of the play *Yankl the Blacksmith*.

Yankl embodies all the qualities of a healthy Jew. He is young and endowed with a dose of *yetser* of both kinds and more. He is not the typical Jewish weakling, bent over a tome of the Talmud, sitting in the study hall all day long, as were many youths of his generation, and who were the typical subjects of the earlier Yiddish theater. Pinski is bringing to the Jewish drama, perhaps for the first time, a new type of Jewish character. Yankl is strong, handsome, and—rare in Jewish theater—a blacksmith, not a scholar or a merchant. He is full of life, vigorous, likes to drink—atypical for a Jew—and he likes to dance and use his body, not his brain, for all that nature created the body for. He is a free spirit, not bound by the restrictions imposed by Jewish laws and tradition. All the girls and women in the village are attracted to Yankl. He dances with them, parties with them in the pub, and shows them a good time. The plot shows us this man in a herculean inner struggle with his demons.

In addition to Yankl, Pinski gives us Rivke, as a female counterpoint. She is a young woman, full of passion, and unhappily married. There is a second woman in Yankl's life, Tamara, whom he courts and wants very much to marry. This is the classic triangle that serves as grist for conflict and high drama in the Yiddish theater, and theater in general. Yankl is pitted against these two women, and he displays a heroic struggle with the *yetser hara*. On one hand he wants very much to be good and abandon the free life and his drunken behavior, in order to win the heart of Tamara. On the other hand, true to his nature, he is attracted to Rivke, who is his real kindred spirit and his equal in drives and passion. The action comes to a head when Rivke insinuates herself in Yankl's workshop and stirs the fire in the forge while at the same time stirring Yankl's passion to the boiling point. The fire in the forge is melting a piece of iron, and, at the same time, Yankl's libido is aroused to the brink. He loses himself in a kiss that proves almost fatal to his fresh marriage, as his wife, Tamara, is in bed in the next room after having given birth to their son. At this point we see the young man's struggle with the *yetser hara*, thus creating a climactic moment of great tension.

The real challenge for the director is in keeping the right balance between these passions while at the same time not losing sight of the spirit of the times in which the play was written. Pinski was a man of the world: born in 1872 in Mogilev, Belarus, he went as a thirteen-year-old to Moscow, where he imbibed prerevolutionary ideas; as a young man he went from there to Vitebsk, Warsaw, Vienna, Berlin, and in 1899 to America; in 1949, he immigrated to Israel where he died in 1959. He sojourned in Berlin in 1896, around the time when Ibsen's plays were performed. It is quite possible that Pinski might have been, if not influenced, at least inspired by the modernistic atmosphere of Germany's capital at that time. He must have visited the theater and seen plays by Ibsen and Hauptmann. Ibsen's characters and their struggles to emancipate themselves from the fetters of societal conventions have a lot in common with Pinski's characters and their struggle for freedom from the constraints of their society.

To take one example, Nora, the main character in Ibsen's play *A Doll's House*, is unhappy and struggles to escape from her marriage and her husband. Like Nora, Rivke too is trying to free herself and escape from an unhappy marriage with an unloved husband. She, in my view, is the tragic hero of Pinski's play. Rivke's options are limited in her small world, dominated by religious traditions. While Nora opts to step into an open world—albeit forbidding—when she slams the door behind her and leaves, Rivke, in her village, has nowhere to run. So, defeated, she returns unwillingly to her unhappy home. We don't know what's to become of her, and she is left with no dramatic resolution. Yankl, after putting up a heroic fight with the *yetser hara*, is almost defeated, but in the end, he is back with Tamara and his newborn child. To live happily ever after? For how long? We don't know. The *yetser hara* is lurking in the wings. After all, we are in the Yiddish theater, and it was too early for a Jewish audience to accept the new current of individual freedom blowing at that time through Europe. Perhaps Pinski made a compromise to his Jewish background. One must not forget that even Ibsen was greeted at first with a cold shoulder.

The theme of the play is the struggle of the characters for emancipation. Of all characters in the play, I am moved by Rivke. Pinski makes her the symbol of the *yetser hara*, the bad impulse, destructive and self-destructive, even physically abusing her husband. At the height of his passion, Yankl compares her to Lilith, the mythical primordial femme fatale. In the twenty-first century, we are more inclined to see her as a victim. She confronts the wrath of the entire shtetl and her predicament is tragic. She loses on all fronts and is defeated by forces too big for her.

If I directed the play, I would emphasize Rivke's plight and tilt the weight of the play toward her struggle and her defeat. Her husband is not really the nincompoop, as he is seen by other characters in the play. He is an astute businessman and would be an adequate husband to another woman who would appreciate him. Tamara, for example. At one point, Rivke even taunts her by making the outrageous suggestion that they switch husbands. However, this is not how proper society works. Life is not perfect, and the best solutions are often unattainable. Theater reflects this reality.

The play has solved the problem of the main protagonists. However, Rivke and Rafael have no such resolution. As a director, I am interested in the personal tragedy of Rivke and Rafael as the contrasting couple. Rivke is the one smitten by her own demons and her unfulfilled drives, which Rafael cannot possibly satisfy. One strong final image comes to my mind that would imprint the impression of their utter incompatibility, versus the image of the harmony attained by Tamara and Yankl at the end of the play; being sent out of Yankl's house by the outraged family members, the representatives of "proper" society, Rivke holds on to the doorpost with all her might, as Rafael waits outside holding her bundle of clothes and pleading with her to come home. On one side, we would see Yankl and Tamara holding their child; on the other side are Rivke and, separately, Rafael with nothing but a bundle of clothes to hold—a perfect symbolic image with expressionist power.

The modern director might want to use music in the play in a Brechtian style, to release the tension and let the audience think about what they are watching. More recent examples of theatrical work rooted in the traditions of folk with its claustrophobic social settings and rough customs and language—possibly comparable to Pinski's Yiddish world—would be, in my estimation, the work of German playwright Franz Xaver Kroetz, or even of the American Sam Shepard; their plays do not shy from depicting the conflicts arising between the impulses of individual freedom versus social constraint.

~

Moshe Yassur was born in Iasi, Romania, where he survived the June 1941 pogrom. His theatrical start was as a child actor in the late 1940s in the world's (revived) original Yiddish theater, and he trained and acted in the Romanian National Theatre. After immigration to Israel, he joined the Hebrew theater as actor, director, and teacher. In Paris, he worked with Jean-Marie Serreau on plays by Eugene Ionesco and Samuel Beckett. In New York since 1971, he has directed in numerous theaters, including the New Federal Theatre, Soho Rep, the Open Space Theatre Experiment, Third Step Theatre Company, and Castillo Theatre. Since 2000, he has directed important premieres and revivals in major Romanian theaters, as well as Yiddish plays for the Jewish State Theatre in Bucharest. His Yiddish credits in New York include adapting and directing works by I. B. Singer and Sholem Aleichem, and the Yiddish world premieres of *Waiting for Godot* by Samuel Beckett and *Rhinoceros* by Eugene Ionesco. In addition, he has published numerous articles about theater.

Yoshke the Musician

(*The Hired Bridegroom, The Rented Bridegroom, The Singer of His Sorrow*)

OSIP DIMOV, REWORKED BY JOSEPH BULOFF

Introduction

I was lucky enough to see Joseph Buloff's last production of *Yoshke the Musician*. It was at the National Yiddish Theatre–Folksbiene in New York, then a semi-professional company, in 1972. Buloff played the title role, which he himself had created half a century earlier; directed, as he had then; and made further changes in the script he had participated in writing. By 1972, he was of an age to play a grandfather not a lover, and he was made up in the nonrealistic masklike style of his youth, but nobody in the audience cared or even noticed. The sad little love story broke my heart. I saw it a second time and brought my husband, who had tears in his eyes though he doesn't even speak Yiddish.

Osip Dimov, or Dymow, whose real name was Yosef Perlman (1878–1959), originally wrote the play on which Buloff's production was based in Russian. Like his parents, Dimov was not involved in Jewish religion or culture, and his early writings for press and stage had no Jewish component. Evidently it was the 1906 pogrom in Bialystok, his hometown, as well as the influence of the thinker Vladimir Jabotinsky, that led him to write *Hear O Israel* in 1907, and subsequently *The Eternal Wanderer*, depictions of Jewish sufferings in the diaspora. Both were extremely successful with public and critics, Jewish and non-Jewish. He continued for some time to write in Russian, though increasingly with the explicit intention that it be translated and published or performed in Yiddish, and eventually he himself wrote in Yiddish. He wrote his last play in English, and it played in New York and London.

Dimov was typical of Yiddish writers in that he was active in various styles and genres: articles, essays, stories, radio plays, a memoir. But above all he was a man of the theater, a wholehearted admirer of the actor's craft. Besides writing many plays, and at least one Yiddish screenplay, he directed. He worked with the great Austrian director Max Reinhardt. He ran a Yiddish drama school. He and the star Rudolph Schildkraut opened a Yiddish art theater in the Bronx, where he produced his best-known play, *Bronx Express*, which also played in English on Broadway. What was definitely not typical of Yiddish plays, however, was the style of *Yoshke*, intensified by Buloff: playful and light, bittersweet, romantically poetic, fantastical—evocative of his French contemporaries Anouilh and Giraudoux.

Yoshke the Musician, *The Hired (Rented) Bridegroom*, *The Singer of His Sorrow* (this last, the original title)—a play with so many titles has obviously had a complicated playing history. In a nutshell: Dimov wrote it in Russian, possibly drawing on boyhood memories of a musician who wandered the streets of Bialystok. That play, which was published in Yiddish translation, is recognizable as an early draft of the play I have translated in this volume. First it was a flop. Then in 1925, a group of idealistic young actors—soon to become famous as the Vilna Troupe—took it on and made it an international smash.

The Vilna Troupe had debuted in 1916, in an abandoned circus building with broken wooden flooring. The actors were cold and hungry, and so were the audiences, but they had a passion to develop an art theater like those of other European cultures. Their mission entailed not only innovative stage practice but also an elevated new Yiddish repertory—not so easy, since Yiddish literature as secular high culture was only two or, at most, three generations old. But the group persevered. By 1918 they had moved from Vilna to Warsaw and were making a name for themselves, and in 1920 they premiered their production of Sh. Ansky's *The Dybbuk*, which made them internationally famous. The Vilna Troupe would go on to tour Europe and America for decades. By then they had splintered, but many of the individual splinters continued to call themselves the Vilna Troupe, and actors who had been part of the original were respected everywhere.

In 1925, Dimov's naive love story, which had already been produced elsewhere without success, was too thin and undeveloped to interest the troupe. But company member Joseph Buloff, only in his twenties but already playing leads, persuaded them to let him approach the plot "as a vehicle toward a completely new piece that I had worked out in my mind.... I had to be a writer, to roll up my sleeves and rework the script to fit it to my own conception." With the poet Yankev Shternberg, he created an adaptation, adding a dream framework; he played Yoshke (as well as the grandmother), and staged the play "as a fantasy," "a childlike vision," "larger and more colorful than real life."[1]

Reuven Rubin, later to become a famous Israeli painter, designed sets and costumes in the angular constructivist style of the period. The chicken vendor was costumed subtly like a hen, for example, and Yoshke's makeup was a clownlike, geometric white mask suggesting the shape of a violin. Even the actors' movements were choreographed expressionistically, less realistic than balletic. This was congenial with much European experimental theater of the period, including the Moscow Yiddish Art Theatre GOSET and the Russian Hebrew-language Habima.

The Vilna Troupe toured constantly. When the new *Yoshke* opened, they happened to be in Bucharest, and there they stayed an entire year, breaking local records for performances of any one play in a single season. Many non-Jews attended. Romanian critics raved, calling it the "epitome of pure art." Buloff later recalled that Eugene Ionesco came to see them and credited them with giving him "the clue to the type of anti-naturalist drama that he was writing." Romanian intellectuals learned to sing "Yoshke with fiddle, Berl with bass." At the hundredth performance of the play, which happened to occur in the Romanian city of Czernowitz, a huge crowd turned out to celebrate. The most dazzling sign of success was being invited to give a command performance for Romanian king Carol II (and his Jewish mistress).

Although some version of the final Buloff-Shternberg script is the only form of the play that has ever been produced since it appeared, it was never published, and in fact the play has always been advertised as

---

1. Luba Kadison and Joseph Buloff with Irving Genn, *On Stage, Off Stage: Memories of a Lifetime in the Yiddish Theatre* (Cambridge: Harvard University Library, 1992), 50.

Dimov's. Dimov is believed to have exclaimed, when told of the Vilna Troupe's hit, "Marvelous! Who wrote it?" Both Dimov and Buloff lived in New York for most of their later lives, moving in the same small and intense theater circle, with no dissension.

The Folksbiene, which produced the play in 1972 and again in 1999—the latter as *A Klezmer's Tale: Yoshke Muzikant*, directed by Eleanor Reissa, probably the most recent production anywhere—preserved two scripts in their archives. One is mostly handwritten, the other typed, but both are scribbled over, pages pasted in and pages crossed out. The texts differ in various ways, large and small. No one now can tell which script comes from which production. The one I have chosen to translate is the one that seems closer to what I remember seeing in 1972, which happens to be the handwritten one. It is also the longer one, and the one that includes more moments of verse, sometimes rhymed, more often loosely or intermittently rhyming. The verses seem to be song lyrics. In fact, the program for the 1999 production includes, in its list of musical numbers, original settings of several of these "poems" by musical director (now the company's artistic director) Zalmen Mlotek; the program also includes folk and theater tunes that may have served as settings for others. (That score is available directly from him.) What I translated was a working script.

I must add that the cast of the 1972 production, mostly veteran members of the semi-professional Folksbiene repertory company (at this writing the longest continuously performing Yiddish theater institution in the world, and entirely professional), was perfection. It's the beauty of the repertory system that Ziporah Spaizman, who played Hodes the chicken lady, later played Mirele Efros at the Folksbiene. Mina Bern, who played Madam Luria, played Hodes in the Folksbiene's 1999 production, described in this volume by its director Eleanor Reissa.

Yoshke has been translated and performed in Hebrew, Polish, and German. In 2014, Target Margin Theater in New York commissioned and produced *The Rented Bridegroom*, "a play by Rinne Groff based on *The Singer of His Sorrows* as adapted by Rinne Groff and Adrian Silver from a translation by Adrian Silver," and this play was presented by Theater J in 2019 under the title *The Red Beads*.

Yoshke the Musician

(The Hired Bridegroom, The Rented Bridegroom, The Singer of His Sorrows)

OSIP DIMOV, REWORKED BY JOSEPH BULOFF

Characters

GRANDMOTHER	Later: SHEYNE.
MADAME LURIA	A widow.
SYEMYONTSHIK	Madame Luria's son, in his twenties or thirties, feckless and weak, handsome, a gambler.
ROYZELE	Madame Luria's daughter, ten years old.
SHEYNE	Madame Luria's servant and distant relative, in her twenties, loves Syemyontshik.
MENDL	A cemetery plot salesman, carries a portfolio.
HODES	A seller of poultry and eggs, vulgar market woman, looks and talks somehow like a chicken.
SHAYKE	A chimneysweep, hands and face black with soot, political, plays drums.
BERL	A water carrier, plays bass fiddle.
YOSHKE	Berl's son, fiddler and leader of the local band, in his thirties or older. Prankster, poetic soul, local letter writer, does magic tricks. Loves Sheyne.
KALEFUTE	The village madman.

BAKER

BUTCHER

YOSHKE'S BLIND MOTHER

REPRESENTATIVE OF THE VILLAGE RICH MEN

RABBI

SEXTON

GOVERNOR

BEGGARS, FIRST AND SECOND

BEGGAR WOMEN, FIRST AND SECOND

FATHER-IN-LAW, MOTHER-IN-LAW, BRIDE

CHIEF OF POLICE, POLICEMEN

JEWS	Workmen, wives, among others.
PLACE	Small village in Russia, seen through memory, with prologue and epilogue in a child's bedroom.
TIME	Around 1900, with prologue and epilogue a generation later.
PROLOGUE/ EPILOGUE	A child's bed or bedroom.
ACTS 1 and 2	Kitchen of Madame Luria's prosperous house, with stairs leading up to the family rooms, sometime in the past.
ACT 3	The same kitchen and later a hallucinatory version of the kitchen.

Prologue, melting into Act 1

GRANDMOTHER and ROYZELE, bedtime.

GRANDMOTHER. These fifty-two cards are like the fifty-two weeks of the year. No matter how you mix them, the number remains the same. Heart, diamond, club, spade are the seasons of the year: summer, winter, spring, autumn. And here are the people. (*Showing cards.*)

ROYZELE. Who are the people, Grandma?

GRANDMOTHER. Who knows? Mute faces, and in them lie all the secrets of what was and what will be. They know all the tricks of the world. Only one thing they don't know: the trick with the five aces. When the five aces meet up, the world shakes, the moon laughs, the stars fall down from the heavens, and great wonders come to pass. And such wonders will happen to you, and this little man with the heart up here on his head will sing for you as he once sang for me.

ROYZELE. Grandma, why is he wearing his heart on his head?

GRANDMOTHER. Because his heart was so big that it couldn't fit in his chest, so he wore it on his head.

ROYZELE. He sang?

GRANDMOTHER. What couldn't he do? They called him Yoshke the Musician. And he knew how to write, too.

ROYZELE. And who is that one with the red nose and the bells on his head?

GRANDMOTHER. Ah, that's just a clown, a nothing. It's Crazy Kalefute. Every village had a fool. He was called Kalefute the First.

ROYZELE. Who was the Second, then?

Clock strikes.

GRANDMOTHER. But listen, the clock is already striking. You have to go to bed.

ROYZELE. No, no, I'll sleep here, but you tell me, tell me everything. Where was he?

GRANDMOTHER. Far, far away. In my little village.

ROYZELE. When was it?

GRANDMOTHER. Long, long ago. Even before the engineers made it so no one had to haul water from the well, you could draw it out of the wall. I was a servant then at my rich aunt's.

ROYZELE. Madame Malka Luria.

GRANDMOTHER. That was her name: Aunt Malka.

ROYZELE. She was mean?

GRANDMOTHER. No. She was good. Only she didn't have any sense. I didn't have too much sense myself. But soon the cards fell in such a way that the aunt stopped being an aunt and I stopped being a servant.

ROYZELE. And where was I?

GRANDMOTHER. You weren't anywhere. But Aunt Malka had a little daughter. Her name was Royzele, and you are named for her. And when Yoshke the Musician and his band used to play, she used to sing with them. I would so love you to learn their song, because I'm getting old and I'm starting to forget. Yoshke with the fiddle . . .

Sleep, sleep, child. I will call Yoshke with his band. Come, come in, little musicians, and stand right here by Royzele. Play her the old song so she learns it in her dream and remembers it when she wakes up.

> YOSHKE, PLAY THE MELODY.
> BERL, THUMP THE BEAT.
> THE TUNE IS SINGING THROUGH THE TOWN.
> IT DANCES DOWN THE STREET.
> LET THE TENDER FIDDLE WEEP,
> LET THE OLD BASS LAUGH,
> AND LET THE MUSIC LIFT MY HEART,
> AND LET IT LIFT MY FEET.

YOSHKE enters.

ROYZELE. Yoshke.

YOSHKE. Shh, shh.

ROYZELE. It's you, you're Yoshke the Musician.

YOSHKE. How did you recognize me?

ROYZELE. Where is your heart that you used to wear on your head?

YOSHKE. I don't know. I gambled it away playing cards.

ROYZELE. Where is my grandma? What did you do with her?

YOSHKE. Don't be scared, she went back to the village, to her rich aunt.

ROYZELE. I fell asleep. She didn't finish telling me.

YOSHKE. Come. I'll tell you. I'm the one who knows the secret of the five aces.

ROYZELE. Where do you want to take me?

YOSHKE. To the rich aunt in the little village. Look, the village looks in through the window. And in the little kitchen, the big oven still stands and the fire on the stove is still dancing the same dance.

Prologue blurs into act 1, set in the kitchen in Madame Luria's house. Oven with chimney above. Table. Window and door leading to street on one side. On opposite side, stairs leading up to the rest of the house.

ROYZELE. Look, who's sitting at the oven?

YOSHKE. That is your grandmother. Don't you recognize her? Oh, how pretty she was then. In fact, they call her Pretty Sheyne.

Sheyne dear, how are you? It's been maybe a hundred years since I saw you last. Do you still remember my letter? Do you still remember my song that I sang for you? "In my heart a little bird sings to you, a little bird with all the most beautiful colors. Ah, my beloved, come back to me. If you don't come, I must die."

ROYZELE. She doesn't hear. She doesn't answer.

YOSHKE. I'll run home and find my fiddle and bring my band. She'll come to life. You stay here, I'll come later. You'll hear something, you'll see something. (*Exits.*)

ROYZELE. Yoshke, don't leave me alone.

SHEYNE. Royzele, what are you doing here?

ROYZELE. I don't know. I thought . . . that Yoshke was standing behind the window.

SHEYNE. Again? I'll pour water on him. (*Looks out.*) Nobody there. What were you dreaming about? What are you doing out of bed so early? And why don't you get dressed? I have enough troubles without you.

ROYZELE. I wanted to tell you something. I forget . . .

SHEYNE. What? Tell me fast.

ROYZELE. I'm mixed up. I don't remember.

SHEYNE. Remember! Did your mama say something about me? Or maybe about your brother Syemyontshik? When is he coming home?

ROYZELE. I don't know. If you want, I can ask Mama.

SHEYNE. Do that, do that, darling, and if you hear something, come tell me. Without anybody knowing.

ROYZELE. I understand. I'll listen in and come tell you very quietly.

SHEYNE. Go get dressed.

ROYZELE. Nobody will know. (*Exits.*)

MENDL. (*Enters with portfolio.*) Good morning. Good morning. Cold, cold. It keeps getting colder. Really winter. Is the madame at home?

SHEYNE. Home.

MENDL. Well, and him, he still hasn't come?

SHEYNE. Who?

MENDL. Syemyontshik.

SHEYNE. Hasn't come. My business.

MENDL. When will he come?

SHEYNE. What do you care?

MENDL. I want to help you.

SHEYNE. How can you help me?

MENDL. If you help me with my business with the madame, I'll help you with your business with her little boy.

SHEYNE. What are you babbling about?

MENDL. I can find you a good job in another rich house, a nicer kitchen, a bigger salary, and less aggravation.

SHEYNE. You think I should leave.

MENDL. Better leave in a nice way than be thrown out in a nasty way.

SHEYNE. What did you say? Talk. I want to know.

MENDL. Oh cold, cold. A glass of hot tea would warm up my tongue a little.

SHEYNE. If you want tea, say so and don't drive me crazy.

MENDL. I will help you in order for you to help me. One hand washes the other.

SHEYNE. What did you say? (*Serves tea.*)

MENDL. Well? A lump of sugar?

SHEYNE. (*Serves. He takes sugar.*) What have you heard? Talk. I want to know.

MENDL. You'll know, you'll know. You need to know, you must know. Better for you to know before everyone else does.

SHEYNE. Enough. The madame counts the lumps every night before she goes to sleep.

MENDL. When does she come down into the kitchen?

SHEYNE. You want to talk to her or to me?

MENDL. To both of you. For her I have a bargain. A brand new cemetery plot. She'd better grab it, because here today and tomorrow: somebody else will snap it up. The grave is four by six. There Moyshe the ritual slaughterer is lying, and there Rabbi Avremele the judge, and on the right, Doctor Pinek. I myself would be happy to lie down among people like that.

SHEYNE. What do I care about the dead?

MENDL. This is for the madame. With you I'll talk about the living. It's been five weeks now since your handsome Syemyontshik went away. Do you know where he went?

SHEYNE. No.

MENDL. Do you know what he went for?

SHEYNE. No.

MENDL. So you know nothing. He went looking for a bride with a hefty dowry.

SHEYNE. Looking for a bride?

MENDL. Looking for a dowry. Only when he found the dowry, there was a bride holding on to it.

SHEYNE. You're lying.

MENDL. If I'm lying, I should lie in the same grave that I want to sell to the madame.

SHEYNE. It's true, my God! What should I do?

MENDL. Ah, once you're asking what to do, we have to do something. First we have to know: are you really Madame's niece?

SHEYNE. I am nothing. Here in the kitchen I am a servant.

MENDL. No, in the kitchen you're the boss. You should have split his head open when he came to you in the kitchen in the middle of the night.

SHEYNE. I was a fool. I loved him and believed him.

MENDL. You really were a fool. Listen, I talked to Hodes the chicken-eater.

HODES. (*Enters.*) Good morning. Ah, Lord of the world, cold. Really winter. Well, what?

MENDL. Nothing. We're drinking tea.

HODES. Oh, lord of the world. And what about what we were talking about?

MENDL. She doesn't want to hear.

HODES. A duck has more sense than you. Why don't you want to hear?

SHEYNE. Because it's a lie. He wouldn't marry anybody else. He promised me.

HODES. Promising and loving don't cost any money. How many men promised me? That's how they are, men. Better not to know them and not to need them.

SHEYNE. He made a fool of me with sweet talk.

HODES. Exactly like my husband Mekhele, rest in peace—May he toss and turn where he lies in the ground. Fut-fut-fut—like a chicken, that's how they are, the men. Before, it's fut-fut-fut, and after it's coo-coo-ree-coo.

MENDL. But Syemyontshik still doesn't want to marry her.

HODES. We have to make him.

SHEYNE. How?

HODES. Give me a glass of tea. I don't talk for free. I have my own sugar.

MENDL. There is sugar.

HODES. If Madame Luria comes in and sees us chewing sugar lumps, she will explode.

MENDL. What do you care? I already have a cemetery plot for her.

HODES. She is so stingy she uses the hair from her comb to stuff the mattress. All the same, I will take a few lumps for later. And you, don't go around like a dead duck. A dead duck can't swim. Why are you bashful? Talk, let's hear.

SHEYNE. I don't want to talk. I don't want to live. I'll throw myself in the river.

MENDL. In the river? Nasty. When a person dies, he should lie in a cemetery, in dry earth.

HODES. You be quiet, let her talk. Let's hear.

SHEYNE. When I was still a child, I heard that somewhere I have a rich aunt Malka. Her picture hung on the wall at home.

MENDL. She means Madame Luria.

HODES. Don't mix in.

SHEYNE. When my parents died, I packed up my little pack and went to look for my aunt.

HODES. Would have been better to find her hanging on the wall.

SHEYNE. She recognized me, asked me to sit down, gave me a glass of tea, and told me to go into the kitchen—to sleep here, do the wash here, and cook, and bake, and clean the main rooms upstairs.

HODES. We know, we understand. But how did the young man come to you?

MENDL. She must have gone upstairs.

SHEYNE. No. He came down here looking for a match for his cigar.

HODES. You should have kicked him out.

SHEYNE. He came right back.

HODES. You should have screamed "no."

MENDL. You should have known that a young man who smokes a cigar . . .

SHEYNE. He was good to me, and the cigar was so becoming, and you could smell his perfume. And once, he brought me a little box of jelly candies.

HODES. That's the way it is. I know those candies. My Mekhl (may he toss and turn where he lies) ruined my whole life with candies like that. Syemyontshik has got to come back home this minute.

MENDL. What do you mean "this minute"?

SHEYNE. He's a thousand miles away.

HODES. We have to send him a letter.

SHEYNE. I can't write.

MENDL. I can throw a few words together.

HODES. Your few words could make him run even further. To bring Syemyontshik here, we need words to pierce his heart like needles. Only one man can write that kind of letter: Yoshke the fiddler.

SHEYNE. That's all I need: for him to know my troubles.

HODES. I met his father, Berl the water carrier, and told him to bring his son.

SHEYNE. Whenever he goes by, he looks in through the window. I've already poured water on him a few times.

MENDL. First let him write the letter, then you can pour water on him again and throw him out.

SHEYNE. I don't want any letter at all.

HODES. If Yoshke writes the letter, it will bring him alive or dead.

MENDL. If he comes alive, you'll have him. If he comes dead, I'll take care of him.

HODES. Yoshke is the only one.

MENDL. So let it be Yoshke.

SHAYKE. (*Enters down the chimney over the oven.*) And I say that certainly a letter must be written, and nobody can write it but Yoshke the fiddler.

MENDL. Get out of here.

HODES. You devil, you black thing, what business is this of yours?

SHAYKE. I jump over roofs, and I hear through the chimneys: someone's laughing, someone's crying, a widow is sitting in tears, a child in a cradle wails and begs for food. But why should a girl who is healthy and good-looking be crying and grieving?

SHEYNE. What do you care, you devil, you black thing creeping in here?

SHAYKE. Black as I am, I am whiter than snow compared to the heart of the one you love.

SHEYNE. Out of the kitchen this minute.

MENDL. I will break your bones.

HODES. Let him go up on the roof, the dark devil.

SHAYKE. If I'm a devil, you are the angel of death. In the hundred years you've been alive, you've slaughtered so many chickens, chopped them up and gobbled them down, till now you're a chicken yourself. Coo-coo-ree-coo.

HODES. Help, help, throw him out.

MENDL. We need to take care of private business.

SHAYKE. The business is not so private as you think.

MENDL. Your tongue should shrivel for saying that.

SHAYKE. Come fly with me over the roofs. You'll hear from chimney to chimney how they talk and talk it over and talk it over.

HODES. Don't listen, don't listen. His words are smoke and chimneys.

SHEYNE. Oh God in heaven, I'll bury myself. Isn't the shame bad enough? What are you creeping around here for? What are you looking for? Who needs you here? Who asked you in?

ALL. We want to help you. Wipe your tears. We want to help you and bring Syemyontshik tied with a rope.

SHEYNE. I love him and I believe him. When he comes, he will throw your lies in your faces, all of you. He will keep his promise. I'll be his wife, just to spite you all.

ROYZELE. (*Enters.*) Sheyne!

MENDL. Shh, quiet, here's another partner in the business.

HODES. The child doesn't belong here.

SHEYNE. What do you want, Royzele? What do you have in your hand?

ROYZELE. There's a whole package waiting for Mama on her table.

HODES. The little one has more sense than the big one.

SHEYNE. What is this thing?

MENDL. An invitation to a wedding. But not to her wedding, only to his.

SHAYKE. Flaming fire! This I did not hear about in the chimney.

MENDL. Now you see that we're right?

HODES. And I say that if there is a wedding, she will be the bride. I'm going to run to the water carrier and bring Yoshke right back here. Shh—here is Berl.

BERL. (*Enters.*) Good morning.

ALL. Good morning.

BERL. Cold, really winter. God's miracle: in summer water turns to steam, in winter it turns to ice. And me, I turn water into my bread.

SHAYKE. Berl, I have news for you.

BERL. I heard, I heard. Some engineer devils are coming from hell. They're going to make the village water come out of the wall. They want to take the little piece of bread from my mouth.

HODES. Why did you come to tell us about your troubles? Where is Yoshke? I asked you to bring him.

BERL. I brought him.

MENDL. Then where is he?

BERL. He's standing outside.

SHAYKE. We need him in here, not outside.

SHEYNE. Let him stand outside.

HODES. He isn't coming for you. He's coming for me. I want him to write a letter for me.

BERL. He's always ready to earn a few groshn.

HODES. I'll pay him. Go bring him in right away.

BERL. I'm going.

SHEYNE. I won't be here. I'm leaving.

HODES. If you leave, he'll think God knows what.

SHAYKE. I'll explain to him.

HODES. You keep your unkosher mouth shut. Not a word out of you. And you, go away, this is no place for children.

ROYZELE. I'm not a child.

HODES. And you sit at the table as if you don't know what's going on.

MENDL. Nobody knows what's going on. Hodes is writing a letter. Shh.

YOSHKE. (*Enters.*) Good morning.

BERL. Good morning. Sheyne, he's here.

SHEYNE. I see. I'm not blind.

YOSHKE. Cold outside. In here it's warm, lovely.

SHEYNE. You don't like it?

YOSHKE. What? I said it's lovely.

HODES. If it's lovely, sit yourself at the table and write me a little letter.

SHAYKE. Not a little letter, a letter! With fire and smoke, it should burn, it should crackle—

YOSHKE. Shayke, why didn't you come last night? The whole band was waiting. How can we play without a drum?

BERL. If you don't come play, the lift goes flat.

SHAYKE. The beat has a solid bash when the lines come together.

YOSHKE. But the band catches the flip or the whole gallop dies.

MENDL. What language are you talking, Turkish? What are Turks doing in a kosher house?

YOSHKE. It's nothing, it's musician language.

ROYZELE. I understand every word. If you didn't play last night, then you can play now for us.

YOSHKE. I came to write, but if you really want me to, I'll play.

ROYZELE. I've never heard you play.

YOSHKE. Neither has Sheyne.

ROYZELE. But now that you're here, you can play.

YOSHKE. With the greatest pleasure. I have composed a new dance, sweet as sugar, you'll lick your fingers. But Shayke and Papa don't have their instruments.

BERL. I'll give you the beat on the broom.

SHAYKE. And me on the chimney.

YOSHKE. And you hold the score. (*Plays.*)

> VILLAGE MUSICIANS, THEY TALK THEIR OWN WAY
> WHEN THEY HAVE SOMETHING IMPORTANT TO SAY.
> EVERYONE DANCES THE MUSIC THEY PLAY,
> BUT NOBODY ELSE CAN SAY WHAT THEY SAY.

WITH A WINK OF THE EYE
AND A TWITCH OF THE CHEEK,
THEY UNDERSTAND EVERYTHING.
NO NEED TO SPEAK.
AND THEY GIVE A BASH—
HEY!

SHEYNE. Help, what does he want from me? Why did he come here to fiddle first thing in the morning?

BERL. Be patient. It's just the first quartet.

MENDL. We called you to do a job, and you stand here and sing.

SHAYKE. Let him, let him. It will lift your heart.

HODES. We don't need any music. We need a letter.

SHAYKE. So put away the bow and take up the pen.

YOSHKE. I only wanted you to hear the wedding dance that Madame Luria up there ordered for the wedding of her precious son and his rich bride.

HODES. Well, that's done it.

MENDL. Who's asking you?

SHEYNE. This minute get him out of here. I'll pour water over him.

MENDL. Pour water over him.

MENDL and HODES. Out!

YOSHKE. Why?

BERL. Why ask why? If they don't want you here, come home.

ROYZELE. Yoshke, I heard you can do tricks.

BERL. Come home.

YOSHKE. Wait a minute, Papa. Since I'm here already, and they won't let me play, and they don't need me to write, I'll show her one of my tricks. It doesn't cost me anything. I'll show you how to lay an egg.

ROYZELE. But I'm not a hen.

YOSHKE. If you were a hen, it wouldn't be a trick. I can even make you into a duck.

> A little duckling goes so sweet
> On her pretty little feet.
> And her little head is bare
> And she waddles here and there.
> "One, two, three, four, five," she quacks,
> And look! An egg falls out—no cracks!

Does a trick, produces an egg.

HODES. That egg is mine. You took it from my basket. You bastard, you thief, I'll smack your face. Now you put it right back in my basket.

YOSHKE. If I'm a bastard, that's my papa's problem, but a thief—here you have your egg, so don't call me thief. Meanwhile, you stole my hat.

HODES. What hat—what cat, what mat—why is he driving me crazy?

YOSHKE. It's not a cat, not a mat, just a plain hat.

HODES. Oh, you scoundrel, you ugly rascal, that egg isn't mine, it's—

YOSHKE. Why are you confusing me with eggs?

> Give—excuse me—a wiggle with your seat
> And look! not one egg but two, that you can eat.

HODES and MENDL. Two! Two!

MENDL. Oh my, I am done for. Three.

BERL. Well, how do you like my son?

SHEYNE. You're proud of him.

BERL. I play bass, he plays fiddle. Why? Because he has the soul of a fiddle.

SHEYNE. Just so you leave my soul alone.

BERL. A decent girl like you and an old bachelor like him could make a good couple.

MENDL. How is he good enough for her? Plenty like him in my portfolio. I can show you his place in the cemetery.

YOSHKE. Why do you need to show it? If God wants, I'll live forever, and you'll never make a groshn from me. Shouldn't I have a wedding?

BERL. So what is there to talk about? I'll give one hundred fifty to one hundred sixty rubles dowry, for you, for him, and for the children if there are any.

YOSHKE. Of course there will be children. Why not?

BERL. On one hundred sixty rubles you can support a whole dozen children in wealth and honor.

YOSHKE. And if one hundred sixty rubles is too little, I'll throw in a hundred sixty thousand.

HODES. A hundred sixty thousand?

YOSHKE. Yes, yes, yes, a hundred sixty thousand. If you don't believe me, I can show you. Papa, should I show them?

BERL. What?

YOSHKE. The hundred sixty thousand.

BERL. What hundred sixty thousand?

YOSHKE. That I bought for forty kopeks.

BERL. Oh, you mean the lottery ticket?

YOSHKE. Here it is.

MENDL. A lottery ticket? Hah?

HODES. You can't buy a plucked hen for that.

YOSHKE. Yes, yes, yes. It can win a hundred sixty thousand someday.

MENDL. Someday when? Once in a hundred sixty thousand years.

YOSHKE. It's not the money, it's the hope of winning. You can only win once, but you can hope all the time. One hundred sixty thousand minutes of hope is worth more than the prize itself.

BERL. Tell us, tell us how you came to buy it.

YOSHKE. What is there to tell? I'm lying in bed one night and I dream that I go out for a stroll down the street. Suddenly I see that a star with a long tail falls down from heaven right on my head. I'm no fool. I put up my hands quick. I catch it; I've got it. Everybody has his own star, and there can be no greater joy than when your star falls into your hands. And whatever my fate is, we both share it, like my mama and papa, like my grandfather and grandmother: what's mine is yours—can there be anything better?

BERL. When he talks, it's like a violin is playing.

MENDL. Stars are fire. It didn't burn your hands?

YOSHKE. In my dream it was fire, but in reality it was a piece of paper.

MENDL. A what?

YOSHKE. A little letter.

MENDL. A little letter, a little piece of paper.

YOSHKE. Yes, that I should buy a ticket for the lottery.

MENDL. A little letter from the sky?

YOSHKE. Written and stamped in plain Yiddish.

MENDL. In Yiddish—such an honor!

YOSHKE. And signed, "Yours truly, Lord God of the World."

BERL. Ha, ha, try to win a debate with him!

SHEYNE. What's going on here? Is this a hen coop? What are you cackling about? What are you quacking about? I don't have time. I have to wash; I have to cook.

HODES. If he wants to write a letter, let him write. I'll pay him and he can leave.

MENDL. Right, until the hundred sixty thousand fall down on you out of the sky. Meanwhile, make a few honest groshn.

SHAYKE. Yoshke, pick up the pen, a fire is burning.

HODES. Sit in your place before I break all your bones.

BERL. Well, no is no. I thought I'd finally bring his blind mama some good news. In that case, I'll take my old buckets and go back to work. And you, write, write the letter.

YOSHKE. All right then. A letter is a letter. We've got paper. Good. I've got my own pen.

SHAYKE. Let's seat him reclining at the table, on cushions, high, like a king at a seder. And you, go sit on the side and be quiet.

YOSHKE. A good pen. Dependable. Well, what kind of a letter should I write? For ten kopeks, for fifteen, or for twenty-five?

BERL. He has three sorts.

SHEYNE. What's the difference?

YOSHKE. The difference is like this: For ten kopeks I can write only what's necessary. Good morning, good year, how are you, how am I, best regards, send a kiss—that's all. For ten kopeks, you get one page, no more. For fifteen—which is the second kind—I add a bit of poetry.

SHEYNE. You add what?

YOSHKE. Po—It's called poetry. As if the words were written not with letters but with musical notes.

SHEYNE. Who needs notes?

MENDL. We don't want you to fiddle, we want you to write.

SHAYKE. The letter is to a devil, black as night—

HODES. Bite your tongue.

SHEYNE. Write. You must know how to start a letter.

YOSHKE. Ah, "Dear, honorable, most distinguished, highly respected . . ."

MENDL. Who are you writing to, a governor? It's only to a Jew: a liar, a deceiver, a seducer.

YOSHKE. Ah. That's something else.

HODES. Wait. The letter is to someone I love, someone dear to me, precious—What would you call him?

YOSHKE. How should I know what to call him when I don't know who it is?

HODES. Write: "I am a miserable orphan; I have no papa and no mama." Write.

YOSHKE. "I have no mama and I have no papa."

HODES. No good. Write with true words that come from the heart, you understand?

YOSHKE. I understand, but if the words come from the heart, it has to be with poetry. For fifteen kopeks. Because a heart cannot talk, a heart can only sing. Like a little bird locked up in a cage.

HODES. Fine, then, let it be with little birds.

ROYZELE. Yes, write with little birds.

SHEYNE. Write for ten kopeks, it'll be good enough for him.

YOSHKE. I'll write for fifteen and charge for ten, all right?

ALL. All right.

YOSHKE. What do I write?

SHAYKE. Write—

HODES. Don't butt in. Write!

YOSHKE. I am writing, but what?

HODES. That he should come back to me this minute. I have no more strength to wait for him.

YOSHKE. Who is waiting?

SHEYNE. I am waiting.

YOSHKE. You're waiting?

HODES. I'm waiting.

YOSHKE. For who?

HODES. For you.

SHEYNE. Is he writing or not?

YOSHKE. What is this? A love letter?

HODES. And so what if it is? I'm not allowed?

BERL. Yoshke, write.

YOSHKE. What should I write?

SHEYNE. Write, "My darling, my dearest—"

YOSHKE. My dearest who?

SHEYNE. Are you going to stop it or not?

YOSHKE. How can I write when I don't know what, how, and who I'm writing to?

BERL. He's right, after all.

MENDL. So write, "My dear Syemyontshik." Write it and forget it.

YOSHKE. "My dear Syemyontshik—" Which Syemyontshik? Syemyontshik from here?

MENDL. No, Syemyontshik from there.

HODES. Why are you sticking your nose in where it doesn't belong?

YOSHKE. Fine. "My dear Syemyontshik." Now what?

SHAYKE. Add a few of your own words. That's what we're paying you for.

SHEYNE. I want him to come back to me.

YOSHKE. "Come back."

SHEYNE. "And besides, I found out you're going around with girls and want to marry somebody else."

YOSHKE. "You're going around with girls . . . marry somebody else . . . the devil take your father's father."

SHEYNE. Why are you writing such vulgar talk?

HODES. God forbid. Why curse? Just write down that he is a liar.

MENDL. A bum, a no-good.

BERL. You could even write a lowlife. But no cursing.

SHEYNE. Erase it.

YOSHKE. Once it's written, it's hard to erase.

SHEYNE. Erase it, I'm telling you.

YOSHKE. Wait, I'll fix it. I'll change "your father's father" to "my father's father was grandson to a rabbi."

MENDL. Oh good. Let him know you're not a nobody.

YOSHKE. Go on.

SHEYNE. "Whole days and nights I think about you."

YOSHKE. "About me." You mean about him.

SHEYNE. But in a letter you have to write "you." "I'm ready to sew shirts for you, wash floors—"

YOSHKE. You don't have to sew for me. Or wash, or cook. I'll do it for you, not you for me. And when my lottery ticket wins, neither of us needs to do a thing except sit and eat and eat.

SHEYNE. What's burning under my heart—that only he knows, and me, and God in heaven—

YOSHKE. No.

SHEYNE. When I say yes, why do you say no? He ran off looking for a bride with a big dowry and left me alone to drown.

SHAYKE. So bring him back, Yoshke. Write, show what you can do.

MENDL. Talk, Sheyne, talk.

YOSHKE. Leave her alone. For this job fifteen kopeks is not enough. Here we need a letter for twenty-five and maybe more.

HODES. Twenty-five kopeks!

YOSHKE. Don't worry. I'll write it on credit and throw a few rhymes in besides. (*The following rhymes inconsistently.*)

> A wind is blowing outside
> And a little snow is falling.
> Oh, my heart is breaking.
> Oh, sorrow and pain.
> At night it is lonesome and dark in the street
> But when I think of you,
> The sun rises at midnight.
> And the universe is radiant.
> Ah darling, my beloved, where have you flown?

>   When I think of you for a moment,
>   The snow melts and cold winds depart.
>   It becomes summer in my heart.
>   Flowers bloom and butterflies dart.
>   Ah darling, my beloved, when oh when will you come?

ALL. Come, come, come.

YOSHKE.

>   There are so many drops in the sea,
>   There are so many stars in the sky,
>   But more than all are my tears
>   Because for me there is only the one I adore.
>   Only one, never more.
>   Oh, may your heart sing forever more.

Sheyne weeps and wipes her eyes with her apron.

MENDL. Why are you spitting, why are you erasing, you're going to ruin the whole letter.

YOSHKE. I did it on purpose. If she is writing and crying, there ought to be a teardrop on the letter. Just wait till he notices.

>   In my heart a little bird sings. See her fly—
>   Fly through the lovely, the colorful, heartbreaking sky!
>   If, God forbid, she no longer sang, I would die.

ALL. Oh sing, sing, sing.

YOSHKE

>   Yoshke with his fiddle,
>   Berl with his bass.
>   This letter is soaked
>   In tears life can't erase.
>   The fiddle will crack,
>   The song will be silenced
>   Until you come back.
>   No one will sing,
>   Not a child, not a king,
>   No man and no bird.
>   No song will be heard.

ALL

> Yoshke with fiddle,
> Berl with bass.

SHEYNE

> My eyes are worn out.
> My face is pale and worn.
> I will wander abandoned
> Through the empty street.
> The tender fiddle will weep.
> The bass will mourn.
> When all-powerful love drives me mad.

ALL

> The fiddle will crack,
> The song will go dumb.
> No one will sing,
> Not a child, not a king.
> No man and no bird,
> No song will be heard.

MADAME LURIA. (*Rushes in.*) Sheyne, Sheyne, what kind of a meeting are you holding here in the middle of everything? Run out and help carry in the baggage. I practically passed out: through the window I see Syemyontshik is here!

ALL. Syemyontshik!

MENDL. The magic of a letter! Barely wrote down "come come come" and here he is.

BERL. Came home. But before he received the letter.

MADAME LURIA. What are you all clustered together for, like a flock of hens on a heap of garbage? Go help carry in the baggage. I'm running upstairs for my valerian.

SYEMYONTSHIK. (*Enters, followed by IN-LAWS and BRIDE.*) How are you, Mama?

SHEYNE. Syemyontshik!

SYEMYONTSHIK. Wait a minute. Not nice. People are coming.

MADAME LURIA. Why through the kitchen?

SYEMYONTSHIK. You have guests. The snow hasn't been cleared away and there's mud by the door.

MADAME LURIA. Oh, I am passing out—so unexpected.

SYEMYONTSHIK. I wanted to surprise you. I brought the in-laws together with the bride.

MADAME LURIA. Good fortune and joy. How do you not let a person know? A person could prepare, clean the mud in front of the door, not to have to bring the in-laws in through the kitchen. (*To in-laws.*) Step in with the right foot, in a good and lucky hour.

SYEMYONTSHIK. The baggage is in the wagon.

MADAME LURIA. Take the in-laws up into the house. And you, Sheyne, comb your hair, fix yourself up, put on your best apron. The table has to be set. The in-laws must be hungry from the trip, poor things. Oh my head, oh my head.

> *Sheyne grabs the letter from the table. Everyone who enters carrying luggage looks for the letter. Royzele searches under the table, bed, and oven. Yoshke is last to enter with luggage and last to search.*

YOSHKE. Where is the letter?

SHEYNE. What do you care? You've been paid for it.

YOSHKE. But I didn't finish.

SHEYNE. Nothing more to do. It's finished.

> *Darkness.*

END OF ACT 1

Act 2

> *Kitchen. Royzele is searching for something. Music under pantomime.*

MADAME LURIA. (*Enters.*) Royzele, what are you doing here in the kitchen? I look at your bed, I see you aren't there, I almost go out of my mind. What are you looking for on top of the oven?

ROYZELE. I was looking for the letter.

MADAME LURIA. What letter?

ROYZELE. That Yoshke wrote for twenty-five kopeks.

MADAME LURIA. Wrote for whom?

ROYZELE. For Sheyne.

MADAME LURIA. What did he write?

ROYZELE. He sang.

MADAME LURIA. To whom?

ROYZELE. To Sheyne. Everybody cried.

MADAME LURIA. Why?

ROYZELE. Because of the little birds.

MADAME LURIA. Everybody knows about a letter, and I don't know anything. Maybe I should also know about that kind of letter. Maybe I should also be looking for that kind of letter.

ROYZELE. You shouldn't have that kind of letter.

MADAME LURIA. Come down from the chimney this minute. I'll tie you to your bed with a rope so you can't wander around all night in a dream. If there was a letter here, I'll find it.

ROYZELE. Even if you find it, you'll never understand it, because Grandmother promised me in my dream that the letter is only for me.

MADAME LURIA. Next time Grandmother promises you something in a dream, you tell her, "I know myself what a letter means when a person needs it." You get into bed this instant, I'm telling you, or I'll I-don't-know-what.

Royzele exits.

HODES. (*Enters.*) Good morning.

MADAME LURIA. Oh, Hodes dear, I practically passed out waiting for you.

HODES. I ran till I'm out of breath.

MADAME LURIA. Calm down. Sit down. Drink a glass of tea, it's keeping warm on the oven.

HODES. Thank you. I have my own sugar.

MADAME LURIA. God forbid, do I begrudge you sugar? There's enough. Take a little for later.

HODES. Thank you, Madame dear. (*Pours all the sugar into her tea.*)

MADAME LURIA. Did you talk to Sheyne?

HODES. I talked.

MADAME LURIA. What did she say?

HODES. She said no. She will not allow the wedding.

MADAME LURIA. Not allow the wedding? Oh my head. That's what she said?

HODES. That's what she said. Take a little valerian pill, Madame dear, you'll feel better.

MADAME LURIA. I need a little lump of sugar.

HODES. Here you are, here you are. (*Takes it out of a pocket in her pants under her skirts.*)

MADAME LURIA. Thank you. Oh, I feel a little better.

HODES. Better?

MADAME LURIA. Yes.

HODES. She said she'll hang herself.

MADAME LURIA. Here in the house?

HODES. Here in the kitchen, on the day of the wedding. Upstairs the guests will be dancing, and down here she will be swinging by a rope from the ceiling.

MADAME LURIA. What does she have against me? What does she want?

HODES. She wants Syemyontshik.

MADAME LURIA. What does she need him for? He doesn't work, he doesn't earn, and he plays cards day and night. Where did she say she'd hang herself?

HODES. (*Points to chandelier in ceiling.*) Right about there.

MADAME LURIA. I must have that nail pulled out of the ceiling before the wedding.

HODES. She says there won't be any wedding.

MADAME LURIA. Oh, I'm passing out.

HODES. Take a little bit more. Better?

MADAME LURIA. Better, better.

HODES. There won't be a wedding.

MADAME LURIA. And I say that there will be a wedding.

HODES. Unless she's the bride.

MADAME LURIA. I'll smack her.

HODES. Won't be a wedding.

MADAME LURIA. We will see.

BAKER. (*Enters.*) Good morning. Excuse me for coming in, I just wanted to ask: Is it true what they're saying, that there won't be a wedding?

MADAME LURIA. Who is spreading such rumors?

BAKER. I don't know. I'm standing, I'm kneading the dough, and my wife stands at the oven.

MADAME LURIA. I heard that already.

BAKER. But why am I kneading and baking if there won't be a wedding?

BUTCHER. (*Enters.*) Good morning, Madame. Ah, I could swear you're here to ask about the wedding, just like me.

BAKER. The madame says there will be a wedding.

BUTCHER. So my wife is crazy.

BAKER. Mine too. I'm standing and kneading the dough; she stands at the oven.

BUTCHER. My wife was at the oven too. What do they hear in the oven?

MADAME LURIA. Why are you driving me crazy with the oven?

BUTCHER. Do I carry bad meat? Fresh, and a bargain. If there's no wedding, why should I slaughter an ox for nothing?

MADAME LURIA. Go tell your wives they can drive themselves crazy. There is going to be a wedding.

BUTCHER. In that case, fine. We can go.

BAKER. I stand and I knead the dough. My wife stands at the oven.

BUTCHER. Mine at the oven too. What do they hear in the oven?

Butcher and baker out.

MADAME LURIA. Well, you hear what they're saying in the village? I won't survive this, and it's all because of you.

HODES. Because of me?

MADAME LURIA. Yes. You know I have a weak heart, and you come driving me crazy with a chandelier. You can go now in good health.

HODES. God forbid. I talked to Sheyne because you asked me to. And she said she's going to hang herself.

MADAME LURIA. Such an old witch.

Hodes exits.

MENDL. (*Enters.*) Good morning.

MADAME LURIA. You startled me.

MENDL. You sent for me.

MADAME LURIA. I need you.

MENDL. I knew you would need me sooner or later. The plot is ready.

MADAME LURIA. Mendl, you can help me.

MENDL. (*Shows cemetery map.*) Here you go. Your husband is lying there, and I'll get you all settled right here.

MADAME LURIA. I realize that you can only be a friend to corpses, but I want you to do me a favor while I'm still alive.

MENDL. By all means.

MADAME LURIA. So listen, I have a bride. Find her a bridegroom.

MENDL. What do you mean? I'm not a matchmaker.

MADAME LURIA. I have the bridegroom too. All you have to do is bring them together.

MENDL. Who is the bride?

MADAME LURIA. Sheyne. My servant here in the kitchen. She is an old maid already. She needs to get married immediately. And Yoshke the fiddler is exactly right for her. I'll provide a dowry. A big dowry. And a trip across the ocean.

MENDL. Will Sheyne agree?

MADAME LURIA. Why not? Yoshke is in love with her. He wrote her a letter with songs, with little birds, with all good things. And it has to be done immediately.

MENDL. I always wanted to do you a good turn, and now that we're finally talking, just take a look.

MADAME LURIA. Mendl, you'll get what's coming to you. My Syemyontshik brought home his bride and the in-laws. The father-in-law is stuffed with money, and he coughs and he wheezes. I'm sure he won't last long. He can be a good thing for you. You can mark a place for him already.

MENDL. Ah. In that case, that's something else. I have a plot. Two by four. You think two by four is enough for him?

MADAME LURIA. You bring me Yoshke.

SYEMYONTSHIK. (*Enters.*) Mama, the in-laws are asking where you are.

MADAME LURIA. Now I'm in the kitchen and soon I'll be there.

MENDL. Not just there but right there.

MADAME LURIA. And all because of you, my jewel.

MENDL. Yes, all because of you.

MADAME LURIA. Mendl, this is not your business. Go and bring Yoshke straight here.

SYEMYONTSHIK. Mama, I don't have a top hat for the wedding.

MADAME LURIA. We're not sure yet that there will be a wedding. When they're dancing up there, she'll be down here hanging on the chandelier.

SYEMYONTSHIK. Who will be hanging?

MADAME LURIA. Your Sheyne. Sheyne.

SYEMYONTSHIK. Sheyne will hang herself?

MADAME LURIA. Talk to her, beg her not to ruin the celebration. If the in-laws find out, they'll run away.

SYEMYONTSHIK. What should I say to her? I can't talk to her.

MADAME LURIA. You used to manage. Why did you come creeping into the kitchen?

SYEMYONTSHIK. I told you twenty times. I only came down once, looking for a match for my cigar.

MADAME LURIA. A match. I will smack you.

Enter Sheyne.

Fine, Syemyontshik, use your judgment. If you want to talk to Sheyne, talk, talk, talk. I have to run up to the in-laws. Sheyne, I'll see you later.

SHEYNE. This is your first time in the kitchen since you arrived.

SYEMYONTSHIK. I couldn't. The in-laws keep watching me and asking where I'm going.

SHEYNE. You could have said you're going down to the kitchen for a match.

SYEMYONTSHIK. I did. The father-in-law had a whole box of matches right on him. Wait, he could come down looking for me. I'll say you're sewing a button on for me. Do you have a needle and thread? Pretend you're sewing on a button. Mama tells me you're mad at me.

SHEYNE. How can I be mad when I love you?

SYEMYONTSHIK. You are sweet, you are good. Forgive me, I thought I heard a step.

SHEYNE. If you're trembling for your bride, go back up to her.

SYEMYONTSHIK. It isn't polite.

SHEYNE. Send your bride back where she came from and stay with me.

SYEMYONTSHIK. I can't stay, I have to run away.

SHEYNE. Take me with you.

SYEMYONTSHIK. I'm not worth anything. I'm not a tailor, or a shoemaker, only a card player. Mama is poor and I've already lost the buttons off my pants playing cards. Sew, sew the button, I'm begging you. They can come down any minute.

SHEYNE. Is it true that you still love me?

SYEMYONTSHIK. It's true, it's true, but what good is the love of a criminal? If they catch me, they'll put me in jail for life.

SHEYNE. Why? What did you do?

SYEMYONTSHIK. Mama sent me to Kiev to take a look at a bride, and when I took a look, I felt sick.

SHEYNE. Why didn't you come straight back to me?

SYEMYONTSHIK. Without a groshn in my pocket? What would I have done with you? Beg house to house? So I decided to try my luck again with cards.

SHEYNE. How? You didn't have any money.

SYEMYONTSHIK. With a check. I signed with a false name.

SHEYNE. And you lost?

SYEMYONTSHIK. Lost. Lost my last groshn. I was just about to break the bank when the other guy came up with an ace, and a second ace, and a third. Three aces against my two kings. I wish they'd burned. I forged three checks. That's enough to sentence me for life. What could I do? I had to consider a bride with a big dowry. Now you know. Now you know everything.

SHEYNE. All I know is that you lost me in a card game.

SYEMYONTSHIK. But it was for your sake I was playing. If I'd had another two kings—

SHEYNE. What good are kings to me? If I can never be your wife, I'm going to pack my things today and go back home.

SHAYKE. (*Enters through the chimney.*) Before you leave the kitchen, I'd really like my glass of milk. I'm hungry and tired. Ah, what's the man of the house doing in the kitchen?

SYEMYONTSHIK. Looking for a match.

SHAYKE. (*Producing match from his pocket with a courtly gesture.*) Allow me to accommodate you.

SYEMYONTSHIK. Thank you. I forgot my cigar upstairs. I'll bring it down. Too many guests in the kitchen. I won't disturb you. (*Exits.*)

SHEYNE. Your milk could have waited. You didn't hear we were talking here?

SHAYKE. Talk is unnecessary. Everything has already been decided. You will be the bride at the wedding.

SHEYNE. Who decided?

SHAYKE. We did, the people of the village.

SHEYNE. Enough, you black ghost. I'm leaving this very day.

SHAYKE. We'll bring you back.

SHEYNE. You won't find me. I'll hang myself. I'll throw myself in the river.

SHAYKE. We will drag you out of the river by your hair and bring you to the wedding canopy.

SHEYNE. Didn't you hear? I can't be his wife.

SHAYKE. There will be no wedding. We'll come like thieves in the night and turn out the lights. The in-laws will dance like ghosts in the dark.

SHEYNE. Enough, enough. You black devil, I don't want to hear any more, I can't look at you. (*Exits.*)

ROYZELE. Why did she run away?

SHAYKE. Don't be scared, she'll be back.

ROYZELE. Shayke, I want to ask you something.

SHAYKE. I don't feel like talking. I worked hard today.

ROYZELE. You were looking for the letter too?

SHAYKE. For you that's work. Whereas I, representative of the toiling masses, ran from roof to roof, chimney to chimney, and turned off the gas so the baker won't bake and the butcher won't slaughter.

ROYZELE. Why?

SHAYKE. Go, go, you don't belong here in the kitchen. Your place is up there, above, with the exploiters. I'm not here, you understand.

MENDL. (*Offstage.*) Why are you dragging along? Move a little faster. The madame is waiting for you.

Mendl and Yoshke enter.

YOSHKE. I'm going, I'm going. Don't you see I'm going?

MENDL. Come in. Nobody here will pour any more water on you. And why hop on one foot like a goat?

YOSHKE. I can't run. A nail from my shoe is sticking in my foot.

MENDL. Then sit down. Wait here. I'll call the madame down.

YOSHKE. Will it take long?

MENDL. All of a sudden you're on fire? All of a sudden you have no time? Sit down under the ground, why don't you?

ROYZELE. Yoshke, I looked for the letter and can't find it.

YOSHKE. Shh, quiet, Sheyne has it. She put it in an envelope and stuck on a postage stamp and hid it in her bosom next to her heart.

ROYZELE. But now that my brother is getting married tomorrow . . . ?

YOSHKE. She'll send the letter to somebody else. Know who she'll send it to? Guess.

ROYZELE. I can't guess.

YOSHKE. To me, to me, may we live and be healthy.

ROYZELE. That's crazy. It would be as if you yourself wrote the letter to yourself.

YOSHKE. That is why I've come.

ROYZELE. Oh, my heart is jumping out. What happened?

YOSHKE. Shh, very quiet. Don't destroy the quiet wonder of your dream. Mendl comes running, says your mama wants to see me immediately. Of course, I understand right away what that means, I know what's going on. But he says first she wants to hear the processional for your brother's wedding. So I ran around looking for the band. My papa was off falling into a well somewhere, Shayke was somewhere jumping over the roofs, and just for spite a nail from my shoe went into my foot. A plague. Do you want to hear the wedding processional?

ROYZELE. My knees are shaking with happiness.

YOSHKE. I begin quietly. By myself. But with meaning. Understand? You know how it always starts, "Weep, bride, weep"? (*Chants a recognizable version of a standard formulaic, roughly rhyming wedding jester's address.*)

> "Oh, dear bride, dear little bride," I'll say,
> "Don't weep, don't weep, don't weep.
> Your bridegroom is so young and handsome and charming and sweet.
> His eyes are like diamonds and his teeth are like pearls,
> And that's why we all wish him to take his bride and go, go, go out into the wide world.
> He should not remain in one place, nor fear the great or the small.
> The Creator of the world should bless them with all—
> Success, blessing, and livelihood—the couple should never lack
> If he goes far, far, far away for a long time and never comes back."
> And that's when the march to the canopy strikes up with a crash.

Music is heard offstage.

ROYZELE. The music is playing. And you didn't pick up your fiddle.

YOSHKE. I don't need a fiddle. The band will play, and the walls, the chandeliers, all the air will be full of the chimes of bottles, glasses, plates, forks, knives, spoons.

ROYZELE. Oh, won't that be lovely! The bride will wear a white dress, with a long train, and the groom a top hat with a white cravat.

YOSHKE. I too will wear a top hat and I too will be a bridegroom. That's why your mama said "immediately." No such thing as a pot without a lid. That is why I came immediately.

ROYZELE. No, no, this is too good even for a dream.

YOSHKE. Here's the story. The wedding won't be all your brother's. It'll be half his and half mine. Quickly, quickly I'll push your brother under the four canopy poles and he'll quickly, quickly put his little ring on the bride. And she her little ring on him. A ring in a ring like a little chain on their hands, and she will take that little chain and pull him to Kiev. Leaving Sheyne here free and alone. So I will stand with her under the four poles—the bridegroom, ready and waiting. And your mama will be the in-law on the bride's side.

ROYZELE. And she'll give you the letter?

YOSHKE. Who else but me? You'll laugh. You won't believe I've already written an answer to her letter. You'll deliver it to her. You'll be the postman.

ROYZELE. No, no. Then she'll have both the letter and the answer, and I won't have anything. Grandmother promised me: I will receive a letter and travel to far lands.

YOSHKE. Oh darling, don't ruin my celebration. I bought you a wedding present too.

ROYZELE. What is it?

YOSHKE. A red kerchief. (*Shows it.*)

ROYZELE. But it's green.

YOSHKE. (*Sleight of hand trick.*) A trifle. One two three, and it turns red.

ROYZELE. No, no, I like the green better.

YOSHKE. Then once again, one two three, and here's your green.

SHAYKE. (*Enters.*) Hold on. It will be not a red wedding and not a green—it will be a black wedding.

YOSHKE. Why?

SHAYKE. We'll turn out the light and switch brides in the dark: up there we'll put Sheyne under the canopy, and for you below we'll bring down the upstairs bride.

YOSHKE. The upstairs bride? What will I do with her?

SHAYKE. You'll sit at the banquet together; you'll eat and drink wine. That is our decision.

YOSHKE. Whose decision?

SHAYKE. Ours, the people of the village

YOSHKE. I also have a voice in this.

SHAYKE. When the village speaks, you have no voice.

YOSHKE. Who speaks, what speaks? How can a village speak?

SHAYKE. I speak for the village.

YOSHKE. In that case I whistle at you and the whole village together.

SHAYKE. You can't whistle that loud.

YOSHKE. Yes, I can. (*Tries to whistle.*)

SHAYKE. No, you can't.

YOSHKE. Yes, I can. (*Tries again.*)

SHAYKE. That's not whistling.

YOSHKE. I'll show you. (*Blows a real whistle.*)

SHAYKE. (*Stops his ears.*) Stop whistling. Be a man.

YOSHKE. I don't want to be a man. I've played a thousand weddings. Half the village brides and grooms I made into mamas and papas. The village is mine as much as yours. And you can't drive me out of the village now.

SHAYKE. Take the noodle pot off your head. The last drops of soup at the bottom will get cold. And why are you wearing one shoe on two feet? Go home and sleep. You'll need to play twenty hours and how can you?

YOSHKE. Of course I can. I can do everything and I have nothing. I do tricks, I write letters. You all have wives and children; I have nails in my shoes. But I'm first violin in the band, and you have to play what and when and where I lead you.

SHAYKE. Nobody will follow. In the name of the village, I say to you: no and no and no.

YOSHKE. Shayke, don't cut my heart with a knife. I'm hanging on by a hair.

SHAYKE. When the masses say no, it's no.

YOSHKE. Shayke, enough that I have a nail in my shoe, don't drive nails into my heart.

MADAME LURIA. (*Enters.*) Who screamed here? What happened?

MENDL. Why stand there in the oven like a Sabbath stew? Come here. Sit down here at the table. You've never in your life had such a piece of luck. Sit down.

MADAME LURIA. Yoshke, I want to pay you for the band. How much will it cost?

YOSHKE. Nothing, Madame. The village doesn't want me to play. I have no band and I have no music.

MADAME LURIA. A wedding without musicians? How can you play such a trick on me? Tell him, Mendl, tell him.

MENDL. Sheyne is the madame's distant relative. She will provide the dowry. If you'll be a decent man and play, you'll receive on the same day both a pretty bride and a rich dowry.

MADAME LURIA. I'll give one hundred rubles.

MENDL. He'll probably want more.

MADAME LURIA. Then I'll give two.

MENDL. Well? Do you insist on three?

MADAME LURIA. I don't even have two. Let it be four, let it be five, just so tomorrow we can make the blessing; they're engaged, get it over with, and done.

MENDL. Did you ever dream such a dream? I've been carrying you in my portfolio for years. Will you play?

MADAME LURIA. You need her and she needs you.

MENDL. Plus five hundred rubles. Will you play?

YOSHKE. I want to ask you something: could they drive me out of the village?

MADAME LURIA. Why wait till they drive you out? Better to go on your own. And for the travel I will add another hundred.

MENDL. Will you play?

MADAME LURIA. Why not? Sheyne is a precious soul. She likes you. She told me about the letter with the little birds. You see I know everything.

YOSHKE. She told you . . .? Can't be.

MADAME LURIA. She showed me the letter.

YOSHKE. Is that true?

MADAME LURIA. I read the letter.

MENDL. And she cried too.

MADAME LURIA. If I'd received such a letter, I'd marry you myself.

YOSHKE. Ah, you there, black cloud. Tell your village that I will play. I myself will play and play so the entire village shakes. Madame, this will be the march to lead the two bridegrooms to veil their brides.

Sheyne enters.

MADAME LURIA. Sheyne dear, where were you?

SHEYNE. I ordered a wagon to come take my things.

MENDL. May my enemies lose their minds. We sit and make plans, talk over the dowry . . .

MADAME LURIA. Let the dowry alone. You're going away? Go in good health. Only if you had told me sooner, I'd have prepared something for you. It's a long way, and it's cold. Wait. Maybe I'll bring down—

SHEYNE. I won't freeze.

MENDL. A girl like you must have a groom immediately, immediately. There you have a readymade groom standing and waiting. (*Off.*)

YOSHKE. If she goes away, you deceived me, Madame.

MADAME LURIA. If you play, I'll pay you.

YOSHKE. If she goes away, who should I play for?

MADAME LURIA. For me, for my money.

YOSHKE. You made a fool of me and laughed at me. All right, laugh, laugh, I don't care. And you, Sheyne, if you go away, go in good health. Only if you should happen to think of me, send me back the little letter you carry next to your heart. And just so you won't have to wait, I've already written you my answer. Here it is.

She tears up the letter and throws it in the oven.

SYEMYONTSHIK. (*Enters at top of stairs.*) Has anyone seen my cards on the table?

MADAME LURIA. Come down, Syemyontshik. Say your good-byes to Sheyne. She's going away.

SYEMYONTSHIK. Mama, I need a little money. I haven't bought a ring to give the bride under the canopy.

MADAME LURIA. I gave you money three times, and you lost it playing cards.

SYEMYONTSHIK. The in-laws keep asking me to take them for a walk and show them the village. That costs money too.

MADAME LURIA. It's good. Better for them not to be around. Take them all the way to the mill outside of town. (*Gives him a coin.*)

SYEMYONTSHIK. That's not enough. I'm out of cigars and the father-in-law keeps asking me for a cigar. It's not nice for me not to have even one cigar.

MADAME LURIA. I'll run up and get a little more money.

YOSHKE. Ha, what kind of cigars does your father-in-law smoke?

SYEMYONTSHIK. Havana cigars.

YOSHKE. Here you are. A good Havana for your father-in-law. And you, don't go out, and don't let her go out either.

SYEMYONTSHIK. Is this a genuine Havana or one of your tricks?

YOSHKE. You don't need any cigar. You're going to play cards. What you need is for me to show you how to break the bank playing twenty-one, sixty-six, or pesha-pisha.

SYEMYONTSHIK. I'm a quick learner. Are you serious? Be a good brother, and where is the cigar?

YOSHKE. Here is your cigar, but please, don't go out and don't let her go.

SYEMYONTSHIK. You don't know my troubles. How can I do that?

YOSHKE. Only for a little while.

SYEMYONTSHIK. Why?

YOSHKE. Sometimes in that little while a miracle might happen.

SYEMYONTSHIK. Why do you drive me crazy?

YOSHKE. I dreamed God sent me a telegram.

SYEMYONTSHIK. A what?

YOSHKE. A star from the sky.

SYEMYONTSHIK. I thought you were crazy; now I see you really are insane.

YOSHKE. Believe what I tell you, keep her from going.

SYEMYONTSHIK. Why can't you keep her from going?

YOSHKE. How?

SYEMYONTSHIK. With one of your tricks.

BAKER. (*Rushes in.*) Yoshke, Yoshke, a great miracle!

SHAYKE. (*Enters from chimney.*) Yoshke, Yoshke, I'm standing on the roof, I see a storm is carrying the whole village into the air.

BUTCHER. (*Rushes in.*) Yoshke, Yoshke, the whole village is looking for you. They've run to your house.

BAKER. Here he is, this way, this way.

MENDL. What happened?

SHAYKE. The whole village is running this way. The town madman Kalefute is running the fastest.

HODES. (*Rushes in breathless.*) If I was a bird, I couldn't have flown faster to bring you the news.

MADAME LURIA. What happened?

HODES. I don't know, maybe it's good, maybe it's bad. Madame, give me your valerian pills.

MADAME LURIA. Lock the door, don't let anybody in.

KALEFUTE. (*Enters.*) Yoshke, Yoshke, you won the lottery.

MENDL. Look at that: Kalefute the madman.

SYEMYONTSHIK. What happened?

KALEFUTE. The doctor told me, "You'll live, Kalefute," he says, "another three days." So before they bury me, I ran to tell you the great news.

ALL. How much? How much?

KALEFUTE. A hundred sixty million.

SHAYKE. Why are you asking a regressive social element? Ask me. Yoshke won the big prize.

ALL. How much, how much?

SHAYKE. I don't know.

BERL. (*Enters.*) Yoshke, help, Yoshke. We are lucky. We're rich. We're millionaires. They delivered it to our house: a silver envelope with a stamp of a golden eagle.

ALL. A golden eagle?

MADAME LURIA. Close the door, don't let anybody in.

SHAYKE. Now you'll sit and drink tea with millionaires. Whereas I, representing the lower classes—

MENDL. Stop up his mouth. The rich people are coming, important people, the landlords of the village. Make way.

REPRESENTATIVE OF THE VILLAGE RICH MEN. (*Enters.*) Reb Joseph, in the name of the wealthy citizens of this village, I have come to congratulate you and make you head of the congregation, ritual director, and chairman of the bathhouse and the Jewish cemetery.

ALL. Amen.

BERL. Make way. The white-haired rabbi and the black-haired sexton are standing at the door and can't come in.

SHAYKE. The sexton carries a lit lantern in bright daylight and can't find the door.

BUTCHER. Let the rabbi in.

RABBI. (*Enters.*) Where is the fortunate one, may his name be blessed? God does not neglect the poor. Congratulations to you, Reb Yoshke, son of Reb Berl the bass player. Congratulations.

All pray.

ALL. Congratulations.

SHAYKE. Make way, here's his blind mama.

MAMA. (*Enters.*) Where is my happy child? Your luck shines in my darkness brighter than the sun of my youth. My child!

BAKER. Make way. The police are coming. The chief of police with the entire fire brigade.

BUTCHER. No, no, the governor.

BERL. All the ministers will come yet. The czar himself will come down (damn him and his father).

GOVERNOR. (*Enters. Speaks first in Russian, mispronounces name.*) Yoshl son of Berl the Bass. Hurrah.

ALL. Hurrah! Hurrah!

MENDL. Shh, quiet. Reb Joseph wants to say something.

ALL. Shhh quiet.

YOSHKE. Where is Sheyne?

ALL. Sheyne! Sheyne!

BAKER. She's here.

YOSHKE. Sheyne. This big fuss interrupted us. I asked you something. And you didn't answer.

SHEYNE. About what?

YOSHKE. Don't go. Stay here. And let's trade. You give me the letter with the poor little bird and I give you the letter with the golden eagle. Together we'll fly like birds over the heads of the village and throw golden coins down to our true friends. Say yes, say yes.

BUTCHER. What letter?

BAKER. Quiet. Shh. Quiet.

Sheyne gives him the letter.

YOSHKE. Jews, you are all witnesses, Sheyne is my bride.

ALL. Congratulations, congratulations. Shayke, show how you can drum.

BAKER. And flowers? A bride without a flower?

YOSHKE. If I have a bride, flowers are not important.

MENDL. Yoshke, pick up your fiddle and show what you can do.

SHEYNE

> EVERY GIRL SEES IN DREAMS HIS FACE,
> HER PREDESTINED ONE, THE ONLY FACE,
> HIS EYES, HIS LIPS, SO SWEET AND FINE,
> HIS SMILE, HIS PERFECT GRACE.
>
> TOMORROW I GO TO THE WEDDING CANOPY.
> WHY IS MY HEART SO HEAVY TODAY?
> TOMORROW I STAND INSIDE THE FOUR POLES.
> WHY IS THE SKY SO DARK TODAY?

WHAT DO I CARE FOR THE FINE WHITE VEIL
WHEN MY HEAD IS BOWED WITH SORROW?
WHAT DO I CARE FOR THE FINE LONG DRESS
WHEN I DRAG IT ALONG IN TEARS TOMORROW?

FOR HE WHO WILL LEAD ME TOMORROW
UNDER THE CANOPY AND BEYOND ON LIFE'S
  WAY
IS NOT THE ONE, NOT THE ONE, NOT THE ONE.
WHAT MORE CAN I SAY?

THERE WILL BE NO RETURNING,
NONE OF YESTERDAY'S DELIGHT,
NO CRUMB OF MY HAPPINESS
WHEN I HEARD HIS VOICE IN THE NIGHT.

THE BAND WITH ITS MUSIC
CANNOT COMFORT MY PAIN
WHEN I HEAR IN THE AIR ALL AROUND ME
HOW HIS SWEET VOICE CALLS MY NAME.

NO, I DON'T WANT THIS ONE. NO, I CAN'T.
HE'S NOT THE ONE I DREAMED OF NIGHT
  AND DAY.
HE'S NOT THE ONE, NOT THE ONE, NOT THE
  ONE.
WHAT MORE CAN I SAY?

I WILL CLENCH MY TEETH SO NO ONE CAN HEAR
MY SOBS AND MY WAILS IN THE DAWN.
NO ONE WILL KNOW THAT MY DREAM
  BREAKS MY HEART
BECAUSE MY BELOVED IS GONE.

ONLY THE STARS WILL HEAR,
ONLY THE HEAVENS UNDERSTAND
MY MUTE HEART SCREAMING.
HE'S NOT THE ONE, NOT THE ONE, NOT THE
  ONE.
WHAT MORE CAN I SAY?

MUSICIANS

> VILLAGE MUSICIANS, THEY TALK THEIR OWN
>   WAY
> WHEN THEY HAVE SOMETHING IMPORTANT
>   TO SAY.
> EVERYONE DANCES THE MUSIC THEY PLAY,
> BUT NOBODY ELSE CAN SAY WHAT THEY SAY.
> WITH A WINK OF THE EYE
> AND A TWITCH OF THE CHEEK
> THEY UNDERSTAND EVERYTHING.
> NO NEED TO SPEAK.
> AND THEY GIVE A BASH—
> HEY!
>
> YAKHTSET, BIKHTSET, BOOKHTSET, BAKHTSET,
> BIKHTSET, BOOKHTSET, BAKHTSET, BAM!
>
> VILLAGE MUSICIANS TALK THEIR OWN WAY.
> THEY DON'T NEED WORDS. INSTEAD
> IT'S A WINK WITH THE EYE
> AND A NOD WITH THE HEAD.
> THEN THEY UNDERSTAND THE TUNE.
> THEN THEY UNDERSTAND THE TIME.
> THEN THE FIDDLE AND THE DRUM.
> THEN A CRASH AND ALL'S FINE.
> HEY!
>
> YAKHTSET, BIKHTSET, BOOKHTSET, BAKHTSET,
> BIKHTSET, BOOKHTSET, BAKHTSET, BAM!

END OF ACT 2

Act 3

Kitchen. Sheyne looks in a hand mirror. Royzele stands on the steps leading up to the family rooms. Sheyne spies her in the mirror.

SHEYNE. What do you want, Royzele?

ROYZELE. Mama invites you to come up and drink tea with cherry preserves.

SHEYNE. I don't have time. In about an hour I'm going away.

ROYZELE. I wish you would take me with you in your carriage with white horses.

SHEYNE. Who told you that nonsense, that I have a carriage with white horses?

ROYZELE. Mama. She talked to Syemyontshik all night. They sat and figured out with a pencil.

SHEYNE. What did they figure out?

ROYZELE. How much is a hundred and sixty thousand rubles. I listened in.

SHEYNE. Why?

ROYZELE. You told me to.

SHEYNE. Now you don't have to listen anymore.

BERL. (*Enters, all dressed up, empty buckets under his arm.*) Good morning.

ROYZELE. Good morning.

BERL. (*To Sheyne.*) Here is an apple for you. (*To Royzele.*) And for you too. And here I brought a present for the children.

SHEYNE. Which children?

BERL. Your children that you'll have, God willing. You'll show them the buckets and tell them who their grandfather was. Forty years I carried them on my shoulders. An oceanful of water. But enough. Now the engineers can come and make water pour out of the walls. I laugh at them. What do you say to that, my old buckets? We laugh at the engineers.

ROYZELE. Buckets can laugh?

BERL. Oh, can they ever. How many years they laughed at me and spilled water over me. But now, I laugh at them. (*Pushes them away with his feet, carries them into a corner.*) Go stand in the corner and croak with thirst. I'm going to take Yoshke's blind mama to a big doctor who will open her eyes. When she sees me, she won't believe it's the same Berl.

ROYZELE. Aren't you going to play in the band anymore?

BERL. What band? No more band. Yoshke dressed all the musicians up like doctors. You should see Shayke.

Shayke comes in through the door, not the chimney.

Ah! Speak of an angel and in comes the priest. What's the matter, Shayke, why are you so depressed?

SHAYKE. I don't feel good.

BERL. If Shayke comes in through the door, he's in trouble.

SHAYKE. I have rheumatism in my feet.

BERL. Go to the doctor.

SHAYKE. I went. He found out that my lungs are stuffed with smoke.

BERL. So who told you to go to the doctor?

SHAYKE. You're right, it was stupid. Now I really do feel bad. Also the doctor ordered me to drink a quarter glass of resin oil, and a half glass of castor oil, and accompany that with a whole glass of mineral water.

BERL. Did you do it?

SHAYKE. Yes, and now I have the entire Ninth Symphony banging in my belly.

MADAME LURIA. (*Enters.*) Sheyne dear, how many times must one invite you to come up and drink tea?

SHEYNE. I can't leave my guests.

MADAME LURIA. Good morning, Reb Berl. Good morning to you, Reb Shayke. Other people, when they go up in the world, they forget their old friends. And I have a present for you, Sheyne. After all, you need something to keep your money in, so I'm giving you a purse.

SHEYNE. Thank you, but I don't carry the money.

MADAME LURIA. Then give it to Yoshke. Does he know how to go around with so much money?

SHEYNE. What did you buy it for?

MADAME LURIA. Did I buy it? I have it from my own grandmother. My grandmother and your grandmother were first cousins.

BERL. Really?

SHEYNE. What do you know.

MADAME LURIA. My heart was always drawn to you. Come upstairs and I'll show you the family album. Your grandmother's sister and Syemyontshik's uncle's brother were—

SHEYNE. I can't leave my guests.

MADAME LURIA. Let the guests come up as well and drink a glass of tea with cherry preserves.

BERL. Cherry preserves. Come, Shayke, tea with cherry preserves. It will bring you back to health.

MADAME LURIA. Come, Sheyne dear.

SHEYNE. I have to fix the bridal veil a bit more.

MADAME LURIA. We'll wait for you upstairs. Come, my dear friends.

BERL. Forgive me, I should have brought a few apples or plums, or pears. Next time I will, please God.

All three off.

ROYZELE. Is this the veil for your wedding gown?

SHEYNE. Yes. Go up to them and stop looking at me with your eyes.

ROYZELE. My eyes are blue, exactly like Syemyontshik's.

SHEYNE. That's why I don't want you looking at me. Go away.

ROYZELE. I'm going. I'll never come down here again. (*Weeps, starts upstairs.*)

SHEYNE. (*Holds her back.*) No, no, Royzele, don't say that. Stay with me, look at me. Stay with me. (*Embraces her.*)

SYEMYONTSHIK. (*Appears on the steps.*) Royzele, Mama is calling you.

Royzele looks at Syemyontshik, then at Sheyne, and then exits.

SHEYNE. What are you doing here? What do you want down here in the kitchen?

SYEMYONTSHIK. A match to light a cigar.

SHEYNE. Why didn't you ask your father-in-law?

SYEMYONTSHIK. I did. Thank God he didn't have any. Mama invited you to come up and drink tea with cherries.

SHEYNE. I'm waiting for Yoshke.

SYEMYONTSHIK. The cards have been shuffled. Now you're the rich lady, and it's not proper to drink tea with a poor boy like me.

SHEYNE. Take your matches and leave me in peace.

SYEMYONTSHIK. You drive me away the way you used to drive Yoshke away from your window, once upon a time.

SHEYNE. What did you come for?

SYEMYONTSHIK. To wish you joy with Yoshke. I gambled you away, and he won you.

SHEYNE. How is that my fault?

SYEMYONTSHIK. It's not your fault. But you can help me.

SHEYNE. How?

SYEMYONTSHIK. Three nights now I haven't slept.

SHEYNE. I know. You sit with a pencil and figure.

SYEMYONTSHIK. How long I'll sit in jail.

SHEYNE. For forgery.

SYEMYONTSHIK. I signed three checks.

SHEYNE. I thought the in-laws would get you out of jail.

SYEMYONTSHIK. They'll take me out of one jail and sentence me to another. I want to get free of them.

SHEYNE. How?

SYEMYONTSHIK. That's what I was figuring with the pencil.

SHEYNE. What did you figure out?

SYEMYONTSHIK. A new system: how to break the bank. Look. (*Demonstrates with cards on the table.*) I figured out that one time in twenty it has to come out three kings, three aces, or three tens. So if I play for small stakes nineteen times, then the twentieth time I break the bank.

SHEYNE. Well, with God's help.

SYEMYONTSHIK. But you know I can't play with empty hands. If you lend me a thousand, I can fix everything.

SHEYNE. Where will I get a thousand?

SYEMYONTSHIK. You have a hundred sixty thousand.

SHEYNE. It's not sixty and not a hundred, it's ten thousand. And the money isn't mine, it's Yoshke's.

SYEMYONTSHIK. I only want to borrow it. I'll pay it back with interest.

SHEYNE. Take your disgusting cards and get out of here.

SYEMYONTSHIK. With that thousand I can win you back.

SHEYNE. Don't talk, don't talk, I don't dare listen.

SYEMYONTSHIK. With that thousand you can rescue me and I can rescue you.

SHEYNE. Go away. Yoshke can come in at any minute.

SYEMYONTSHIK. I'll say I came down for you to sew a button on.

SHEYNE. I'm not sewing any more buttons.

SYEMYONTSHIK. When you loved me, nothing was too hard for you. But I never stopped loving you. Why would you drive me away if you love me?

SHEYNE. What do you want from me? You want a thousand?

SYEMYONTSHIK. The thousand is a loan, but you I'll keep forever.

SHEYNE. Forget about me. You'll get your thousand.

He embraces her. Enter Hodes.

SYEMYONTSHIK. Come in, Hodes, I was just saying good-bye to Sheyne.

HODES. I want to say good-bye to her too.

SYEMYONTSHIK. Fine, then. So come up and we'll drink tea with cherry preserves. I'll wait for you. (*Exits.*)

HODES. Are you done?

SHEYNE. Hodes, I swear, he only came down to ask me to do him a favor.

HODES. The same favor that my husband Mekhele asked for. (May he toss and turn where he lies in the ground.) Get out of the kitchen before I throw you out.

SHEYNE. I'm waiting here for Yoshke.

HODES. Wait outside.

SHEYNE. It's cold out.

HODES. But in here it's hot. In here a fire is burning. Go, go.

MENDL. (*Enters.*) Good morning. Is Yoshke here? I've torn my shoes running around and can't find him. Can I talk to the bride about business?

HODES. Your business can wait. Go, Sheyne, go where you ought to go.

Sheyne exits.

MENDL. What was the reason for that? Why drive away my customer?

HODES. Up there you have plenty of customers.

MENDL. Up there they're paupers compared to Yoshke. This plot is only fit for a millionaire. Take a look. Here lies Doctor Pinek. Here lies Rabbi Avremele the judge. A lovely spot, covered with grass, refreshing.

HODES. Stop it. Enough. I think someone's coming.

YOSHKE. (*Enters all dressed up, carrying packages.*) Good morning, Hodes. Quick, quick, put water on for tea. (*Sneezes.*)

HODES and MENDL. Good health, good health, a healthy year.

HODES. (*Spits to keep away the evil eye.*) Tfoo! I thought for a minute that Rothschild walked in.

YOSHKE. (*Sneezes.*) I used to go around barefoot in the worst of winter. Today for the first time I put on a fur coat and I get a cold in the nose. (*Sneezes.*)

HODES and MENDL. Good health, good health, a healthy year.

MENDL. Listen, now that you've started sneezing, we need to talk seriously. I was looking for you and couldn't find you.

YOSHKE. I was running around buying presents for Sheyne. I bought a few pretty pairs of combs, a box of perfumed soap—smell! I know Sheyne likes beads, but I don't know which, so I bought red and green and yellow and she can pick. But the main thing is I bought her a gold ring with a diamond as big as a pea. And for myself a watch. Oh my, it's already seven o'clock, where is Sheyne? I have to get our dance tune ready.

MENDL. It hasn't struck four yet.

YOSHKE. Must be running fast.

MENDL. So catch it.

YOSHKE. (*Puts watch to his ear.*) It's standing still.

MENDL. Shake it. It'll go.

YOSHKE. Ah, it's going. Ah, it stopped again. Now it goes, now it stops. So what time is it?

MENDL. It's late. Let's finish our business. I already showed you. Clean and dry as a feather bed. Doctor Pinek here, Rabbi Avremele the judge there.

YOSHKE. I don't care who's lying there. I'll buy it. Here's a hundred. (*Puts down the money.*) I pay the money, and the plot is yours.

MENDL. What would somebody like me do with a plot like that?

YOSHKE. What's wrong with it? Clean and dry. A doctor on one side, a rabbi on the other side.

MENDL. How do I belong next to rabbis and doctors?

YOSHKE. If you don't want it, give back the money.

MENDL. Who says I don't want it? Only I have a wife and children. Who can think about presents?

YOSHKE. You don't want it? Give the money back. (*Starts to take the money back, but Mendl doesn't let him.*)

MENDL. God forbid. What is it for, the rushing, the running, the flying, if not for a place to rest? Only when it comes with no warning, suddenly, out of a clear blue sky, all ready and waiting, just go and lie down in it—that's a shock to the heart.

HODES. There you have it. Runs after a living, his feet hurt; somebody gives him a living, his heart hurts. Take your plot and go home in good health. Let live people talk a little.

MENDL. It's not the money. Only to come to my wife and say that I'm already taken care of . . . And if I refuse the gift, will the gift refuse me?

HODES. You're going or you aren't going?

MENDL. Of course I'm going. Everyone goes. Everyone has to go. You're taken, and you go. That's how it is. No more rushing, running, flying, all for a place to rest. Four by six. On one side Rabbi Avremele the judge, on the other side Doctor Pinek. I don't know the judge; I don't know the doctor. Crawl in and stretch yourself out, there's an end of it, shh, quiet. (*Exits.*)

YOSHKE. Maybe I shouldn't have?

HODES. Don't take it to heart.

YOSHKE. I've already reserved places on a ship. Right after the wedding, Sheyne and I travel to the other side of the ocean. There, they say, everyone has gold teeth and lives to be a hundred and seventy. So why would I need a cemetery plot?

HODES. Don't worry about him. He has what he wanted, and you don't need to cross the ocean in order to find what you want.

YOSHKE. Ah, you old fool. I still need more than I have. Maybe there are certain things, certain secrets that a bridegroom wants to know, needs to know, must know. So tell me, you old chicken gobbler. Don't be shy, nobody will know. Because I didn't forget you either. I bought you a nice present—a pair of warm panties. (*Unwraps long, warm underpants decorated with lace.*)

HODES. Lord of the world! How did you know what I need?

YOSHKE. But now where is Sheyne? I need to arrange our bride and groom dance.

HODES. You can arrange the bride and groom dance with me.

YOSHKE. With you? Old busybody.

HODES. Shut your mouth, you good-for-nothing turkey. This old busybody has already forgotten what you haven't even tried yet. Come dance with me before I knock your teeth out.

Sheyne enters. Hodes hides the pants.

YOSHKE. Darling, where were you?

SHEYNE. I went for a walk around town

YOSHKE. You're all frozen.

SHEYNE. I'll warm myself by the oven.

HODES. She'll drink a glass of hot tea. I already put it on.

SHEYNE. My aunt invited me to drink tea upstairs with the guests.

YOSHKE. If she invited you, it isn't nice to refuse. But before we go up, guess what presents I brought you.

SHEYNE. I can't guess.

HODES. Let her alone now, tomorrow is another day.

YOSHKE. Tomorrow she won't be my bride anymore. Tomorrow she'll be my wife. So guess—guess.

SHEYNE. I can't guess.

YOSHKE. What's something you'd wish for? For example—the biggest, the best, the most expensive?

SHEYNE. If I had a little money—

YOSHKE. How much money?

SHEYNE. A thousand.

YOSHKE. That's all? Some big business— (*Takes out money.*) Here you have a thousand. One hundred, two, three—

HODES. What do you need the money for?

YOSHKE. Don't mix in. Three hundred, four hundred.

HODES. For a thousand rubles you can buy the entire world.

YOSHKE. Don't mix in. Now you confused me. Five hundred, four—I don't have the strength to count. Take the whole thing. So what if you have one hundred more.

SHEYNE. You're a good boy.

YOSHKE. Not a boy, a bridegroom, and tomorrow a husband.

SHEYNE. I have to go upstairs for tea. They're waiting for me.

YOSHKE. So take the money and let's go up.

HODES. Let her go by herself, and you stay with me.

SHEYNE. I'll be right back.

HODES. Yoshke, you were not invited. I'll give you tea.

YOSHKE. I don't want any tea. I want to go with you.

Sheyne off.

HODES. (*Holds him back. Secretly*) Yoshke, before you go, let me run to the apothecary and buy a medicine.

YOSHKE. What kind of medicine?

HODES. You know how my Mekhele (may he toss and turn where he lies in the ground) made a fool of me? He put a love potion in my tea. And once I swallowed it, I couldn't spit it out for eighty years. So when you go up to drink tea, take a potion along with you.

YOSHKE. A love potion? Oh, you old witch. I don't need any potion. I don't need to trick Sheyne.

HODES. You're always doing tricks.

YOSHKE. But now I don't need them anymore. I don't need to wait for a star to fall from heaven. I'm in heaven right here. All of heaven came down to me. In the morning I take a walk in the blue air, and at noon I ride on a cloud. And at night—oh, hold me, hold me, I am dazzled with joy.

> *Music. In-laws and Bride come down from the family rooms. They are agitated and disappointed, almost embarrassed. The Father-in-law leads out first the Bride and then the Mother-in-Law. Buttons his fur coat, goes over to the door leading to the family rooms, spits hastily, and runs off. Yoshke remains a while at the door.*

Hodes, are you sure that the potions work?

HODES. I don't know. Maybe it's already too late for a potion.

YOSHKE. What do you mean?

HODES. Sheyne didn't take the thousand for herself.

YOSHKE. For who then?

SYEMYONTSHIK. (*Enters, standing on steps.*) Yoshke, I want to thank you for the thousand you lent me.

YOSHKE. Hodes, run and bring me the potion.

> *Hodes off.*

SYEMYONTSHIK. Yoshke, I'll pay back the money to the last groshn. If you don't believe me, I'll sign an IOU.

YOSHKE. I gave the money to Sheyne, not you.

SYEMYONTSHIK. She rescued me. I'm a free man now. Tomorrow I travel to Kiev and I'll stake my thousand and break the bank. I figured out a new system. Let's say (*demonstrates with the cards*) nineteen times you get a better hand. The twentieth time you get a king and I get a queen. I put down the thousand—

YOSHKE. (*They're both at the table.*) Where is the money?

SYEMYONTSHIK. I've got it here.

YOSHKE. Why don't you put it down, then?

SYEMYONTSHIK. For real?

YOSHKE. (*Takes out his money and puts it on the table.*) Here's the bank.

SYEMYONTSHIK. I'm a player. I'll stake the whole thousand.

YOSHKE. Let's see.

SYEMYONTSHIK. You're going to lose.

YOSHKE. Don't you worry about me. Shuffle the cards. Deal.

SYEMYONTSHIK. Deal means deal. (*Shuffles and deals.*) I am going to take your money. (*Yoshke shows his hand. Syemyontshik screams.*) Four queens.

YOSHKE. Three would have been enough to beat you. You lose. (*Runs toward the stairs.*)

SYEMYONTSHIK. Can't be. It's some kind of trick.

YOSHKE. Your cards, you shuffled, you dealt.

SYEMYONTSHIK. I promised Sheyne to pay my debts with that money, and not play anymore.

YOSHKE. You promised her a lot of things.

SYEMYONTSHIK. I would have kept all my promises if you hadn't come and bought her with your money.

YOSHKE. That's a lie. Sheyne loves me.

SYEMYONTSHIK. If she loves you, why did she kiss me and cry when she gave me the money?

YOSHKE. When?

SYEMYONTSHIK. Before, up there. If not for you, Sheyne would be my bride today. If not for you, I would be her husband today and the father of her child.

YOSHKE. Is that true?

SYEMYONTSHIK. Go up and ask her.

YOSHKE. Why didn't you tell me before?

SYEMYONTSHIK. What?

YOSHKE. That you want to be the father of her child.

SYEMYONTSHIK. I came down to tell you but somehow, before I could, you won the money.

YOSHKE. Don't cry, don't carry on, the game isn't over yet.

SYEMYONTSHIK. I don't have any more money.

YOSHKE. I'll take an IOU.

SYEMYONTSHIK. With my signature?

YOSHKE. Here's a thousand. I'll hold the bank.

SYEMYONTSHIK. I'll shuffle the cards.

YOSHKE. Shuffle, but fast. Somebody could come down.

SYEMYONTSHIK. Oh, what a hand. Can I raise you for two thousand?

YOSHKE. Even three. Your word is good with me.

SYEMYONTSHIK. Three thousand. (*Yoshke gives him another two cards and himself two cards.*) What do you have?

YOSHKE. Four queens again. (*Starts to take the money.*)

SYEMYONTSHIK. Not so fast. It's not always your birthday party. I have four kings.

YOSHKE. (*Gives him money.*) You have one and three—four thousand.

SYEMYONTSHIK. You lose. I beat you, my friend. See, all I need is one good hand. It's what I told Sheyne: I'll just keep losing till I win.

YOSHKE. Wait, you haven't won yet. What do you raise me?

SYEMYONTSHIK. Let me see a card. (*Yoshke deals him a card.*) How much is the pot? Two thousand?

YOSHKE. I double the two thousand to four and the four to eight. I raise you everything I've got.

SYEMYONTSHIK. With a hand like this I'd bet a million. But I'm not playing. I'm scared.

YOSHKE. You lost Sheyne playing. Win her back. Take the card. You have an ace.

SYEMYONTSHIK. I'll play if you put me down another card.

YOSHKE. Another ace.

SYEMYONTSHIK. Two aces. Wait, yes . . . no. No I'm scared. I don't dare lose. Because of Sheyne. I don't dare. I don't want to. Let me see what you've got.

YOSHKE. (*Opens his cards.*) King of hearts, king of spades, king of diamonds, king of clubs—four kings.

SYEMYONTSHIK. No, no. I said I didn't want to, I didn't dare.

YOSHKE. Open your cards. You have two aces.

SYEMYONTSHIK. No, no, how can I beat you with four kings? Even if I— (*Opens a card.*) An ace. (*Opens a second card and then the other two.*) An ace. Four aces. Ha, ha, ha. It's my money. A slam is a slam. Who ever heard of a slam like that—not even in Kiev, nobody's ever heard of a slam like that. The system works! (*Grabs the money and runs upstairs screaming with joy.*)

BERL. (*Comes downstairs with Shayke.*) Yoshke, where were you? I am flooded with tea. Delightful. Where were you, my son?

SHAYKE. (*Sees the cards scattered on the table.*) He was playing cards. I could swear Syemyontshik won all his money.

BERL. Won all his money?

SHAYKE. He has lost it, lost it.

BERL. The money. The money. So fast—the money gone. The card player cheated all his money away from him. Help, everybody! Help!

MADAME LURIA. (*Enters from above.*) Shh. What is all this noise? People are going to come running.

BERL. I'll turn this house upside down. I'll smash down the walls. (*At window.*) People, come! All the money stolen. Robbed. The money, the money.

SHAYKE. You kept pouring tea into us up there so down here Syemyontshik could take away Yoshke's money.

MADAME LURIA. Out of my house.

BERL and SHAYKE. We won't go. Give back the money, the money. Let go of the money.

YOSHKE. Shh. Quiet. You'll frighten her.

SHEYNE. (*Comes downstairs with the money in her hand.*) I ripped the money out of Syemyontshik's hand. Because I know your tricks. You can win and you can lose. Yoshke, here is your money back.

YOSHKE. No, no, I didn't lose to him, I lost to you.

BERL. Take it back, Yoshke. Your mother is blind, I am old. Take it back.

SHAYKE. Take it back. Till the new world order! Meanwhile, a man must have some money of his own.

SHEYNE. Take it, Yoshke. I won't be your wife no matter what. If you tied me up with ropes, I would tear them off somehow and run to him, because I love him and I belong to him, only him. Forever, forever.

MADAME LURIA. Come, Sheyne, come. People are waiting. It isn't nice.

YOSHKE. Take it, Sheyne, and go. You'll be late for the wedding.

SHEYNE. You are a fine and a good man. Maybe better than him. Yoshke, my dear, forgive me. I will remember you forever. I take your letter in my heart, and I will never forget the sweet song you used to sing under my window.

Music.

Listen. The song still floats around in the kitchen. The fire in the oven sings it while the clock beats the time. Yoshke dear, I will not be your wife, but I will rock my child to sleep with your song.

Sheyne and Madame Luria off. Yoshke lies at the foot of the steps with his head buried and weeps.

SHAYKE. Yoshke, what will happen to me now? You dressed me up like a parasite. No more crawling through chimneys: just go to doctors and drink cordial. Instead of giving your money to the poor masses, you gambled it all away. I'll smear my face black again, I'll climb back up through the chimneys and out onto the roofs, and I will scream, "Traitor, traitor! Yoshke the plutocrat is an exploiter. Traitor, traitor."

BERL. Yoshke, what have you done? It was a miracle from heaven, but you ripped heaven apart and darkened the stars. No mercy on your old father, didn't spare your blind mother. Oh, you cursed buckets, come on then, settle yourselves back, come ride on my shoulders. Back to work, old workhorse. Back to drawing water, back to hauling water. Till we fall down together in the middle of the street.

KALEFUTE. (*Enters.*) Yoshke, don't you recognize me?

YOSHKE. Kalefute.

KALEFUTE. I thought you might want to see me.

YOSHKE. But you died from the cold a week ago. Tell me, are you dead or are you alive?

KALEFUTE. You yourself came to my funeral.

YOSHKE. How did you come here?

KALEFUTE. Up there nobody pays attention. I grabbed on to a falling star and *whoosh* jumped down here into the house, and in through the wall.

YOSHKE. Look, they've got me locked up here. I want to run away too, but I don't know where and how.

KALEFUTE. Die. Come with me.

YOSHKE. I don't know how to die. Don't they let in any live people?

KALEFUTE. What would a live person do there?

YOSHKE. I can write letters.

KALEFUTE. They don't have a post office.

YOSHKE. I can play the fiddle.

KALEFUTE. No use, only the angels play. On harps.

YOSHKE. How does a plain man like me manage there?

KALEFUTE. A plain man is in trouble. Look at me.

YOSHKE. You're still wearing the same rags.

KALEFUTE. Maybe you have an old shirt, a cap, a vest? Brrr. It's very cold there.

YOSHKE. My fur coat might suit you.

KALEFUTE. Oh my, my, my! God himself would love to have a coat like that. Thank you. I'm sorry I can't take you with me.

YOSHKE. I can't leave here. Upstairs is the wedding, and I forgot to give Sheyne the ring.

KALEFUTE. Give it here. I'll carry it up to her. I can go right through the wall.

YOSHKE. Oh good, that's what I need. Wait, I'll make you a top hat so you look like an in-law on the bridegroom's side. Wish them *mazl tov* from me.

Music. Enter BEGGARS.

KALEFUTE. Look. See.

FIRST BEGGAR. I drag myself through the streets like a dog. I was counting on your wedding: something to drink and something to eat and maybe a little present.

FIRST BEGGAR WOMAN. Yoshke, I heard you went crazy. You gave away all your money.

SECOND BEGGAR WOMAN. I want my child to go to school so he can write letters just like you. If you could help me out with a little money . . .

SECOND BEGGAR. My little boy plays on a broom something wonderful. Why can't he play a fiddle like you?

FIRST BEGGAR. Why not share your luck with the people who wished you well?

FIRST BEGGAR. I'll scream at Heaven. I'll curse. I'll burn down the stars.

SECOND BEGGAR. Wait. Maybe he's cheating. Maybe he's still got something hidden in his pockets.

SECOND BEGGAR WOMAN. Let's look.

ALL
> Give me something.
> Give me a little.
> Give me what you have left.
> Don't give her.
> Give me, give me.
> Give me your collar, your necktie,
> Your pants,
> Your vest,
> Your shirt, your shirt, that's good too.

YOSHKE. No, I won't, not that.

FIRST BEGGAR. I have it.

ALL. What is it?

SECOND BEGGAR. A piece of paper.

FIRST BEGGAR WOMAN. The lottery.

SECOND BEGGAR WOMAN. Lost everything and held on to a piece of paper.

FIRST BEGGAR. To cheat us all, to fool the poor people.

FIRST BEGGAR WOMAN. I'll tear it all up and burn it. I'll destroy the whole world.

YOSHKE. No, no.

SECOND BEGGAR. Quiet, let him talk. Let him say something.

Yoshke weeps.

SECOND BEGGAR WOMAN. There you have it, another Kalefute on our hands.

FIRST BEGGAR. Ha, ha. Kalefute died, Kalefute lives.

SECOND BEGGAR. Long live Kalefute the Second.

ALL. Crazy, get out.

ROYZELE. (*Enters, chases them out.*) Out of here this minute. I'll call my grandmother, and she will scratch out your eyes and break your hands. Out, get out.

Beggars exit.

Come, I'll hide you. I'll disguise you as my grandmother. Here is where she keeps her clothes. Change your clothes, I'll just pull the curtains.

YOSHKE. But if your grandmother comes in, she'll think we're playing like children.

ROYZELE. I know now that your letter will never come to me. It's torn up and blown away. Oh Grandma, Grandma, hold me, I'm falling out of a dream.

GRANDMOTHER. Sleep then, sleep quickly. I will knit you socks and sing you the little song so you won't forget it—God forbid—when you wake up.

> SOON, SOON YOUR SLEEP
> WILL MELT AWAY WITH NIGHT
> AND YOU'LL WAKE FROM YOUR DREAM—
> ALL A DREAM—FROM YOUR FLIGHT,
> AND YOU'LL TELL THE SWEET TALE,
> ALL THE JOY, ALL THE SORROW.
> FOR I'M HERE IN THE DARK
> BY YOUR SIDE TILL TOMORROW.
> WHAT JOYS AND WHAT PAINS
> WILL THE SUN BRING TOMORROW?
> TOMORROW, TOMORROW.

Darkness.

The End

Notes

Act 1

As I explain in my introduction to the play, some of the passages that are printed in verse format may have been written specifically for the 1972 Folksbiene production. Some rhyme consistently; some rhyme loosely and intermittently; all are simple and folky. I have tried to reflect the writer's intention and basic pattern in each case.

Probably many, or all, of those versified passages were intended to be sung. Certainly the verse that starts with musicians Yoshke and Berl comes from a familiar old folk song, though I have tweaked it in translation. The best-known version of that song, with melody by Abe Ellstein, runs through the charming Yiddish film *Yiddle with His Fiddle* (1936). The other passages printed in caps are the ones I feel surest were meant to be sung. The score for the Folksbiene's 1999 production was developed and orchestrated by Zalmen Mlotek from folk music. He also composed settings for some of the poetry. His score is available; he can be reached at the National Yiddish Theatre–Folksbiene, where he is artistic director.

Musicians' jargon was only one of the varieties of Yiddish language specific to certain occupations, such as the jargons of horse traders in Alsace and of underworld thugs in Warsaw. Very little of these specific vocabularies has remained current—in fact, the great preserver and analyst of Yiddish, Professor Mordkhe Schaechter, in 1987 produced a lexicon of botanical terminology that included many words that have virtually disappeared. Some of the musicians' words in act 1 were actually translated for me by current klezmer musicians, while others are simply our joint guesses.

It was a familiar custom that the bridal party, especially the young couple's parents, be accompanied as they moved in more-or-less formal procession from the ceremony to the place of celebration. Pieces of music were composed with this specific moment in mind, generally a lively march.

Weddings are traditionally performed under a canopy, which is usually, though not always, made of cloth. A common way to refer to a wedding is a *khupe*, meaning simply a "canopy." Because the canopy is supported at its corners, another way to refer to it is "standing between, or among, the four posts."

Act 2

It was very common for communities to form volunteer committees to take care of communal needs. Thus the bathhouse, for example, which served not only for hygiene but also for ritual bathing on stipulated occasions, would be run by a committee, among whose duties it is to raise money to pay its expenses.

Pesha-pisha is a card game.

Eleanor Reissa: Director's Thoughts

In 1999, Zalmen Mlotek and I were in our second year as artistic directors of the Folksbiene Yiddish Theatre, a theater company that had produced plays uninterrupted for over ninety years. (The theater is now called the National Yiddish Theatre–Folksbiene, with Zalmen as artistic director.) By 1999, the Folksbiene was no longer amateur or even semi-professional but strictly professional, and Zalmen and I were newly challenged to bring a new audience to the ever-ailing Yiddish theater. Since both of us were native Yiddish-speakers with experience in Yiddish as well as non-Yiddish theater, we wanted passionately to make this a theater that would inspire and reinvigorate. We hoped to bring the company into the twentieth century by producing Yiddish works: both classic plays and new works of worth and depth.

Our first offering was a play I wrote in Yiddish called *Zise Khaloymes* (*Sweet Dreams*), a modern musical set in New York City about a contemporary young woman, the daughter of Holocaust survivors, who is trying to make a life for herself, while being plagued by the ghost of her dead mother. We decided that our second offering should be more classic and come from the Yiddish theater oeuvre. We looked into many possibilities and ultimately decided that *Yoshke Muzikant* was magical and moving and would still resonate today. We saw its potential to combine many worlds: modern yet classic; earthly yet mystical. The language was beautiful and poetic, and the tale could be transporting.

There were a few different versions of the play by Osip Dimov. The actor and director Joseph Buloff had great and many successes with his own version(s) of the play, which he adapted and readapted over the years. We ultimately decided to use primarily one of the Buloff versions as our base. His draft was theatrical and bold. It had a touching preface that would bookend the play and provide a storytelling device: the granddaughter would dream of Yoshke, who would magically visit her in her dreams. It was like in *Peter Pan* where Wendy tells the story of Peter Pan to her own daughter.

We would call our version *A Klezmer's Tale: Yoshke Muzikant*. We would add music because the folksiness of the piece would be enhanced by Yiddish folk tunes, developed and orchestrated for the production by Zalmen to heighten the events of the play. Also, of course, musicals have a tendency to sell better than straight plays.

Our biggest charge would be to find the actors—talented performers who also had a proficiency in Yiddish. Getting nonnative speakers to speak Yiddish dialogue in a way that sounds natural always adds a special difficulty. And now that we've added music, we would need actors who could also sing!

Who would we get for Yoshke—the part that Buloff made famous and vice versa? I can't remember now where or how we found him, but a young actor, the opposite of the older Buloff—tall, lean, and lithe—came in to audition for us. Spencer Chandler's ear for Yiddish was very, very good. He played the violin, juggled, did magic(!), and sang.

The love interest came next. An excellent actress, also with a good ear for Yiddish, with an honest romantic soul, was Rachel Botchan, whom I was to work with many more times over these more than twenty years. For the character women, we had the classic comediennes Mina Bern and Shifra Lehrer: Mina as the poultry seller Hodes and Shifra as the more elegant Madam Luria. Both were major artists in the world of the Yiddish theater, from Poland to Argentina to Uganda to Israel to the United States. They were the grandes dames of the Yiddish world. Between them they knew more about acting and the Yiddish theater than all of the rest of the cast combined. They would help set the high bar for everyone else. The other actors included Allen Lewis Rickman [who wrote the essay on *Mirele Efros* in this volume] as the sneaky, creepy, greedy Syemyontshik. It was a wonderful company.

Vicki R. Davis designed a colorful set practically out of a storybook, with a dreamy, magical realistic look that was a pleasure to play on and helped place the world of the tale and tell the story. It was as poetic as the dialogue. The costumes by Gail Cooper Hecht were warm and rich and lush—seeming to come directly from Russia of the 1890s. Together with the onstage band of musicians, the world of Yoshke was created.

The *New York Times* review by Lawrence Van Gelder called it a "colorful, melodic, funny, bittersweet, and surprising musical folk tale . . ." That was precisely what the play called for and exactly what we had intended.

Fluent in both English and Yiddish, Eleanor Reissa is director/cocreator and performer in Carnegie Hall's Migration series *From Shtetl to Stage*. Her directing debut on Broadway resulted in two Tony Award nominations, including Best Direction of a Musical for *Those Were the Days*, which she also choreographed and starred in. Her diverse directing credits include: *Cowgirls* (Outer Critics Circle nomination), *Echoes of the War* (Drama Desk nomination), *The Soldier's Wife* (two Drama Desk nominations), Sholem Asch's *Got Fun Nekome* (*God of Vengeance*), and John Galsworthy's *The Skin Game*. She is slated to direct the premiere of Paddy Chayefsky's *The Tenth Man*, which she was commissioned to translate into Yiddish by National Yiddish Theatre Folksbiene.

As an actress, Reissa recently appeared on Broadway in Paula Vogel's *Indecent* and regionally in Wendy Wasserstein's *The Sisters Rosensweig*. She just completed filming an independent feature, *Minyan*, directed by Eric Steel, and will be seen next season on the HBO miniseries *The Plot Against America*, based on the novel by Philip Roth. As a singer, Eleanor has headlined in every major concert hall in New York City. For the past decade she and Grammy-nominated Frank London have rocked Yiddish festivals around the world, as well as stages all over the country. Recently they performed their new show *Kurt Weill in New York* at the Weill Festival in Germany.

Reissa's original plays have been published in an anthology, *The Last Survivor and Other Modern Jewish Plays*. Her play *Thicker than Water* has just been optioned for Off-Broadway, and her translation into Yiddish of Paddy Chayefsky's *The Tenth Man* opened in 2020, under her own direction.

Scenes

Uncle Moses

SHOLEM ASCH

Introduction and Notes

Sholem Asch (1880–1957) wrote the novel *Uncle Moses* in 1918. It was dramatized several times but never published as a play. The version below, a typed and scribbled-over playing script, comes from the YIVO archives of the papers of the star-manager Maurice Schwartz. Schwartz dramatized it in 1930 for production by his Yiddish Art Theater, with himself in the title role. Later that same year he starred in a film based on his dramatization.

Sholem Asch was a major figure in Yiddish literature and also in the larger European and American literary world. He wrote many novels and a number of plays, of which the best known are *The Messianic Era* (1906), *The Sanctification of the Name* (1919), and *God of Vengeance* (1907). He was a controversial figure because of *God of Vengeance*, which shows prostitutes and lesbians, and also because he was interested in Christianity and wrote several novels, sympathetic in tone, related to Jesus and Mary.

The story begins when Masha, as a child, stands up bravely to her weak father's boss, known as "Uncle" Moses, and persuades Moses not to fire him. Moses is a coarse man, driven only by his desire for money and power, though with a paternal attachment to his sweatshop workers who come from his own hometown. He has mistresses but cares for no one in the world. But the child Masha charms him, and as she matures, he loves her more and more, showering money and favors on her and her family. Finally, Masha does marry Moses for her parents' sake, but she leaves him in the end, taking their child and leaving him a broken man.

I drew from act 2, scenes 2 and 3, which follow each other immediately, in order to construct one cohesive scene. I also borrowed a few lines from a partial script in the same archive.

The suffice *-ele* is an affectionate diminutive, turning Masha into a pet name.

The Merry Widow is an operetta by Franz Lehar. It has been popular since its debut in 1905 and is revived to this day.

Uncle Moses

SHOLEM ASCH

DRAMATIZED FROM THE NOVEL BY MAURICE SCHWARTZ (1930)

(FROM ACT 2)

Characters

MASHA   Pretty seventeen-year-old girl.

MOSES   Prosperous, vulgar, used to giving orders. Middle-aged, rather portly. In love with Masha.

PLACE   Apartment in a Lower East Side tenement, early twentieth century.

TIME   Early twentieth century.

Masha is fastening the collar of Uncle Moses. The collar is stiff and tight, so she is having difficulty. Both are dressed up for an evening at the theater.

MOSES. Take your time. If we miss the first act or two, it's not so terrible.

She struggles.

Pinches, hah? But it feels good. Oh such little hands! Never in my life have I seen such little hands. I have hands (*Puts out a paw.*) but yours are like . . . a rabbi's daughter. Masha, I love you. I feel you love me too. Your little heart is jumping like mine. Yesterday I was standing in Brownsville on the roof of one of my houses, and I heard you calling me. I almost leaped off. "Mashele," I yelled out, "Mashele!"

MASHA. You're so strange today, Uncle, that I can't even laugh.

MOSES. Strange . . . (*Pours self another cognac.*) Masha, I am happy that you are here alone with me.

MASHA. Please, Uncle, don't drink so much.

MOSES. It's nothing, it's cognac, Masha.
Don't call me Uncle; all the hands in the shop call me Uncle. Call me by my name, Mashele. It's more than a year now since you came to the shop to call for your father. You called me "Beast," "Dog." I can still hear you. (*Smiles.*) "Beast." "Dog." More than a year, and for me every day has been a year. Every day I've watched you grow—no evil eye—become a woman, I've felt that there is a God in the world. You're seventeen now, you're not a child, and I want you to know that not once in all this time—you hear me? not once, I swear it—have I thought of you the way men do. May I die like a dog in the street if I've even given one thought like other men. Say in a restaurant, with the men, a nice woman, a good lunch, drink a cognac, a cigar, you feel a twinge, a pull—not me. I knock the thought out, I bite it back with my teeth. "Shh!" I catch myself, "Don't think about it. Don't think about it. Wait: Mashele is growing up." Mashele . . . Mashele. Forgive me. It's hard for me to talk about these things.

MASHA. Come, let's go, Uncle.

MOSES. I'm a hard man. I want respect, people have to do what I say. I like to be the boss. If I stopped bossing people, I wouldn't be Uncle Moses. But with you I'm different. The opposite, I want you to give me orders. Make me run for you into the earth, crawl for you on the ground like a worm. Kiss the earth under your feet. Because Masha, I love you. I love you. Love you. Now make me happy and say one word: Uncle, I love you too.

MASHA. I've already told you that I love you, many times.

MOSES. No, that kind of love—everybody loves me that way. The good uncle, the rich uncle. (*Yells.*) No, I want a different love, that kind that hurts, like it hurts me. Love that you don't sleep. Day and night, you're thinking. Your mind is dried up from thinking. Like mine. Come to the point, the point. I bought an apartment for you. Two apartments put together, big, right in this building. Six months ago already. It's all ready for you. All fixed up. A bedroom set, blue—everything matches. Six months already there's an apartment, all ready for you. All fixed up. A music room, with a player piano, a phonograph with the prettiest records: *The Merry Widow*, operas, everything. And upstairs a separate apartment for your parents: three rooms, new carpets, beautiful! A sofa—your mother can sit like a lady.

She has started to cry.

You're crying, you're crying. Well, you don't have to cry. Nobody's forcing you, God forbid. What I've poured out on you, on your family—they're from my town, they're family. So another ten thousand to hell. (*Drinks.*) But why didn't anybody tell me? You're not a child. At sixteen you were as smart as at seventeen. You saw I was crazy about you. You saw I was dressing myself up, I spray myself to hell with perfume. I was already going to shave off the moustache, turned my heart inside out, to hell with it. You didn't see? Your parents didn't see? Why give a man useless hopes? "Uncle Moses, eat." "Uncle Moses, potatoes with sour cream." "Uncle Moses, next year we celebrate, all New York will ring with it, the in-laws will dance and the little bride will shine in her wedding gown." "She's just shy, Uncle Moses." (*Breaks his glass.*) Why fool me? Swindlers! I will not forgive the swindle. Playing with a person's heart? Playing with a heart? Why raise a man's hopes? Come, Masha darling, I'll take you home.

MASHA. You're taking me home?

MOSES. You think I want to go to the theater? (*Rips tickets.*) To hell, that's where I want to go. I'll go to a doctor, to cure my heart, that's where I'm going. She thinks a year of hopes is nothing. Come, Masha.

MASHA. I don't want to go home, Uncle. Please, take me somewhere else, wherever you want—theater, a restaurant—all night, all night, only not home.

MOSES. You talk like a child. Come, the car is waiting. I'll take you home.

MASHA. No, not home. Papa and mama can't know what happened between us. They are happy. Everybody is happy at home. The table is set with the most expensive food. Papa pays by check. My sister is going to school. The neighbors are celebrating. I can't go home.

MOSES. Come, come, come, Masha. Papa is waiting. Mama is waiting.

MASHA. No, Uncle, no. (*Kisses his hand.*) No, I won't go home. I want your home to be my home. Today I'll talk to you, Uncle. Until now Papa and Mama talked to you. Today I will do it.

UNCLE. Mashele, sweet girl. Now you make me happy. (*Takes off his coat.*) Take, Mashele, take something. Please take something. A little cognac, a piece of chocolate, take something. My God, my God, what can I do for you? Wait a minute, wait a minute. I want you to see something. (*Puts coat back on, turns out the lights.*) Shh, come, darling come.

> *They exit. Reappear in a dark room*

Wait a minute, wait a minute, I'll put on the lights.

> *They are in a big elaborate bedroom, walls and furniture painted blue, very big bed in center. The lights are bright and have fancy effects.*

Maybe too dark? A different light is better? (*He switches on other lights.*)

MASHA. No, no it's good, very good.

MOSES. Something to drink, a sandwich? You see the bed hasn't been touched. I don't sleep in this room. No, a promise is a promise. I made myself a promise that till my dear bride is here, I'll—

MASHA. I am here, Uncle.

MOSES. Ha, ha. I mean after the wedding

MASHA. (*Frightened.*) The wedding.

MOSES. After the wedding. Mashele, may my hands wither if I meant, God forbid—

MASHA. Come here, Uncle, sit down.

MOSES. I can stand. I have enough strength. Don't worry.

MASHA. Let's get married right away.

MOSES. I don't understand. You were—and now this rush. I don't understand.

MASHA. I didn't understand you, Uncle. I loved you, I loved you very much, as an uncle. I heard Mama talking, Papa talking, and I understood what they meant. But I kept quiet and waited to hear what the uncle would say. The uncle who was so good to me. Like a father, and I loved you like—

MOSES. Like a father? Talk, talk, don't be ashamed. I can take it. Don't be ashamed and talk to me openly. "Uncle, I can't. Uncle, I like Charlie better." I know you go out with him a lot. Mashele, no one is angry at you. Don't be embarrassed. Tell your parents, say to them, "I want a young man. We'll go to Coney Island and play ball on the beach. He'll talk fine talk to me."

MASHA. No. Uncle Moses— (*Corrects herself.*) Moses, let's get married right away.

MOSES. Masha?

MASHA. Right away. Right away. Let's go tell Mama and Papa.

MOSES. You want to marry me, Masha? You love me?

MASHA. You're so good to me, how can I help it?

MOSES. Like a father you love me. Like an Uncle Moses.

MASHA. (*Looking straight into his eyes.*) No. I love you like a man, like a man I want to marry.

MOSES. When you look at me, straight in the eye, and you tell me that, what are the houses, with the property, the Bowery Bank—what are they? Nothing. Nothing compared with you. You make me a new man, a brand new soul. Masha, come, let me show you your whole home. Let me show you, Masha. Come.

END OF SCENE

Homeless

JACOB GORDIN

Introduction and Notes

The action begins when Bas-Sheve, with her old father and young son, arrives to join her husband Abe, who has been in New York long enough to go to night school and get some education. There he met Bessie, clearly a perfect match for him, but they were honorable and resisted the attraction; he remained faithful and sent for Bas-Sheve. But Bas-Sheve is a simple, ignorant, superstitious woman. She cannot cope with big city life, let alone a whole new country and language. She can't protect her adolescent son from falling in with juvenile delinquents in the tenement where they live. She is so uneducated that she tries a love potion to hold on to her husband's love.

Although there is a temporary improvement in the marriage, in the end Bas-Sheve collapses and goes to an insane asylum. Though Bessie could bring stability and happiness to Abe and the boy, she leaves, refusing to build her happiness on another woman's tragedy.

Bas-Sheve was a big role for Bessie Tomashefsky, known for her ability to seem perfectly natural onstage. The play was later made into a film, with the comic duo Dzigan and Shumakher, but the whole story is so changed that it is practically unrecognizable.

Bessie is right about the grammar, of course. Yiddish, like many European languages, and like older forms of English, distinguishes between two forms of address to a single person: second-person plural, which is formal, and second-person singular, which is intimate. It is common for dialogue to include bits of languages other than Yiddish. This is realistic: in fact, most Yiddish-speakers knew more than one language. Language shifts and misunderstandings, especially in immigrant settings, are often a source of comedy. Bessie and Bas-Sheve both use English words without particularly noticing: cent, tenement, hurry up, shop, factory, supper. (So do Uncle Moses and Khantshe in other plays in this volume.) The common shifts of diction and vocabulary reflect the importance of Hebrew for pious quotations and indeed most religious allusions and practices, the contemporary bias that German sounds classier than Yiddish, and the Slavic flavor and vocabulary of rougher populations.

Seders take place the first night (or two nights) of the Passover holiday, which usually falls in April. The ceremony commemorates the exodus from Egypt, telling the story with prayers and songs and incorporating a festive meal. It is a major event in every observant Jewish home; there are Jews who make or attend some kind of seder even though they observe virtually no other custom.

For decades, *tsaytbilder* (literally, "pictures or scenes of the times") were among the most popular genres on the American Yiddish stage. Although as twentieth-century tastes developed, *tsaytbilder* tended to be domestic dramas rather than melodramas, they retained the characteristic mix of sorrow and comedy. Even as avant-garde expressionism became familiar to intellectual Yiddish audiences, the popular Yiddish theater kept such nineteenth-century qualities as a propensity and appreciation for evoking tears.

I made very few changes. I removed another few characters who come on and off the stage, and I added a few lines from an earlier scene. This scene, in a version of this translation, was part of a revue called *Vagabond Stars*, for which I wrote the book, Raphael Crystal the music, and Alan Poul the lyrics. It opened at the Berkshire Theatre Festival in 1978 and then ran at the Jewish Repertory Theatre in New York City, directed by Ran Avni.

For information about Jacob Gordin, see the introductions to *Mirele Efros* and *Safo*.

Homeless

JACOB GORDIN

(1898)

(from act 2)

Characters

BAS-SHEVE RIVKIN   Mid-thirties, dressed as in old country.
ABE   Her husband, Americanized.
HARRY   Their son, Americanized, about eleven.
BESSIE   Thirties or a bit younger, Americanized.

PLACE   Lower East Side tenement.
TIME   Around 1900.

Kitchen of Rivkin apartment. Bas-Sheve is setting the elaborate seder table. BESSIE enters.

BESSIE. You're Mrs. Rivkin? I'm Bessie Steinberg. The girl who took down your address told me you were crying. So I came to see.

BAS-SHEVE. You came to see me crying?

BESSIE. I hope nothing further has happened, God forbid.

BAS-SHEVE. No, nothing further. Just my husband is gone. A man leaves his wife and son—is that nothing further in America?

BESSIE. Yes, I heard just a few days ago.

BAS-SHEVE. Your mailman is that slow? It's eleven days since he left us.

BESSIE. Eleven days?

BAS-SHEVE. Eleven days. Why act so innocent? You don't know it?

BESSIE. I know you feel bitter. I don't hold it against you.

BAS-SHEVE. (*Putting something away on a shelf, banging the plates.*) Hold it against me, I don't mind.

BESSIE. If this is your attitude, I can't understand why you would want to see me.

BAS-SHEVE. Today is the first seder. You're probably an enlightened person, a real American, like my Abie is now. You probably don't bother with the holidays, and you don't know what it means to have a holiday spoiled. At first, I thought I'd die sooner than go to you. But I couldn't bear it any longer. Maybe he's been hurt, God forbid. Where is he?

It's getting dark outside.

BESSIE. I don't know where he is, and I wonder why you think I would know.

BAS-SHEVE. Because I think it's your fault he is not happy with me; he's like a stranger in the house. I wouldn't have believed it. But now I do. He told me himself that he respects you very much. (*Examines her. Sarcastically*) Now I see that there's something there worth respecting.

BESSIE. Mrs. Rivkin, if you—

BAS SHEVE. (*Interrupts.*) Yes! Yes I know that he spent years here alone while you got cute and cozy with him.

BESSIE. Why do you need to speak to me like that?

BAS-SHEVE. (*Doesn't hear.*) You've been seen together very often lately. And anyway, the night before he left, something came over me and I gave in and read the letter you sent him. That is, somebody translated it for me. I still can't read English. Go ahead and laugh, I'm an old lady who sits by the fire, not a saleslady.

BESSIE. I don't understand.

BAS-SHEVE. (*Angrily*) No? But to sign a letter "truthfully thine own"—that you understand, hah? When you've gotten to the stage of calling another woman's husband "thine" and "truthfully thine," things must have gone pretty far. Everything in this country is "hurry-up."

BESSIE. (*Smiles kindly.*) You say we've been seen together often lately. That is not true. We belong to the same literary club, and when I attend a meeting, which is very seldom, we go out afterward—all the members together—to drink tea in a restaurant.

BAS-SHEVE. Those restaurants should burn to the ground. More than one poor woman sits alone at home.

BESSIE. A member of our literary club has caught consumption.

BAS-SHEVE. Sure, a literary complaint. What else would you catch in a literary club?

BESSIE. (*Laughs.*) You know, you're much cleverer than you think.

BAS-SHEVE. I know he thinks I'm a fool. I'm tongue-tied around him.

BESSIE. Mr. Rivkin and I were appointed to a committee to raise money to send our friend to a sanatorium in Denver. We arranged to meet at Butsik's Restaurant.

BAS-SHEVE. The letter said Butsik's. And meanwhile supper stood here on the table.

BESSIE. But I happened to get sick. And . . . and . . . I'll tell you the truth: I thought it would be better for us not to meet. So I simply wrote that I was busy and couldn't come. (*Laughs.*) But I did not sign the letter "truthfully thine own." Whoever translated for you doesn't know English.

BAS-SHEVE. I gave it to my son to read, and you guessed right: he doesn't really know English yet.

BESSIE. I signed that letter "sincerely yours," which means "honestly yours." "Yours," not "thine." In modern English, there's no such word as "thou" or "thee" or "thine." "You" is what you use to a lover or a horse, to a wife or to the cat.

BAS-SHEVE. A lover, a horse, a cat, a wife—all the same.

BESSIE. Yes, and it's only a form for signing a letter, like "respectfully" or "humbly." In Russian they write "your devoted servant," but they don't mean it, they just write it like that.

BAS-SHEVE. Without a meaning, it doesn't mean anything. (*Friendly*) So then, you want me to believe that my husband was never tied up with you.

BESSIE. (*Laughs.*) He certainly was not. I don't deny that while he was here alone, we did become good friends. We were boarders together.

BAS-SHEVE. So much unhappiness comes from the years men spend alone here without their wives, boarding together.

BESSIE. But when I saw that our friendship was taking a dangerous direction for both of us, I advised him to send for his family right away. I lent him the hundred fifty dollars to bring you over, and I myself moved all the way to the Bronx. I lost almost my entire work connections, but I decided to stay far away, and that's what I've done.

BAS-SHEVE. Yes, he said a friend helped him bring us over. Did he pay you back the money?

BESSIE. Every cent. I lent him the money because I knew it was safe. I work very hard, very hard for my dollars.

BAS-SHEVE. (*Looks at her hard.*) You're not a bad person, I see it in your eyes. And not a liar either, I think. I see it and feel it. Hm. Tell the truth: you like my husband, don't you?

BESSIE. Yes. That is the truth. And still today. I don't want him to know, but I can tell you. Because of him I can't think about getting married. I'm an old maid and a practical person. I hate to make a fool of people, or to make a fool of myself with impossible fantasies. I work hard and make a good living. But I have no home. In the ten years I've been in New York, I've worked in different shops and factories, I've wandered from tenement to tenement. I still do. I have no home, and I don't believe that I ever will.

BAS-SHEVE. All these years without a home? Ah, America! A pretty young woman has no home. Youth and beauty go to waste here and nobody knows for what or for who. You live, that's all. Admit it, wasn't it better back home? Ah, it's bitter to be homeless. Even more bitter when you do have a bit of a home and it becomes broken and ruined.

It grows darker.

Oh my. It's almost night. We have to get ready. (*Puts out plates, wine, glasses, two candlesticks.*) It's getting dark. I have to set the table.

I shouldn't have opened your letter. I threw it at him when he walked in the door that night, and I shouted at him. You know how he never raises his voice. He said to me, so coldly, "It's enough you make me a stranger in my own home, with your old wives' cures, and your prayers and superstitions. My son," he said, "you want to make him like his great-grandfather back in the Old Country and not like me, and now you have him spy on me to read my letters. You can shout at me all you want," he said. "I'm leaving." And he left.

BESSIE. I felt so bad for you when I heard what happened. I dropped everything and came to see you. He hasn't written in all this time?

BAS-SHEVE. The first day, in the morning. I had waited for him all night. Sat by the door and waited till dawn. Dozed off on the chair. How I cried that night. In the morning this came, a few words in pencil on a scrap of paper. (*Takes note from her pocket.*) You won't be able to read it, it's blotted from tears. He says, "You don't need to know where I am. But as soon as I find work, I'll send money for you and the child." No word since. Eleven days already. My boy put a letter to his father in the Yiddish paper.

Gives Bessie the newspaper. She reads it, drops it, and starts to cry.

BAS-SHEVE. (*Goes to her, hugs her head to her, and says quietly.*) Oh, sister, it hurts me so badly. (*Indicates her heart.*) I am wounded here, a deep wound. My head gets confused, the thoughts get mixed up, and it seems to me I'm losing my mind.

Both weep. HARRY enters.

HARRY. Aw, gee. Crying again.

BAS-SHEVE. No, no, Harry, just a very little bit. Bessie, you'll stay for supper with my boy and me. Yes, don't say a word, we'll make a seder together. Bessie, it would be very good if we took rooms together. I'd take good care of you. And me, I am lonesome, I don't have a friend. (*Quietly*) And if he comes back, he would stay home, Bessie, for your sake. I know I can't please him. I'm sick, I'm ignorant. I won't have any more children. (*Controls herself.*) Harry sweetheart, just look how late it is. Isn't grandfather going to synagogue?

HARRY. No, he's praying at home. He says it's time to light candles.

BESSIE. Can I help?

BAS-SHEVE. Yes, Bessie, just finish wiping these few dishes.

> *Bessie takes a towel and wipes dishes.*

I think that's all. Now you'll excuse me, Bessie, I'm an old lady and I have to bless the candles the way my mother did. Just look: no time even to change my clothes. And no mood for it either, God forgive me. Who should I dress for? (*Puts silk kerchief on her head, becomes solemn.*) Well, three years Pesach in America. (*Strikes match, lights candles. Spreads her hands over the candles, tries to speak but chokes with tears. Finally masters herself and quietly begins praying. We hear the first few words.*) Dear God, in your holy house, the holy fire is never extinguished, so let my child's life never be extinguished, the life of all those I love, all those, dear God, because— (*Suddenly bends toward the candles, covers her face and weeps with a bitter wail.*)

> *Bessie covers her face with a kerchief and weeps. The women do not hear a quiet knock on the door and don't see Harry open it. Abie enters.*

ABIE. Boy, did you call me home? Oh my boy. My boy! (*Catches boy in his arms and weeps.*)

End of Scene

Safo

JACOB GORDIN

Introduction and Notes

The story goes that, visiting backstage once, Gordin saw the beautiful Bertha Kalish in her dressing room brushing her hair. "Write a play for my hair," she coaxed coquettishly. And Gordin, who did tailor some of his work to specific actors on the Lower East Side, wrote several roles especially for her, including Sofia/Safo. (Kalish later starred in several plays on Broadway, including a translation of another Gordin play.)

Sofia is an enlightened young woman, who in act 1 publicly refused to marry her lover Boris, though she was pregnant by him, because she discovered he actually loves her sister. Now a single parent, she has just met Apolon, newly returned from studying piano in Paris. They have just met at a family party; he is engaged to her silly, shallow cousin Manitshke.

As the story continues after this scene, Apolon does marry Manitshke but continues his relationship with Sofia, who is clearly his soulmate. Sofia brings up her own child while Apolon and Manitshke live together and have children of their own. But finally, years later, Sofia's sister dies, and Sofia marries her first love Boris, breaking off with Apolon at last, in order to unite Boris with his daughter and to bring up her sister's children.

Sofia works in a photography shop. A large proportion of photographers and photography shop owners in Russia in this period were Jewish.

Gordin was typical of the wave of Russian Jewish intellectuals who arrived in America in the late nineteenth century. They generally spoke Russian to each other—rather than, or as much as Yiddish—and considered themselves part of Russian high culture, a distinct community among American Jews. It is natural that these characters quote the poetry of Lermontov to each other. Earlier in the play, Boris sings a Russian folk song, accompanying himself on the guitar.

Music and musicians were important on the Yiddish stage. A character who was a musician could provide an excuse to introduce music into the action in some plausible way. Also, a character who was a musician—professional or even amateur—was felt to possess spirituality, or to represent some such element.

Sofia's father is a dandy, a would-be man-about-town who constantly touches her for pocket money. Her uncle Shtempl, the fish merchant, talks constantly in terms of fish. Their verbal tics and obsessions are a kind of shorthand identification and a running gag, a venerable stage convention still in common use on sitcoms.

Among Gordin's missions was to educate Yiddish masses about Western culture. Dialogue in Gordin's *God, Man and Devil*, for example, explains the character of Faustus. Here, early in this play, for the benefit of the audience, Sofia and Apolon Sonenshayn (i.e., Sunshine) discuss the origin of his name—Apollo, Greek god of music and the sun—and he connects her name, Sofia, with the ancient poet Sappho. (See the introduction to *Mirele Efros* in this volume for a more thorough overview of Gordin as reformer of the Yiddish stage.)

Safo

JACOB GORDIN

1901

(from act 2)

Characters

SOFIA   A "modern" woman in her twenties, works in a photographer's studio, supports herself and helps support her parents.

APOLON   A pianist.

PLACE   A Russian city near the sea.

TIME   Around 1900.

Street. Summer evening. Sofia and Apolon stroll in.

SOFIA. Here's my palace. You offered to wait with me at the bus stop, and we ended up walking the whole way. Do you know, it must be almost four miles! Thank you. Good night.

APOLON. Four miles! I didn't even notice.

SOFIA. We were talking. Mr. Sonenshayn, they must be wondering where you are. Good night.

APOLON. I told them I had to stop by and visit some people. And I do have some visits I should pay, now that I'm back from Paris. But to tell the truth, it was much pleasanter to walk you home.

SOFIA. You remember our agreement: no compliments. Besides, for me it was not so pleasant when we left the party together. My aunt Frade must be sharpening her tongue back there.

APOLON. You're afraid of Auntie Frade?

SOFIA. I'm not afraid of any aunts, or any uncles, or anybody in the world. But I am afraid of making trouble. Go home and sleep well.

APOLON. Good night. You may not believe me, but I feel as if we didn't just meet tonight. I feel as if I've known you a long, long time.

SOFIA. Well, no matter how long you know me, you're not going to discover any hidden virtues. No hidden flaws either. You've found plenty of flaws already, right? without having to look for them. Go home, go home. I have to get up early for work. You don't want me to be miserable in the morning.

APOLON. God forbid. Have a good night. I wish you peaceful, happy dreams. (*He starts out.*)

SOFIA. I wanted to ask you—all night I kept wanting to ask you: are you in love with my cousin Manitshke?

APOLON. What can I tell you? When I was younger, the difference between us wasn't so great. And now—my training has cost your uncle Shtempl a lot of money. He bought himself an expensive son-in-law. He can afford something showy. And he's been paying in advance for years. I stayed away at the conservatory, I put off the wedding, and I hoped for a miracle. But I'll have to go through with it in the end. You see how your uncle's fish business supports art; without it I couldn't play Beethoven sonatas.

SOFIA. Don't you think that someone with a strong character might have handled things differently? You intend to be a good husband, but I'm afraid you're not going to manage it. Manitshke is going to be unhappy with you. You mask your true feelings around her. That means you're deceiving her already. That's my opinion. Excuse me. I may be wrong. And good night to you.

APOLON. No, stay. You've touched the most important question in my life. I need to think it out clearly. I have no one to advise me. Can you at least believe that I want to behave honorably? Let's sit down here a minute. The night is so lovely, the sky is so blue. Listen, I think I almost hear the ocean. I could sit here all night and let you scold me. A scolding from a sincere heart can't offend anybody. It's harmonious, like music. Tell me, do you have a piano? I'm in the mood to play the Moonlight Sonata. Or, you know what, if you weren't so tired, I'd invite you for a stroll in the park. They say it's beautiful this time of year.

SOFIA. The park? Now? When silvery moonlight pours down over the trees and throws great dark shadows on the pond? Come on then. The night is really beautiful. It's been so very long since I had anyone to stroll with and talk with. (*Quotes Russian poem by Lermontov.*)

> "In solitary wastes,
> I wander alone
> Where through the mist
> the gray road stretches on . . .

APOLON. (*Continuing the quotation.*)

> The night is still.
> I hear the whispering of stars.

BOTH. (*Complete the passage together.*)

> Under the dark blue sky,
> the warm earth slumbers on."

SOFIA. Give me your arm.

They stroll out together.

END OF SCENE

Carcass

PERETZ HIRSCHBEIN

Introduction and Notes

From his first serious play, Peretz Hirschbein (1881–1948) showed his concern with the suffering of the lower levels of society; for instance, *Miriam* is the sad story of a girl who is drawn into the terrible life of prostitution. (A translation by Joel Berkowitz and Jeremy Dauber appears in *Landmark Yiddish Plays*, published by State University of New York Press in 2006.) Plays aiming to reveal characters in deprived and miserable situations, often Jewish paupers who starved and coughed their lives away in damp cold cellars, were in Yiddish known (half-jocularly) as "cellar plays"; the young Hirschbein soon earned the nickname of "cellar poet." Most often, cellar plays concentrated on character and situation rather than plot, and therefore did not develop at greater length than one act. Hirschbein wrote a number of one-acters, in this vein and lighter as well.

Carcass demonstrates Hirschbein's participation in the theatrical currents of his time. In 1888, Andre Antoine, pioneer of naturalism, had hung bloody, dripping carcasses onstage for his production of *The Butchers*; in 1902, Gorki's *Lower Depths* opened—and was presented almost immediately in Yiddish translation. But Hirschbein wrote a body of plays of many types, experimenting with more than one avant-garde style. Moreover, he founded the first Yiddish art theater. Founded in Odessa in 1908, the Hirschbein Troupe lasted only two years—not bad for an adventurous company in any language—but was definitely influential. It presented new plays by new Yiddish writers and developed a cadre of serious young actors, integrating Yiddish theater into the larger art world.

Hirschbein wrote *Carcass* in 1905, in Hebrew, and then rewrote it in Yiddish. In this transition, he was part of a larger movement, encouraged by I. L. Peretz, of young writers casting their lot with the newborn modern Yiddish literature. Later, like many other Yiddish writers, he tried a wide variety of styles and forms. (For his biography, see the notes in this volume to *Between Day and Night*, which shows a startlingly different sensibility and intention.)

    I added some words and phrases (*my son, married a drunk*) to clarify relationships between the characters. Similarly, although Avrush talks a lot about his daughter—who was adopted in childhood by people of a higher class and now disdains him—I took out those references because they seemed confusing, too much backstory to explicate. In place of his laments for his beautiful lost daughter and Brayne's brutal replies, I substituted his laments for the beautiful horses he once trained—laments that he actually makes elsewhere in the play.

    Like English, Yiddish integrates elements from several distinct language streams. In the case of Yiddish, the dominant elements are German, Hebrew, and Slavic languages. In this scene, many of the curses are Hebrew words: *carcass, plague, misery, pig, bastard, robber, murderer*. Their unself-conscious use is analogous to the English assimilation of the word *kindergarten* from German and *chic* from French. The *Garden of Eden* is naturally also Hebrew.

    Also, like English, there are many types and levels of Yiddish, differentiated by geographical region, by social class, and by how formal the occasion is or how much the speaker respects the person spoken to. There is lingo specific to a trade, such as musicians, street criminals, or Alsatian horse traders. One variable lies in the proportions of Slavic or other local languages and of Hebrew. These characters speak a rough street Yiddish.

    As in many other European languages, Yiddish verbs distinguish between formal and informal address. Reyzl uses the formal *ir* (you) to Mendl—a deliberate distancing—while he, loving her, replies with *du* (more intimate, or for a child).

    In 2013 an English-language version by Ellen Perecman and Mark Altman was produced by Ellen Perecman's New Worlds Theatre Project at HERE Arts Center in New York.

The play ends when Mendl, maddened by Reyzl's rejection of him and his sense of himself as uneducated, doomed to nothing better than the despised work of flaying hides, starts to flay himself.

Carcass

PERETZ HIRSCHBEIN

1924

(from act 1)

Characters

AVRUSH	An old drunk who used to be a respected trainer of aristocrats' horses.
MENDL	Avrush's son by a first marriage, strong but inarticulate, who lives by flaying carcasses for their hides; he stinks of meat and blood.
BRAYNE	Avrush's second wife, a ragpicker, harsh and angry.
REYZL	Her daughter by her first marriage, who's been flirting with a local thug called Berl the Pig.
PLACE	Cellar in a big Polish city.
TIME	Early twentieth century.

Filthy, impoverished basement room. Avrush lies on a pallet, half-drunk or hallucinating. Door leads to hallway.

BRAYNE. Who's out there?

MENDL. (*Rushes in, closes door behind him. Carries a big sack on his back.*) That bastard. Berl the Pig! I'll get him. He practically strangled me.

BRAYNE. Nice convenient place for a fight. Scared me to death.

AVRUSH. Mendl?

MENDL. Yes, Mendl. So what?

AVRUSH. Mendl, my son. Mendl.

MENDL. What?

BRAYNE. Give him something for a little brandy.

MENDL. If I want to give him, I'll give him, and I don't need to ask permission from a stepmother.

BRAYNE. You can bang your heads on the wall, both of you, father and son, what do I care. I went and married a drunk.

AVRUSH. (*Goes to sack, opens it.*) A hide! You skinned it yourself?

REYZL. He dragged another carcass into the house.

AVRUSH. You're a carcass yourself. This is a good five rubles, right here.

REYZL. Soon he'll drag a whole dead horse into the house. (*To Brayne.*) I told you not to marry the drunk.

MENDL. An aristocrat. My aristocrat. (*To Avrush.*) Married a queen, got her daughter the princess. Barefoot princess.

BRAYNE. (*To Reyzl.*) What was Berl the Pig doing here?

REYZL. I don't know.

BRAYNE. I will bury you alive. You hear me, bastard?

REYZL. Give me back my shoes.

BRAYNE. I'll take your shirt, too, and lock you in the house. I'll go away and lock you in the house. You're gonna know I'm your mother. Your father's dead and buried, and I'll take care of you.

MENDL. Reyzl! I'll buy you shoes. You want? Tell me.

BRAYNE. And I'll buy you misery, all of you. Went and married a drunk.

MENDL. She thinks anyone's afraid of her. Ha! (*Drags his sack over to Avrush and opens it.*) Look, Dad, what a hide.

REYZL. (*Runs over, pushes Mendl away.*) Put it back, I'm telling you. I'm gonna smash your head. Just try taking it out.

AVRUSH. Slut.

MENDL. Get out of here, you barefoot bitch.

AVRUSH. Forget it, son. She's no better than her mother. This is a good five rubles right here.

Reyzl keeps cursing.

MENDL. (*Closes the sack.*) Oh so ladylike. Your highness. This hide is cleaner than you and your mother put together. (*Pause. Mendl sits in corner, upset.*)

AVRUSH. Oh my beauties, my horses. Driven out of the Garden of Eden, driven out. They must miss me. How I took care of them, how they loved me. Don't they miss me?

Mendl doesn't answer.

Hah? Mendl?

MENDL. Leave me alone.

Each person by himself in a corner. Avrush stands up and lowers the flame in the lamp.

BRAYNE. The Garden of Eden in a stable, you drunk. Isn't it dark enough in this house already? What are you doing? Why are you turning the lamp down?

AVRUSH. We're not doing anything anyway.

BRAYNE. Save money on brandy, not on light. Worthless!

AVRUSH. (*Returns to his place muttering.*) Robber. Murderer. Robber.

BRAYNE. And I'm supposed to feed you? Food for worms, that's you. (*Wanders around the room as if looking for something.*) I don't know what I was going to do. (*Remains standing in the middle of the room.*)

Reyzl exits. Brayne throws herself at the door after her.

Where are you going, you lowlife?

By now Reyzl is out of the door.

MENDL. (*After a while, to Brayne.*) You think I'm afraid of you? That's what you think? What are you to me? Nothing. I just want to ask you one thing, just one thing.

AVRUSH. Don't bother with her, my child.

BRAYNE. You pig, you slobbering pig.

MENDL. I'm not afraid of her anymore. I just want to ask her one thing, just one thing: why does she hit Reyzl? Why? A grown girl, and she hits her? She took away her shoes, a mother does that? If you were my mother, I would strangle you. Now you can bang your head against the wall ten times a day. But Reyzl, tell me, why do you hit Reyzl? Tell me.

BRAYNE. (*Frightened.*) Reyzl?

MENDL. (*With crazy agitation.*) I'm going to tell Reyzl—I'm going to tell her that I won't let you hurt her. I won't let you. I'll smash your head. I'll buy her shoes. I'll buy them with my money. And we're going to knock your teeth out. Tell me, why do you hit Reyzl? Why?

AVRUSH. Driven out of the Garden of Eden, driven out. My beauties. Elegant. Beautiful.

BRAYNE. Drunk. They kicked you out of the stables. You were bad for the horses.

AVRUSH. No. They loved me, my beauties. They loved me.

BRAYNE. You poor old drunk. Couldn't feed them a carrot.

AVRUSH. Like in a dream, everything gone. Like a dream.

Reyzl enters, stands in middle of room, looks around where to sit. Mendl looks at her feet.

MENDL. Reyzl?

BRAYNE. What about Reyzl? What's Reyzl to you?

REYZL. (*Confused.*) What do you want from me? What do you want?

MENDL. (*Gets up.*) Come to me, Reyzl, don't be scared, what's the matter?

AVRUSH. Let her alone, she's no good.

BRAYNE. (*Screams.*) You carcass!

MENDL. (*Confused by Brayne's scream.*) Reyzl! Listen, she isn't your mother, I'm telling you. I'm telling you, she'll kill you yet, Reyzl. Spit in her face, Reyzl, spit. I'll buy you shoes, me, Reyzl. I won't let her hit you. You'll see, Reyzl. Spit in her face. (*Pulls at her sleeve.*)

REYZL. (*Moves away.*) What do you want?

BRAYNE. Carcass! Die! Out of my house, carcass! (*Picks up the sack with the hide and drags it to the door.*) Out of here, together with your corpse. Out! (*Taps her feet.*)

Mendl tears the sack from her.

BRAYNE. (*To Avrush.*) You, get out of here with your son the carcass.

MENDL. (*Opens the sack.*) I'll show you. I'll show you who Mendl is. I'll show you what this is. (*Wants to take the hide out of the sack.*) Here in the middle of the house.

REYZL. Close the sack. Close it, I'm telling you.

MENDL. (*Throws the sack, mutters something, looks pityingly at Reyzl.*) Reyzl, do what I'm telling you, she is not your mother, she isn't. Spit in her face. Knock out her teeth. Tomorrow I'll buy you shoes—shoes for three rubles I'll buy you. And you'll go where you want. Here's money, Reyzl. (*Searches in his pockets feverishly.*)

REYZL. (*Confused. Looks at Mendl resentfully.*) What do you want from me. What am I doing to you? (*Weeps.*) What do you have against me?

AVRUSH. From Eden, driven out.

MENDL. Spit in her face. (*Spits at Brayne.*)

BRAYNE. (*Throws herself at Reyzl, starts hitting her on the head with both fists.*) I am her mother. I am a mother. I am allowed to hit. I am allowed. I am allowed.

REYZL. Save me!

Mendl runs to her. General scuffle.

BRAYNE. (*Hitting.*) I am a mother. I am a mother. Ha. Ha! Ha!

Avrush looks on, his mouth open and hands outspread.

END OF SCENE

Between Day and Night

PERETZ HIRSCHBEIN

Introduction and Notes

This play is part of the current of symbolism that fascinated the European avant-garde in the early twentieth century. Some examples include August Strindberg's *Ghost Sonata* (1907) and William Butler Yeats's *At the Hawk's Well* (1916). Unlike typical symbolist pieces, however, which primarily wield emotionally charged abstractions, this play combines a floating poeticized tone and vocabulary with real-world references and a political idea. Ellen Perecman, producer of the New Worlds Theatre Project that presented this play in English in 2009, found and translated this relevant passage from Hirschbein's memoirs:

> The post-natal pain that followed the revolution of 1905 did not leave me in a very good mood. In the end, "spring" became a long autumn for me. The notion of a "sunrise" promised by the Revolution evaporated, I was overcome with a feeling of being in a twilight between day and night, and the days of my life were thrown into anxious sadness.*

The play opens in a mysterious house in the woods, where a passionate philosopher lives with his father, his little daughter, and an older daughter, the young woman Tomer. His long-lost brother Heyman suddenly appears. Heyman seems to have a mysteriously evil past; his brother and father are afraid of him. At the end of this scene, Tomer runs off to carry to the world her father's mystical message of universal love. However, at the play's final curtain, Heyman carries in Tomer's corpse, explaining that she was trampled to death and that her father sent her to die for false notions.

In order for this scene to stand alone, I rearranged speeches and actually added several that are spoken elsewhere in the play. I also eliminated most references to Tomer's father: in the original, Tomer praises him and Heyman scorns him, but that is confusing and unnecessary when presenting only the one scene.

Hirschbein, whose father was a miller, grew up in an isolated household in the woods, very attached to his spiritual mother and intensely aware of nature around him and all its mystical beauties. He was typical of Yiddish playwrights in that he was raised in a small town in Eastern Europe and received a traditional Jewish education. He left home, starved, studied Talmud and increasingly secular literature in several languages, and lived by tutoring—altogether a very common early biography for Yiddish writers. Also typical was that he wrote his first play and poems in Hebrew but, encouraged by Isaac Leib Peretz, switched to Yiddish. He soon made a name for himself, even founding the first Yiddish art theater. His range of subjects, forms, and styles was enormous. His best-known play is *Green Fields*, a charming pastoral romance. He wrote several more plays in that vein as well as symbolist plays, naturalist plays, and one-acters that are both touching and folky. A great traveler, he recorded his travels, and an account of his childhood, in vivid memoirs. Hirschbein lived his last years in California, where he loved to take long walks in woods and fields.

An English-language version of this play by Ellen Perecman and Mark Altman was produced by Ellen Perecman's New Worlds Theatre Project in New York in 2009, under the title *Dammerung*.

Between Day and Night

PERETZ HIRSCHBEIN

1906?

(from act 3)

Characters

TOMER	A passionate young woman.
HEYMAN	Her mysterious uncle, recently returned to his family and their home deep in the forest.
PLACE	Outside a little house in the woods in Eastern Europe.
TIME	Early twentieth century.

Tomer comes out of the house and goes toward the forest. Heyman comes out of the forest and blocks her path. She tries to pass.

HEYMAN. Wait. Don't hurry off.

TOMER. Let me go, Uncle, let me go.

HEYMAN. Go where?

TOMER. The moment has arrived. I take on my father's mission, the mission my soul has yearned for. Everything must happen tonight. I can wait no longer.

I must run, and fall at the feet of all humanity, and beg them, weeping, "Throw off your ancient war between brothers." I will awaken in them an ocean of love and mercy. I am ready to thrust forth my breast so they may pierce it with spears—but no, that will never be. They will not harm the heart that brings them love. Come with me, come. Come help me bring the earth a beautiful new dawn.

HEYMAN. Your father's foolish ideas. My foolish brother. The people of the earth will drown in their own blood. The last survivor will eat his own flesh out of bestial hunger and will drink his own blood with devilish thirst.

TOMER. Is it because God has punished them that people walk around with blood in their eyes, angry as wild animals? I am ready to die for them. I will spread my arms wide. I will run amid all the people. I will call out with all my strength, "Have mercy on one another, my brothers and sisters." One has only to remind them.

HEYMAN. My child, you, together with your tears, won't bring that beautiful new dawn. Even a thousand of your sisters all weeping together—nothing will rise from them but a sorrow-chorus, an ugly death rattle.

TOMER. How hard your heart is, how hard and evil. Let me go. I am afraid of you. In your eyes burns a wildfire. I am afraid of it.

HEYMAN. I have come to save your life, because you were raised in the same nest where I spent my youth. Come with me.

TOMER. I hate you like the angry snake. Your eyes burn like an angry snake.

HEYMAN. My eyes are lit by my heart, and my heart is lit by the sun, which rises daily on the peaks of the highest mountains where clouds never reach.

TOMER. But don't you understand what is going on among the people? Their souls struggle. They lack love, they lack mercy. One must remind them. Come with me, and love and mercy will embrace the whole world. Listen to me. People will become like angels.

HEYMAN. Love and mercy! (*Laughs.*) "Mercy." Worms thought that up. As they lay trampled underfoot, with tears in their eyes, they begged, "Mercy, mercy." False prophets have dirtied the earth. They have dragged down to earth the soul of humanity that yearned toward heaven. False prophets will bury your pure soul in earthly filth. Come, I'll tear you away from this place so that your soul can be purified anew.

TOMER. My father knows better. The new dawn that will light the world with love and mercy is already upon us.

HEYMAN. My child, it won't be blind moles with claws that bring on the new dawn. People will create that dawn, human beings lifted to the heavens by pride. And their hearts will storm with yearnings. (*Laughs.*) Worms drag themselves around searching for rays from suns extinguished long ago. They pick fallen stars out of the mud. That dawn will be lit by a sun that life itself created, a sun created by the human heart alone.

TOMER. Look how beautiful the sunset is tonight.

HEYMAN. The rays search for their young queen. They want to protect her from the evil, wild night that comes ever closer.

TOMER. Have mercy on me. Let me do my father's will. Let me go to unhappy humanity. Newborn, naked fledglings, they lie in their cradles and wail. They call for their mama, "Mama, Mama," they scream. They stumble along, begging for love and mercy, wandering without mama and papa. Orphans, a whole world of orphans. People, dear ones, I run to you. Soon, soon I am coming. I bring you my heart, full of love, yearning for love. Let go of me, let go of me. I've overslept. I'm late. There they are waiting for my love. There is still time. I am coming to you. I am hurrying. (*Runs into the forest.*)

HEYMAN. The night will go on and on. It is now between night and day. It will go on and on until the last poor soul is annihilated, is trampled by his brother like a disgusting worm. I will save her life against her will.

End of Scene

Mishke and Moshke; or, Europeans in America

(*Mishke and Moshke; or, The Greenhorns*)

JOSEPH LATEINER

Introduction and Notes

Yosef (Joseph) Lateiner (1853–1935) was one of the first professional Yiddish playwrights. He began his theatrical career as actor and prompter, soon started translating and "Yiddishizing" plays from Romanian and German, and eventually turned out hundreds of shows, many of which were very popular, though relatively few were published. His audiences particularly favored intensely dramatic melodramas and historical operettas.

The main plot of this play involves young lovers named Karl and Charlotta. Moshke is Karl's uncle. Mishke and Moshke, with their low comedy jokes and slapstick, function as comic subplot. Note that the romantic characters have higher-class European—specifically Germanic—names, and they also speak a higher-class, German-flavored Yiddish. By contrast, Mishke and Moshke have Jewish/Slavic names and their diction is vulgar to match. Nevertheless, the elderly clowning couple so captured the audience's affections that the play was known as *Mishke and Moshke*. The public's darling, comedian Zelig Mogulesco was a sensation as the old lady Mishke, holding out a skinny arm to be vaccinated. The play concludes, naturally, when the young lovers are united.

I edited this scene to cut out extraneous characters and, for the original puns and malapropisms, I substituted others that would be comprehensible in English. The short section of dialogue about digging down to America is excerpted and adapted from act 3 of Fishl Bimko's play *American Thievery* (or *America the Thief*), published in 1936. Bimko (1890–1965) wrote many stories and plays. One of his best-known plays is *Ganovim* (*Thieves*), published with a glossary of underworld slang in one of his many volumes of collected plays and stories.

Mishke and Moshke; or, Europeans in America
(*Mishke and Moshke; or, The Greenhorns*)

JOSEPH LATEINER

1896

(from act 2)

Characters

MISHKE and MOSHKE — Elderly couple from a village in Eastern Europe.

PLACE — Shipboard, en route to America.

TIME — End of the nineteenth century.

MISHKE. (*Leaning over deck rail, sick.*) A black year on Columbus. Moshke, I'm dying.

MOSHKE. Die, Mishke, die, and they'll throw you overboard to the cats. You're just seasick.

MISHKE. What do you mean: "sea sick"? I see you just fine—there's nothing wrong with my eyes, God forbid. What I see is, I see you thinking that when I die, you can marry some young girl. Wait, you bum. As many years as I don't die, that's how many years you should become a chandelier: hang by day and burn by night. I'm going to stay alive just to spite you. This is what happens when you trust a man. You couldn't pick out a real ship to spend our money that I slaved for, no, he had to have a kind of rocking horse. This is a ship? You march in and make them turn this rocking horse around and ride me back to Kishinev. March in and tell him, that one wearing the red pot on his head—

MOSHKE. The captain, you mean?

MISHKE. Yes, the one with the red cap on his head.

MOSHKE. The captain.

MISHKE. Kaplan, Goldberg, whatever his name is. Tell him I want to go home.

MOSHKE. Maybe you want them to fill in the ocean for you so you can just walk across?

MISHKE. Why not? When I was a little girl, they used to talk about building a bridge so you could ride the streetcar to America. But Moshke, if America is on the other side of the world, all you should really have to do is dig down to it. There was a man in Kishinev tried to dig to America from his cellar. He was sure that if he only kept digging, he'd get there in the end. But water kept flooding in.

MOSHKE. Couldn't he figure out some way to pump out the water?

MISHKE. The more he pumped, the more the water ran in. The whole town could have drowned. He had to fill in the hole.

MOSHKE. If it was as simple as that, anyone could get to America.

MISHKE. You wouldn't need papers from the consul.

MOSHKE. Or a ship.

MISHKE. Or Ellis Island.

MOSHKE. If a letter didn't come, let yourself down by rope to America: "Yankl, you owe me a letter." If the money didn't come, down on the rope to America.

MISHKE. With someone holding on to the end, of course.

MOSHKE. Naturally.

MISHKE. If at home America is underground, then when you're in America—

MOSHKE. (*Traditional inflection for Talmudic reasoning.*) —then in America, you're really in the cellar at home.

MISHKE. Yes, but it's over your head.

MOSHKE. For the ones who don't write letters, America is further than under the ground.

MISHKE. Help, Moshke, the ship is sinking. Why are all those people running around on the *drek*.

MOSHKE. The deck, in English it's deck. They're going to be inoculated.

MISHKE. Let them do it to the herring. I already was *immoculated* and *immeasle-ated* and shot.

MOSHKE. But America is a new land, and whoever comes to America is a new person and needs a new inoculation. When they say shot, it's shot. So come on.

MISHKE. Where?

MOSHKE. To get inoculated.

MISHKE. Moshke!

MOSHKE. No, no, that way, over there.

Chase, struggle.

Mishke dear, please, you see what this sign says?

MISHKE. Who can read that? It's written backwards.

MOSHKE. It says that anyone who refuses to be inoculated in the arm gets shot in the tongue.

MISHKE. A plague! What am I going to do?

MOSHKE. What will you do? You won't say a word. The doctor will walk in, roll up his sleeves, take out his little knife, and go *pik-pik*.

MISHKE. May you own a hundred houses, you and your captain and your doctor together, and in every house a hundred rooms, and in every room a hundred beds, and may you be shaken with fever from bed to bed and room to room and find no rest, every year that nobody gets near me with his *pik-pik*. And what are you going to do about it?

MOSHKE. I'm not going to do a thing about it. Only without your shot they won't let you into America. See how all the people are strolling around the deck. They've had their shots and they're already healthy.

Chorus sings happy song.

END OF SCENE

Khantshe in America

NAHUM RAKOV

Introduction

Nahum Rakov (1866–1928) left Lithuania in 1885 and lived in Denmark and London before arriving in the United States early in the twentieth century. By then he had started in theater as a prompter, but in America he went on to write over sixty very popular melodramas and operettas. Their titles give a taste: *The Women's Nation*; *Love and Hate*; *Forbidden Fruit*; *Hello, New York*. When plays with "green" (meaning "greenhorn," i.e., newly arrived in America) in the title were the craze for a while, Rakov wrote many, including *The Green Bachelor*, *Green Girl*, *Green Wife*, *Green Father*, and *Green Children*. The role of Khantshe was originally played by the box office favorite Bessie Thomashefsky.

The operetta included many catchy musical numbers, including a rousing suffragette anthem, by Joseph Rumshinsky (1881–1956). Rumshinsky's melodies were crucial to the success of many popular Yiddish shows. In 2017, the operetta *The Golden Bride*, book by Lateiner and score by Rumshinsky (restored by Ronald Robboy), was very successfully revived in New York, where it won two Drama Desk nominations. (That plot is even less realistic than *Khantshe*'s: a poor girl in a village in the old country discovers that she is an heiress, falls in love, finds her long-lost mother, goes to a costume ball, and lives happily ever after.)

The following scene puts together two scenes, much compressed, from act 1. In act 2, Khantshe disguises herself as a man and takes a job as chauffeur with the Goldhendler family, where she/he flirts with all the women in the household. Farcical complications ensue, but in the end, she gets her Isidore.

Khantshe in America

NAHUM RAKOV

WITH MUSIC BY JOSEPH RUMSHINSKY

1913

(from act 1)

Characters

KHANTSHE MOTELZON	Lively young woman.
GITL	Her friend and coworker at a paper box factory.
SAM	Elevator operator in love with Khantshe.
ISIDORE	Khantshe's fiancé.
KHANTSHE'S FATHER	Cheerful and lazy.
PLACE	Tenement apartment on the Lower East Side of New York City.
TIME	Early twentieth century.

KHANTSHE. (*Walking with Gitl into the kitchen of her family's tenement apartment, where her FATHER is sitting. To Gitl.*) The nerve of that clown! If you girls hadn't held me back, I'd have smacked him. Did you see him shake when you said, "If Khantshe goes, we all go"? Nobody steps on us like rags, not even the boss. We're women, not ducks, not geese, but women with our own will, with free thoughts and with women's rights. (*Yells out window.*) Long live women's rights!

FATHER. What are you doing home so early?

KHANTSHE. Don't ask, Papa, just yell, "Long live women's rights."

FATHER. You got the sack.

GITL. I'm going back to the picket line and keep the scabs from taking our jobs. (*Exits.*)

KHANTSHE. Maybe I won't go back to making paper boxes anyway. Maybe I'll just get married instead. You're scared you'll miss my few dollars? Never mind, my Isidore will give you your dollars. Papa, you should have seen how I poured a bucket of fresh pulp over the foreman's head. It dripped from his head into his mouth, from his mouth into his beard, from his beard down his neck.

FATHER. You're right. You're not going back.

KHANTSHE. What do you want? Should he say, "Khantshe, take your things and go to the devil" and I should keep quiet? Oh no, Khantshe does not keep quiet. (*Yells out the door.*) Women's rights forever!

SAM enters as she yells.

Papa, this is Sam, the elevator man at the factory. The boss sent you?

SAM. No, Miss Motelzon.

Father exits.

As soon as I took you down, I went straight to Mr. Goldhendler, and I quit.

KHANTSHE. Oh Sam, I don't want you to suffer.

SAM. I already have a better job, in the elevator in an apartment house on Riverside Drive. You understand I stayed in the factory only because you were there. If you're not there anymore, for me it's—And now that I have such a good job, I'm not afraid anymore to say—I can get you a job as a maid in the same building. And then together we can make a nice living.

KHANTSHE. And what should I do with the bridegroom I've got?

SAM. With who? With Isidore? I'll knock him down the stairs. He's no good.

KHANTSHE. Sam, not a word, you hear?

SAM. I don't care, you can knock me down the stairs and I'll still say— That is, I won't say anything bad, but—I'll say.

KHANTSHE. What will you say?

SAM. Isidore, so long as he was a little bookkeeper, he was all right. But as soon as Mr. Goldhendler made him a little private secretary, he—That is, I won't say anything bad about him. But I have to say that he is no good, a drinker, a card player, and he—He doesn't love you, he loves Miss Goldhendler, and she loves him too.

KHANTSHE. It's a lie.

SAM. I did an errand to Goldhendler's house. I went past the parlor, I saw how Frances sat at the piano playing "There Where Love Dwells." And he stood next to her, and he turned the pages. And he—

KHANTSHE. It's a lie. You get out of here, you hear?

SAM. Oh Miss Motelzon, Khantshe, I will make you happy, believe me. Until the baby we would take two rooms, that's enough, and if you don't want to be a maid you don't have to, I'll earn.

KHANTSHE. You shut up, you troublemaker. Look, he's coming. You'd better get out now.

SAM. Oh Miss Motelzon, Khantshe, I will make you happy.

Exits as ISIDORE enters. The two men meet briefly in doorway.

KHANTSHE. Isidore? Why stand so far away? Isidore, take me and squeeze me till I taste the taste of Eden. I've been longing for a kiss the way a drunk longs for a little brandy. Maybe you're jealous because you found the elevator boy here? Don't be silly, just come and give me a kiss. Well, I see that today it's all women's rights, and I have to be the first to step up and take what I want.

ISIDORE. Stop it, Khantshe.

KHANTSHE. You're upset by what happened at the factory. But I couldn't help it. "Take my things and go to the devil." If he'd spoken to me differently, I'd have acted differently. You should have seen him with the bucket of hot pulp on his head. What is the matter with you today?

ISIDORE. I came to discuss a serious matter.

KHANTSHE. Well, discuss.

ISIDORE. Lately I've been looking at my future and I've realized that I'm wasting time.

KHANTSHE. See that? I think so too.

ISIDORE. I'm sorry. You don't understand.

KHANTSHE. It's time to get married; that's what I want too.

ISIDORE. You don't understand, Khantshe. I want you to set me free.

KHANTSHE. Set you free?

ISIDORE. How would we end up? I am poor and you are poor. It makes no sense to get married just to be miserable together.

KHANTSHE. That's what you came to discuss? Oh, I understand what you came for. Here, take it. (*Throws him her ring.*)

ISIDORE. No, I'm not such a bad person. I understand that this is hard on you, and I want you to let me make you compensation.

KHANTSHE. Compensation?

ISIDORE. Yes. (*Putting money on the table.*) There you have—

KHANTSHE. Compensation? The rich Miss Goldhendler must have given it to you so you could buy the heart of a poor paper box maker. Did you tell her that when you arrived in America, alone, we took you in because you were from our village, and we gave you something to eat and drink? Did you tell her how the box maker made you your first American suit, behind her father's back? And now you give me money? Here, take your dirty compensation. Take it and go.

ISIDORE. Since you drive me away— (*Exits.*)

Father returns.

KHANTSHE. Papa, I've gotten the sack again. My boss fired me from the factory and now my bridegroom has fired me from being his bride.

GITL. (*Rushes back in.*) Khantshe, we've won, we've won the strike! We're picketing outside like this, out comes the boss and says we can all come back to work tomorrow. You too!

KHANTSHE. All right, good luck to you. You can go back to work. But I'm not going. I'm not making any more paper boxes. Now I'm going to build some wooden boxes and bury a few of those men who play with the hearts of poor working girls like us.

END OF SCENE

Riverside Drive

LEON KOBRIN

Introduction and Notes

Leon Kobrin (1872–1946) began writing in Russian, and in his long career wrote stories, novels, memoirs, and plays in various styles. He greatly admired Jacob Gordin, who in turn helped him become known. Kobrin's first big success was *Yankl Boyle; or, The Village Youth*, a highly colored drama about a "child of nature," a Jewish fisherman who lives mostly among Russians and loves a Russian peasant girl, though he fears the ghost of his disapproving father. Kobrin's realist play *Minna; or The Ruined Family from Downtown* was another of his big hits, as was *The East Side Ghetto*, dramatized from his own novel.

In this scene, the old couple Shloyme and Rivke have just arrived from their peasant village deep in Russia. They are virtually in rags, having escaped a pogrom in which they lost everything and traveled by primitive trains and steamship. They have come to live with their son, whom they haven't seen since he left for America at least twenty years before. Now he is successful, married to the American daughter of a cultured German-born rabbi. Their daughter-in-law, her family, and the grandchildren do not speak Yiddish, and their religious practice is modern liberalized Reform (associated with German culture), which is barely recognizable as Judaism to the pious old couple. But everyone resolves to make the old couple welcome. This scene from act 1 shows them at the end of their first day in America.

However, from act 2 we suspect that this family reunion will not work. The daughter-in-law finds the couple alien, stubborn, and ignorant; the three grandchildren (a child, an adolescent, and a marriageable girl) find them alien and scary. The old people long for a relationship with the grandchildren, feel patronized and humiliated by the daughter-in-law, and disapprove of her parents. The son is grieved but cannot make things right. In the end, despite the son's pleas, the old couple move out.

This play is written in three languages. The couple speak only Yiddish, and their son speaks Yiddish with them. The grandchildren, daughter-in-law, and her parents speak only English. An old worker whom the son hires to help the old people feel at home speaks an immigrant jumble of Yiddish mixed with so much English that it is incomprehensible to them. Naturally, the audience gets it all. (For uses of language on the Yiddish stage, see the introduction to *Homeless* in this volume.)

In 1931 Maurice Schwartz produced and starred in the play at his Yiddish Art Theater. In the cast were Joseph Buloff and Stella Adler. Schwartz then toured it internationally under the title *Nakhes fun kinder* (a common expression meaning the glowing contentment a parent feels from successful and loving children). It was very popular with amateur groups, for example, a South African group that put it on in 1947. It was published several times, most recently in 1952 in Kobrin's collected dramatic works. This scene, in a version of this translation, was part of a revue called *Vagabond Stars*, for which I wrote the book, Raphael Crystal the music, and Alan Poul the lyrics. It opened at the Berkshire Theatre Festival in 1978 and then ran at the Jewish Repertory Theatre in New York City, directed by Ran Avni.

Baron Ginsberg and Brodsky were very rich Jews, often used (like Rockefeller) as emblematic of great wealth.

Blessings to end Sabbath. This ceremony, called *havdala*, is described in notes to *Mirele Efros* and *Yankl the Blacksmith* earlier in this volume.

Riverside Drive

LEON KOBRIN

1930

(from the end of act 1)

Characters

RIVKE and SHLOYME	An elderly pious couple, who arrived only that day from a rural village deep in Russia.
PLACE	An apartment on Riverside Drive in New York City.
TIME	1931.

Bedroom of luxurious apartment. Twin beds. Lamp or overhead light. Shloyme has a beard and earlocks; Rivke's head is covered with a kerchief or snood the whole time, and she will sleep in it. Their clothes are poor, old-fashioned, and old country. They are getting into bed.

RIVKE. So, what do you think, Shloyme?

SHLOYME. What do I think about what?

RIVKE. A palace, ha?

SHLOYME. Ay, ay, what then? A palace.

RIVKE. Who, would you say, at home, lives in a house like this?

SHLOYME. At home? Maybe Baron Ginsburg, maybe Brodsky. Maybe the czar himself.

RIVKE. I somehow can't believe it, Shloyme.

SHLOYME. What can't you believe?

RIVKE. That it's true. After the pogrom, after the misery on the ship.

SHLOYME. Ay, ay, ay, a paradise.

RIVKE. Will you know how to make it dark, Shloyme?

SHLOYME. Why ask such stupid questions? The same push as on the ship.

RIVKE. So, give it a push, Shloyme.

SHLOYME. Wait a little while longer. I want to take another look at the light. A whole different kind of electricity from at home. Like a red cloud hovering over us. And man thought these wonders out, with his own intelligence!

RIVKE. Intelligence comes from God, Shloyme. Shloyme? Shloyme, are you asleep?

SHLOYME. No.

RIVKE. Our daughter-in-law, Shloyme, what do you think, ha?

SHLOYME. What?

RIVKE. Such an aristocrat, and she helped me bathe with her own hands.

SHLOYME. She is a diamond, and from a very good family too, an American rabbi's daughter.

RIVKE. And she sprayed me with a sort of spices.

SHLOYME. With spices even?

RIVKE. They were fragrant, a pleasure. In fact, when I put my hand near my nose I can still smell them. Here, smell, if you're not too lazy.

SHLOYME. (*Gets out of his bed and goes to her bed to smell.*) It's true. It smells just like spices for the blessings to end Sabbath. (*Returns to bed.*)

RIVKE. Oh, it's not bad at all to come to a rich son. How about the grandchildren, Shloyme, what do you think?

SHLOYME. Aristocratic children, may they be healthy.

RIVKE. Please God, they should only keep growing so beautiful and bright a hundred twenty years.

SHLOYME. Amen. Only it hurts that we don't understand them. Hodl— (*Corrects himself from Yiddish name to English.*) Adele is mute for us. Mordkhele— (*Again corrects himself.*) Mortimer is mute. Little Tatele—

This time Rivke corrects him: Tede.

Teddy is mute. Even our daughter-in-law is mute. English!

RIVKE. Talk and talk, to our daughter-in-law and to them, and it's like talking to the wall.

SHLOYME. It's a good thing our Hershl still understands Yiddish after all these years in America.

RIVKE. It is kosher here, though, isn't it, Shloyme?

SHLOYME. What do you mean, silly? She said to us herself: "kosher." We heard her.

RIVKE. That's true, she said that.

SHLOYME. A rabbi's daughter would not deceive us.

RIVKE. God forbid.

Pause.

SHLOYME. You know, Rivke, they are not going to stay mute for me. I used to have a good head. I am going to get hold of this American language. Starting tomorrow. And you'll see—Are you asleep? (*Turns out light.*) Ay, ay, ay. (*Murmurs prayers.*)

END OF SCENE

The 200,000

(*The Big Prize, The Big Lottery, The Jackpot*)

SHOLEM ALEICHEM

Introduction and Notes

Under its various titles, *The 200,000* has played in Yiddish theaters all over the world. The Moscow Yiddish Art Theatre's production of this play, as well as of Sholem Aleichem's *Tevye the Dairyman*, kept going even during the dark Stalin years, when an affectionate portrayal of prerevolutionary bourgeois Jewish society was dangerous. It helped that the story emphasizes the evils of capitalism and glorifies love and honest labor above money, and the working class above the rich. In the 1940s and '50s, when attachment to Jewish culture could get a person sent to Siberia, Sholem Aleichem's play kept playing in Moscow, to packed houses, and Jews who passed the star, Shlomo Mikhoels, in the street would recognize him and might greet him with "Hello, Comrade Shimele!"

In greeting Shlomo Mikhoels as Shimele, his admirers were not only applauding the most famous Shimele in the world, they were greeting "God's plain Jew"—the character Shimele himself—and the beloved, beleaguered culture he represented. Mikhoels was a great actor—in addition to roles in classical and newly written Yiddish plays, he won international recognition for his portrayal of King Lear—but perhaps his greatest role was as head of the Moscow Yiddish Art Theatre. Eventually, during the 1940s, he became the face of Soviet Jewry and de facto leader of the Soviet Jewish community. Not long after 1948, when his bloody body was found in the snow, the theater's doors were locked. Binyomin Zuskin, the company's other major star, was tortured and then executed on August 12, 1952, together with another twelve of the surviving great figures in Soviet Yiddish culture; that date is still solemnly commemorated annually as the Night of the Murdered Poets.

The 200,000 shines in a variety of approaches. From its founding in 1923, the Moscow Yiddish Art Theatre's performance style was balletic, robotic, nonrealistic. Makeup, costume, scenery, and movement made the characters into cartoonlike emblems of their social roles. Eventually, Soviet pressure on artists, in all of the arts, to reject formalism, expressionism, nationalism, and pessimism—now declared to be alien to proletarian culture—and to embrace Soviet realism, changed all that. Outside the Soviet, the play has been a perennial favorite, lending itself primarily to brisk realism and broad comedy. A production, with music added, and with Joseph Buloff in the cast, filled a Broadway theater in 1973. The most recent production that I know of was the Troïm-Teater's in Paris, Lyon, and Metz in 2012.

By 1915, when Sholem Yankev Rabinovitsh (1859–1916) wrote this play, he was already a famous writer. Under his facetious pseudonym Sholem Aleichem, which means literally "Peace upon you" but is a common greeting as ordinary as hello (which is why Eti-Meni finds it laughable), he wrote many novels, stories, and vignettes. Like very many of his contemporaries, he began his career writing in Hebrew, but switched to the newly developing Yiddish literary language. In addition to *Tevye the Dairyman* (dramatized from a collection of Sholem Aleichem's stories, as was the musical *Fiddler on the Roof* a generation later), his other best-known play was *Hard to Be a Jew* (*The Bloody Joke*), 1914. He himself adapted that play from his own novel, in which a young Russian aristocrat and his Jewish friend trade identities, with painful legal and romantic repercussions. *People*, or *Staff*, is a short play that we would now describe as "upstairs/downstairs": a young maidservant in a prosperous Jewish household is seduced and ruined; the other servants sympathize but the employers do not. This play was in the initial repertory of the very first Yiddish art theater, established by Peretz Hirschbein in Odessa in 1908, featuring the very young Jacob Ben-Ami as a sad, elderly servant. In 2011, the New Yiddish Rep created a comedy, *Agents*, from Sholem Aleichem's play plus several of his short stories. Sholem Aleichem's many marvelous monologues are actually little dramas published as short stories; Rafael Goldvaser with his LufTeater, based in Strasbourg, currently performs Sholem Aleichem monologues as a moving and elegant one-man show.

This play begins in Shimele Soroker's tailor shop. His two hardworking young apprentices, dear friends, are both in love with his daughter Beylke. But when Shimele wins the lottery, rich suitors pursue her. There are complications, and Beylke even runs away from home to escape the cold-hearted aristocratic society she is now supposed to enter, but at the end of the play, the swindlers relieve her father of all the money. Now Beylke is a poor tailor's daughter again. She is happy to marry the apprentice she has loved all along, and Shimele is actually more comfortable back home with his "shears and iron," to cut and stitch among "God's own plain people."

"Shears and iron" and "God's own plain people" are Shimele's beloved catchphrases. I am not entirely satisfied with my translation of either one. "Shears and iron" are weighty, physical, images that suit him. But they are not as strong in English, and at first hearing may not even call to mind a tailor. So instead of a literal translation, I substituted "cut and stitch." And what I translated as "God's own plain people" is a single word, *amkho* (actually a Hebrew word whose literal meaning is simply "your—i.e., God's—people"). But that is extra syllables, and a director might consider shortening it to "God's own." In direct contrast to honest, working-class *amkho* are the phony, fancy Russian names the family go by when they are rich, and also the honorific Herr, reflecting the attitude that German is higher-class than Yiddish.

I edited this scene by cutting out a number of characters, such as a suitor for Beylke, who keep interrupting Shimele's business with the swindlers.

The 200,000

(The Big Prize, The Big Lottery, The Jackpot)

SHOLEM ALEICHEM

1922

(from act 2)

Characters

SHIMELE SOROKER	Good-hearted tailor who has just won the lottery, in his forties or fifties.
ETI-MENI	Shimele's wife, as simple as he but no dope.
YOKHEVED	Shimele and Eti-Meni's maidservant.
VIGDORTSHUK	Hustler, former theater fiddler, now in the business of showing silent movies.
RUBINTSHIK	Hustler, former wig-maker, now in the business of showing silent movies.
PLACE	Russian city.
TIME	Early twentieth century.

Richly overdecorated parlor with a sofa, a writing desk, an iron strongbox. SHIMELE and ETI-MENI are wearing richly overdecorated clothes. She is covered with jewelry.

ETI-MENI SOROKER. Shimen. Shimen?

He is reading, doesn't hear.

Shimen! Shimen?

SHIMELE SOROKER. (*Tears himself from his book, imitates her.*) "Shimen. Shimen." Semyon Makarevitsh, not Shimen.

ETI-MENI. Semyon Makarevitsh, what time is it on your gold watch?

SHIMELE. (*Takes out watch.*) Eleven forty-five. Why?

ETI-MENI. Just asking. Three weeks ago, at this hour, we still didn't know our lottery ticket would win the big prize. (*Cracks her knuckles, admires her reflection in her diamond rings.*) Shimen! Shimen?

SHIMELE. Again Shimen? You've got the memory of a cat. How many times a day do I have to knock it into your head: Semyon Makarevitsh, Semyon Makarevitsh.

ETI-MENI. Excuse me, Semyon Makarevitsh. What are you doing?

SHIMELE. You see yourself I'm reading.

ETI-MENI. I see you're reading. I'm asking what you're reading.

SHIMELE. And if I tell you, will you know? I'm reading a story, that's what I'm reading.

ETI-MENI. What kind of a story are you reading?

SHIMELE. Not exactly a story, a kind of a description, a—a—critique. And let me alone. (*Can't tear himself away from his book.*)

ETI-MENI. Looks like you got up on the wrong side of the bed today. You're so mad, I'm afraid that you're reading and don't even know what you're reading.

SHIMELE. You can be perfectly sure that I do too know what I'm reading. I am reading a critique by this clown who makes fun of the whole world. Calls himself Sholem Aleichem.

ETI-MENI. Sholem Aleichem. Well, when there's nothing else to do, I guess that counts as work. What does he have against the world?

SHIMELE. Against the world he has nothing. But here he's describing some tailor, who used to be a pauper seven times over and suddenly goes and gets rich.

ETI-MENI. Well, and then what happens?

SHIMELE. And then nothing. He clowns around about the tailor and his wife. A real devil, that Sholem Aleichem, a regular guy.

ETI-MENI. My sorrows on his head. What does he have against the wife?

SHIMELE. You can sprain yourself laughing at what he makes of them both. But her, the tailor's wife, the devil makes her a real dummy.

ETI-MENI. A plague on him. Tfoo. I wouldn't hold such a nasty thing in my hands. And besides, what kind of business is this—a grown man sits down in the middle of the day and reads a little book, just like Sabbath afternoon after dinner. And sways over it like he's praying!

SHIMELE. So what? I'm going crazy. I've got to have something to do. I am—I was—a tailor, I'm in the habit of working.

ETI-MENI. You've worked enough. Let your enemies work instead. (*Pause.*) Shimen. Tfoo, I mean Semyon Makarevitsh. Where are we going this evening?

SHIMELE. Maybe you'd like to go to the three-ater?

ETI-MENI. Three-ater—fooey. (*Yawning.*) It's ridiculous. I don't understand a word. If they would play in Yiddish, at least. Let's better go to the luminations.

SHIMELE. You mean the cinematograph? Wait a while, as soon as I make my business deal with the film company, then we'll go, and go every night, and go for free without paying a groshn.

ETI-MENI. You won't get mad? I've got something to say.

SHIMELE. Me mad? Am I mad so very often? If it's something reasonable, go ahead and say it.

ETI-MENI. I don't like the company with the two crooks that you're company-ing with.

SHIMELE. Have you ever met them, the ones you're calling crooks?

ETI-MENI. It's just because I don't know them is the reason that I'm afraid they'll fool you.

SHIMELE. Me? Fool me? Garbage! No one deceives me. I'm making a good contract with them. I've got them nailed down good. Twenty-two clauses. Strong like a tailor's shears and iron.

ETI-MENI. Twenty-two clauses? And at the twenty-third they'll take all your money, by the handful.

SHIMELE. Bite your tongue. Listen to what you're saying. Do you even know what you're saying?

ETI-MENI. That is exactly the trouble with you, that nobody can talk to you. Right away you get angry.

SHIMELE. Eti-Meni, don't drive me out of my mind. (*Walking back and forth.*) You're forgetting who you're talking to. You think you're talking to Shimele the tailor. You forget that I'm no longer a plain man. No more shears and iron. No more cut and stitch. Today I am Semyon Makarevitsh Soroker, one of the biggest, if not the biggest, aristocrat in this town. (*No longer angry.*) Go listen to what they say about me. And the people who come to see me. And the business deals they offer me. Plain good people! God's own plain people!

ETI-MENI. For me you are the same as you always were.

SHIMELE. That is exactly the trouble. You ought to have a little more respect.

ETI-MENI. Soon you'll want me to take my hat off in your presence.

SHIMELE. (*Waves her away.*) What's the use of talking to you? (*Pause.*) Where is Beylke, I mean Izabeletshke?

ETI-MENI. What do you need Beylke for, I mean Izabeletshke?

SHIMELE. I'm her father. And I want her to read the mail.

ETI-MENI. Mail again? More mail?

SHIMELE. And how. (*Shows her the heap of unopened letters on his desk.*)

ETI-MENI. Important letters. Naturally, from a Jew that they drove out of his village with his wife and children, and from a widow whose husband hanged himself, or from a girl who wants to get married but doesn't have a dowry—

SHIMELE. Well, it's really a shame about her, that girl.

ETI-MENI. So in other words, you have to look out for the whole world?

SHIMELE. As far as I can.

ETI-MENI. And that's why God gave you the big prize?

SHIMELE. Why else? So we could eat soup and kasha?

ETI-MENI. How long can you keep it up?

SHIMELE. Silly, the deal with the film company will take care of everything. The whole town envies me. It will probably come to a half million or more. But what do you understand about millions?

ETI-MENI. It's nice that you understand. Because you, after all, grew up among millionaires.

SHIMELE. All the same, you know . . . (*Sits back down in his place, shakes himself. Back into his book. Pause.*) Eti-Meni. (*In half a minute again, louder.*) Eti-Meni.

ETI-MENI. Since when am I Eti-Meni to you? He's got to be called Semyon Makarevitsh, and I'm still only (*Imitates him.*) "Eti-Meni. Eti-Meni."

SHIMELE. (*Crestfallen.*) True is true. I'm sorry. I totally forgot that now you're called Ernestina Yefimevne.

ETI-MENI. And you say I have a cat's brain.

SHIMELE. You're right. I beg your pardon. Do you know what I wish you would give me, Ernestina Yefimevne?

ETI-MENI. Well let's hear what you wish I would give you, Semyon Makarevitsh.

SHIMELE. (*With a pathetic expression.*) A little bit of preserves.

ETI-MENI. Now all of a sudden he wants preserves. (*Yells at the top of her voice.*) Maid!

YOCHEVED. (*Enters.*) Are you calling me?

ETI-MENI. Who do you think I was calling—the rabbi?

YOCHEVED. That's the only name I've got is Maid?

ETI-MENI. What's the matter with Maid if you're a maid? (*Gives her keys.*) Bring the head of the household some preserves from the tub that's covered with a shawl and tied around with a kerchief.

YOCHEVED. How much should I bring?

ETI-MENI. You said you worked for rich people. You must know how much preserves a rich man eats.

YOCHEVED. There are all kinds of rich people. There's the rich man who eats like a little bird. And there are, if you'll excuse me, rich pigs who, no matter how much they eat, it's never enough. (*Stops in doorway.*) My name is Yocheved.

ETI-MENI. Yocheved? Good thing you told me. Yocheved, go get the preserves, Yocheved.

YOCHEVED. The little big shots are waiting in the front room.

SHIMELE. Which little big shots?

YOCHEVED. From the three-ater.

SHIMELE. (*Puts down book.*) Vigdortshuk and Rubintshik? My partners in the film company? Why don't they come in?

YOCHEVED. Because I didn't let them in.

SHIMELE. What do you mean, you didn't let them in?

YOCHEVED. That's the way the rich do it. When somebody comes, if he's dressed poorly, you give it to him good and you throw him out. And if he's well dressed, first you have to let the people know. And after that, if they say to let him in, you let him in.

SHIMELE. (*Silent. To wife.*) Ernestina Yefimevne, what do you say to that?

YOCHEVED. So what should I tell them?

SHIMELE. Who?

YOCHEVED. The big shots.

SHIMELE. Don't tell them anything. Send them in here.

YOCHEVED. (*On her way out.*) Next time you want to call me, my name is Yocheved.

In come VIGDORTSHUK and RUBINTSHIK. Dressed artistically, shaven artistically, top hats in hand, wearing gloves and artistic neckties.

SHIMELE. Here are welcome guests. Have you brought the contract all written out?

ETI-MENI. That girl is in the kitchen eating up the preserves. (*Exits.*)

SHIMELE. Let me look at the contract. That is, my daughter will look at it. At writing, I'm just beginning Hebrew school. But God blessed me with a daughter: intelligent, my entire bookkeeper, legal advisor, everything. Reads and writes and figures like water.

Mr. Vigdortshuk sir, Mr. Rubintshik sir, try these cigarettes. These are some cigarettes. (*He hands around cigarettes in a silver box. They take with two fingers.*) So where were we? Yes, tell me, my dear Vigdortshuk, my dear Rubintshik, I want to ask you, how comes it that two young people like yourselves—excuse me for speaking so plainly—how comes it that you know how to do a golden business, like films?

VIGDORTSHUK. Oh, that's a whole story . . .

RUBINTSHIK. Which can be told in three words. We are, as you can see—

VIGDORTSHUK. I'll tell you in three words. What do you need to know to do the film business? Turns out you need nothing.

RUBINTSHIK. It's a laugh.

VIGDORTSHUK. (*Catching himself.*) In other words, you need to know a lot, but what you need to know is a very special knowledge.

RUBINTSHIK. Very special.

SHIMELE. I want you to know that we are big fans of the luminations. Even when we were not like today, when we were ordinary people, every week we went to the luminations. And now, since God made us happy with the big prize, almost never a night goes by when we don't go. So I'd really like to know, especially now since I'm putting money into it, the—the . . . the . . . the sense of it. The way it works. There must be some trick to it, some—some—

VIGDORTSHUK. Naturally there is a trick to it.

RUBINTSHIK. And what a trick.

VIGDORTSHUK. (*Using hands a lot to show turning.*) I'll explain the whole thing. Have you noticed that opposite the show, over the door, there's a lantern with a wheel? And the wheel turns. And on the wheel, which is turning up there by the lantern, there's a long celluloid, a long ribbon?

RUBINTSHIK. It's called film.

SHIMELE. Forgive me, I want my wife to hear this. (*Opens door. Eti-Meni was just walking in with a tray of preserves, carafe of brandy, little glasses.*)

ETI-MENI. Here you have brandy, there's preserves. You can take if you want.

SHIMELE. They'll take, certainly they'll take. (*Pours. To Eti-Meni.*) You have to hear how the lumination works, how it turns and we see everything on the sheet. Sit down, you'll hear something. You love it. You'd spend day and night there.

ETI-MENI. (*Sarcastically*) Oh and you hate it. (*Sits at the side on a soft sofa, props herself on a heavily decorated, multicolored little silken cushion, positions her hands so as to make sure all her jewelry is visible.*) All right, let's hear.

VIGDORTSHUK. (*Facing her but talking to Shimele.*) Now where were we? Here you have a screen.

RUBINTSHIK. We were explaining the film, how the wheel turns next to the lantern.

SHIMELE. (*To Eti-Meni.*) Above the door, exactly opposite the sheet, you've seen the lantern. (*Using his hands a lot to show the wheel turning.*) There's a wheel there and it turns. Let it keep turning, meanwhile a drink. (*Stops to pour more brandy.*) To life. May God keep giving. (*All drink. To Vigdortshuk.*) Now don't stop.

VIGDORTSHUK. So again. In brief. Here you have a screen.

RUBINTSHIK. An ordinary screen.

VIGDORTSHUK. Nothing on the screen. And on the other side of the screen also nothing.

RUBINTSHIK. Also nothing.

ETI-MENI. Tell that to your granny. What do you mean nothing on the screen? We go to the luminations. You think it doesn't cost us money? Somebody else would be glad to have that money. And they say there's nothing on the other side of the screen! We're not children for you to tell bedtime stories to.

VIGDORTSHUK. (*Smiles.*) Pardon me, Madame, we are specialists. We work day and night. We pour into it our health and our life.

RUBINTSHIK. It is our profession.

VIGDORTSHUK. So in other words: nothing. The main thing is the wheel that's there by the lantern. (*His hand gestures demonstrate turning.*) There where the ribbon is turning—

RUBINTSHIK. In other words, film—

ETI-MENI. And the contract, Shimele?

SHIMELE. There's one more point that my wife absolutely insists on. (*To Eti-Meni.*) Ernestina Yefimevne. I want the contract to say, in so many words, that you and I and our friends have the right to go in any three-ater we want, whenever we want, day or night, free, without paying at all.

ETI-MENI. You mean that's not in the contract already?

RUBINTSHIK. Madame, our word is our bond.

ETI-MENI. That's what you say. And later, when it comes down to it, you'll say you don't remember. We know your kind of people. We know what's what.

SHIMELE. I say so too. Put it in. (*To Rubintshik, gestures to desk.*) Better roll up your sleeves, excuse me. You know my writing is not so fancy. And write it in.

VIGDORTSHUK. (*Writes, reads aloud.*) "We, the undersigned, hereby add the clause that the honorable Herr Soroker, Madame Soroker, and any member of their family, has the right, day or night, to enter and take a seat in any of our cinematographic theaters free, with no charge." Satisfactory? (*Shimele looks at Eti-Meni.*)

ETI-MENI. I want it to say in the contract, my sister Feygl too.

VIGDORTSHUK. Madame, the contract says "the Soroker Family."

ETI-MENI. Her family is not the Soroker family. Her family is the Vishkrobenko family.

RUBINTSHIK. The Madame is correct.

SHIMELE. In that case, write in "all friends and acquaintances."

ETI-MENI. Acquaintances? He's afraid of being stingy. A plague on them, they can stay healthy and pay their own way.

RUBINTSHIK. The Madame is absolutely in the right. (*To Vigdortshuk.*) Write in Madame Vishkrobenko with her children.

ETI-MENI. No. Her yes, the children no. They should all disappear. Each one a bigger bum than the next.

RUBINTSHIK. The Madame is absolutely and entirely correct. Write Madame Vishkrobenko, and get this over with.

ETI-MENI. What Madame? Some Madame. Poor thing, she's a pauper, a beggar, it would break your heart for her.

SHIMELE. Eti-Meni, it's down there, it's down, and enough. Now we take care of business. (*Puts on glasses, rolls sleeve, goes to table.*) A delicate job. And done. (*Signs his name. Then they sign.*) And now we give you the sugar candy. (*Goes to iron strongbox.*) But I have to tell you, my dear partners, that there are no coins at all in the iron box. I don't keep that kind of money here at home. You understand, that's what banks are for. (*Opens box, takes out checkbook.*)

The Official Commercial Bank. There's where I keep my entire capital, and when I need, whatever I need, I write out a check and they give it to me. (*Checkbook on table.*) But, though, when it comes to writing Russian, I'm just beginning Hebrew school. That's why I have a daughter, who is my entire bookkeeper. (*To Eti-Meni.*) Call Beylke in here for a little minute.

ETI-MENI. Izabeletshke? I don't think she's home. I'll go look. (*Exits.*)

SHIMELE. Believe me, it's no good when a person is blind. When he can't write Russian, it's worse than needing glasses. (*Pause.*) But wait, you know what? Maybe we'll manage. If you would be good enough—If you have pen and ink—Would you mind writing the check yourselves? Which of you writes nicer?

> *Both rush to desk. Vigdortshuk takes pen and ink. Shimele puts on his glasses, runs his finger across checkbook like a man who knows all about using checks.*

Right there, on the right-hand side, you see? If you don't mind, put down the number fifteen thousand. One, with a five, with three—yes, with three zeroes. That's it. That's it. Did you put it? Now if you don't mind, give me the pen right here, and now we do the job again. (*Rolls up his sleeves again and carefully signs. Sits.*) Oof! Exhausted myself with writing. (*Waves check in the air to dry.*) And whose fault is it? After all, nobody's fault but my father's, rest in peace. He didn't want me to learn to write. If I'd learned to write, I would have been some writer.

VIGDORTSHUK. You have a rare talent.

RUBINTSHIK. A talent. An extraordinary talent.

SHIMELE. (*Very pleased, squeezes their hands.*) Really? A sin my wife isn't here to hear what people say about me. (*Gives Vigdortshuk the check.*)

> *Rubintshik looks at it. Vigdortshuk pokes Rubintshik in the ribs with his elbow, puts the check into his wallet and fastens it. Becomes noticeably nervous.*

VIGDORTSHUK. We've taken up so much of your time.

RUBINTSHIK. Your valuable time.

SHIMELE. What are you talking about? We did business, with God's help.

VIGDORTSHUK. And good business.

RUBINTSHIK. Wonderful business.

SHIMELE. And in that case, we'll drink another glass of brandy before you go. (*Pours.*) Wishing that the half million won't wait very long, and the town will know what God's own plain people can do.

Clink glasses, drink standing.

Now you can go in good health and be well. (*Accompanies them out.*)

END OF SCENE

Appendix

How to Pronounce Yiddish Words and Names

There is a clear, simple system for transliterating Yiddish phonetically:

ay = as in the English *sky*
ey = as in the English *hey*
i = as in the English *ski*
e = as in the English *hen* (never silent, though at the ends of words closer to *i* as in *it*)
tsh = as in the English *match*
kh = guttural *h* (often rendered in English as *ch*)

There are no silent letters. The name Kalefute has four syllables (ka-le-FOO-te), Mirele and Bas-Sheve have three (MEE-re-le and bas-SHE-ve), and Sheyne has two (SHEY-ne), as does the noun *khupe* (KHU-pe).

Reb simply means Mister. It does not mean Rabbi. It is polite, but it is not an honorific and does not suggest particular holiness or learning.

A further note is that Hebrew words and phrases are not pronounced in the Sephardik mode, as spoken in modern Israel. Modern Sephardik pronunciation would be incongruous. When embedded in Yiddish speech, Hebrew sounds like Yiddish. Directors can hear the appropriate sound from Yiddish speakers or on YouTube. (Pronunciation varies radically by region of origin, but any Yiddish pronunciation will sound better here than the modern Sephardik Hebrew.)

www.ingramcontent.com/pod-product-compliance
Lightning Source LLC
Chambersburg PA
CBHW020733160426
43192CB00006B/212